Opening Schools and Closing Prisons

The book covers the period from 1812, when the Tron Riot in Edinburgh dramatically drew attention to the 'lamentable extent of juvenile depravity', up to 1872, when the Education Act (Scotland) inaugurated a system of universal schooling.

During the 1840s and 1850s in particular there was a move away from a punitive approach to young offenders to one based on reformation and prevention. Scotland played a key role in developing reformatory institutions – notably the Glasgow House of Refuge, the largest of its type in the UK – and industrial schools which provided meals and education for children in danger of falling into crime.

These schools were pioneered in Aberdeen by Sheriff William Watson and in Edinburgh by the Reverend Thomas Guthrie and exerted considerable influence throughout the United Kingdom. The experience of the Scottish schools was crucial in the development of legislation for a national, UK-wide system between 1854 and 1866.

Andrew G. Ralston, a student at Glasgow University in the late 1970s, was encouraged by the late Geoffrey Finlayson, author of the definitive biography of Lord Shaftesbury, to take an interest in the history of the treatment of destitute and delinquent children in nineteenth-century Scotland. Having completed a degree of D.Phil at Balliol College, Oxford University, he has subsequently co-authored more than twenty successful school textbooks.

Routledge Studies in Modern British History

A full list of titles in this series is available at: www.routledge.com

5   **Origins of Pan-Africanism**
    Henry Sylvester Williams, Africa, and the African Diaspora
    Marika Sherwood

6   **Statistics and the Public Sphere**
    Numbers and the People in Modern Britain, *c.* 1800–2000
    Edited by Tom Crook and Glen O'Hara

7   **Public Health in the British Empire**
    Intermediaries, Subordinates, and the Practice of Public Health, 1850–1960
    Edited by Ryan Johnson and Amna Khalid

8   **Disability in Eighteenth-Century England**
    Imagining Physical Impairment
    David M. Turner

9   **British Student Activism in the Long Sixties**
    Caroline M. Hoefferle

10 **Philanthropy and Voluntary Action in the First World War**
    Mobilizing Charity
    Peter Grant

11 **The British Army Regular Mounted Infantry 1880–1913**
    Andrew Winrow

12 **The Chartist General**
    Charles James Napier, The Conquest of Sind, and Imperial Liberalism
    Edward Beasley

13 **The Great Church Crisis and the End of English Erastianism, 1898–1906**
    Bethany Kilcrease

14 **Opening Schools and Closing Prisons**
    Caring for Destitute and Delinquent Children in Scotland 1812–1872
    Andrew G. Ralston

Opening Schools and Closing Prisons
Caring for destitute and delinquent children in Scotland 1812–1872

Andrew G. Ralston

LONDON AND NEW YORK

First published 2017
by Routledge
2 Park Square, Milton Park, Abingdon, Oxon OX14 4RN

and by Routledge
711 Third Avenue, New York, NY 10017

First issued in paperback 2018

Routledge is an imprint of the Taylor & Francis Group, an informa business

© 2017 Andrew G. Ralston

The right of Andrew G. Ralston to be identified as author of this work has been asserted by him in accordance with sections 77 and 78 of the Copyright, Designs and Patents Act 1988.

All rights reserved. No part of this book may be reprinted or reproduced or utilised in any form or by any electronic, mechanical, or other means, now known or hereafter invented, including photocopying and recording, or in any information storage or retrieval system, without permission in writing from the publishers.

Trademark notice: Product or corporate names may be trademarks or registered trademarks, and are used only for identification and explanation without intent to infringe.

British Library Cataloguing in Publication Data
A catalogue record for this book is available from the British Library

Library of Congress Cataloging in Publication Data
Names: Ralston, Andrew, author.
Title: Opening schools and closing prisons : caring for destitute and delinquent children in Scotland 1812-1872 / Andrew Ralston.
Description: New York : Routledge, 2017. | Series: Routledge studies in modern British history | Includes bibliographical references and index.
Identifiers: LCCN 2016027957| ISBN 978-1-138-22172-7 (hardback : alk. paper) | ISBN 978-1-315-40973-3 (ebook)
Subjects: LCSH: Juvenile delinquents—Rehabilitation—Scotland—History—19th century. | Juvenile delinquency—Scotland—History—19th century. | Prisons—Scotland—History—19th century. | Reformatories—Scotland—History—19th century. | Trade schools—Scotland—History—19th century.
Classification: LCC HV9147.A5 R35 2017 | DDC 371.9309411/09034—dc23
LC record available at https://lccn.loc.gov/2016027957

ISBN 13: 978-1-138-32995-9 (pbk)
ISBN 13: 978-1-138-22172-7 (hbk)

Typeset in Bembo
by FiSH Books Ltd, Enfield

Printed in the United Kingdom
by Henry Ling Limited

He who opens a school closes a prison.
      (A saying attributed to Victor Hugo, 1802–1885)

Contents

List of figures and tables ix
Preface x

1 Punishment, reformation and prevention: changing attitudes to juvenile crime in mid-nineteenth century Britain 1

2 'The lamentable extent of youthful depravity': the Tron Riot of 1812 24

3 Stirrings for change: developments in Edinburgh, 1812–1846 34

4 'An intermediate step': the Glasgow House of Refuge, 1838–1854 44

5 Prevention is better than cure: the Aberdeen industrial schools, 1841–1854 57

6 Ragged school rivalry: the Original versus the United Industrial School in Edinburgh, 1847–1854 75

7 'A better model': the influence of the Scottish approach in England 91

8 The emergence of a national system (i): reformatory and industrial schools legislation, 1854–1872 112

9 The emergence of a national system (ii): the effects of legislation on individual schools 129

10 Schooling for all: industrial schools and the 1872 Education Act   154

11 Change and continuity: nineteenth-century approaches in context   162

Bibliography   168
Index   176

Figures and tables

Figures

0.1	Children outside the entrance to the Edinburgh Original Ragged School	xii
1.1	'Oliver amazed at the Dodger's mode of going to work': one of George Cruikshank's illustrations for Charles Dickens' *Oliver Twist*	5
2.1	New Year's Eve at the Tron Church	25
4.1	The Glasgow House of Refuge	52
5.1	Sheriff William Watson	59
5.2	Alexander Thomson	61
6.1	Rev. Dr. Thomas Guthrie	80
6.2	The Edinburgh United Industrial School	85
8.1	Alexander Murray Dunlop	113
9.1	Connections between institutions in Aberdeen	135

Tables

4.1	Admissions to Boys' House of Refuge, 1851	50
7.1	Agencies providing education in Scotland, 1851	107
8.1	Children sentenced to Scottish industrial schools, 1862–1867	124
8.2	Number of juveniles detained in reformatory and industrial schools from 31 December 1859 to 31 December 1874	126
9.1	Children on the roll of the United Industrial School, Edinburgh, 1847–73	151
10.1	Number of children in Glasgow under fifteen brought before magistrates charged with crime, 1860–80	159

Preface

> Piecemeal, fragmented solutions don't work. Instead, you need to see how an individual's problems link together, and intervene in the right way. So while we've got the opportunity that prison presents, we need to be far better at dealing with and at addressing prisoners' illiteracy, addiction and mental health problems'.[1]

These words come from a February 2016 speech on prison reform by former Prime Minister David Cameron, announcing what was claimed to be 'the biggest shake-up in the way our prisons are run since the Victorian times'. Yet the same issues were being debated throughout the United Kingdom more than 150 years earlier. At that time a new understanding was emerging that the problem of crime could not be dealt with unless the social conditions which produced it were also addressed. One key aspect of this was intervention to support vulnerable children before they became caught up in a cycle of reoffending, and numerous attempts were made to supplement and, later, replace the imprisonment of young offenders with a programme of education and training for work.

In pre-industrial Britain the law had made little distinction between offenders on the grounds of age, and treatment was essentially punitive in function. As one Glasgow advocate put it in 1818, 'It matters nothing in the eyes of the law whether the prisoner is nine or sixty years of age'.[2] By the mid-1850s, however, a different system of dealing with young offenders had been established.

Two distinct types of institution emerged: the reformatory school for convicted offenders, and the industrial (or 'ragged') school whose role was primarily a preventive one, targeting children in danger of falling into crime.

These initiatives were based on the belief that dealing with problem youngsters would have a positive effect on the whole of society, the assumption being that, as one social reformer put it, 'a penny spent on teaching will save a pound on punishing'.[3] Young offenders were no longer seen as criminals responsible for their own misdemeanours and deserving of punishment, but as victims of circumstances over which they had limited control. In other words, juvenile delinquency had ceased to be regarded as a penal issue and had become a social problem.

Scotland made a number of significant contributions to the development of this new approach, both by pioneering efforts such as the Glasgow House of Refuge and the system of industrial schools set up in Aberdeen and Edinburgh, and by publicising the benefits of a strategy based on reformation and prevention. Scottish ideas fed into the creation of a national system embodied in legislation from 1854 onwards. This book will examine the Scottish contribution, assessing its importance in the context of the UK as a whole and seeking to explain the differences between Scotland and England by reference to existing penal procedure, educational tradition and welfare provision.

A convenient starting point for this story is the Tron Riot of 1812, when gangs of youths attacked the crowds gathered to celebrate the New Year in the streets of Edinburgh. This created considerable public concern about the problem of juvenile crime but the response of the authorities was to make an example of the ringleaders and strengthen the police force, rather than to adopt a new approach. In the next twenty years, however, some attempts were made in Edinburgh to set up a reformatory institution for young offenders, but it was in Glasgow in 1838 that the most ambitious institution of this type was founded. Meanwhile, in Aberdeen, a different strategy was developed, focusing on prevention rather than cure. Here, the efforts of Sheriff William Watson (1796–1887) led to the establishment of a system of day industrial schools where children received meals. Rev. Dr. Thomas Guthrie (1803–1873) extended Watson's idea to Edinburgh and became a prominent figure nationally, gaining a reputation as 'the apostle of ragged schools'.[4]

Recognising the value of such efforts, the state passed legislation in the 1850s allowing children to be committed to the schools by magistrates and providing financial support dependent on certification and inspection. However, this process inevitably altered the character of the industrial schools, as it led to an increasing degree of standardisation and institutionalisation. In an ironic twist, by the 1870s they were being compared to prisons, leading in turn to a renewal of interest in the concept of day industrial feeding schools as originally set up in Scotland. This book ends by looking briefly at the treatment of destitute and delinquent children in the period after the 1872 Education Act which provided for universal schooling, and suggests that today's welfare-based and child-centred policies owe much to the pioneering efforts of nineteenth-century reformers.

★

Reformatory and industrial schools have received relatively little attention from historians of crime and social policy. Various seminal works from the 1970s and 1980s continue to provide an essential starting point. For example, J.J. Carlebach's *Caring for Children in Trouble* provides a short survey of the history of the treatment of young offenders in Britain from the establishment of the Philanthropic Society of 1788 to the approved schools of the 1960s. Carlebach concludes that 'the approved school system is a closed system in the sense that, so far, it has functioned with very little reference to allied and associated areas of child care and has carefully avoided identification with the penal system'.[5] This was not, however, the case with the historical antecedents of these schools, which brought together many features from other social agencies, both within and outside the penal system, as will be shown in detail using Scotland as an example.

Figure 0.1 Children outside the entrance to the Edinburgh Original Ragged School
Source: *Ragged School Rhymes* by Alexander Maclagan, Edinburgh, 1851

This 'joined-up' approach was recognised by David J. Rothman, who put forward a theory of the inter-relation of institutions dealing with diverse social problems in an American context in *The Discovery of the Asylum* (1971). Rothman contends that 'The almshouse and the orphan asylum, the penitentiary, the reformatory, and the insane asylum all represented an effort to insure the cohesion of the community in new and changing circumstances'.[6] Michel Foucault explored this idea further in *Discipline and Punish* (English edition, 1977), an unconventional study of French prisons which argues that the prison,

> in the central position that it occupies ... is not alone, but linked to a whole series of 'carceral' mechanisms which seem distinct enough – since they are intended to alleviate pain, to cure, to comfort – but which all tend, like the prison to exercise a power of normalization.[7]

One of the few books dealing specifically with the Scottish context is Olive Checkland's *Philanthropy in Victorian Scotland* (1980), which examines the importance of the voluntary principle in all areas of health, education, housing and welfare and includes a chapter on reformatories and ragged schools.

Another influential contribution to the history of criminology was made in 1985 by David Garland's *Punishment and Welfare: A History of Penal Strategies*, a study of the connections between criminal justice and social regulation in Britain in the twentieth century which traces the origins of current approaches to the 1895–1914 period. Garland argues that in these years a 'new logic of penal-welfare' was established, 'with its new agencies, techniques, knowledges and institutions'.[8] While acknowledging that many of the aspects of penal policy that emerged during the early stages of the welfare state had their roots in the Victorian period, Garland places little emphasis on reformatory and industrial schools, which he considers to have 'formed a reformative example on the margins of the system'.[9]

In 1988, in an article entitled 'The Development of Reformatory and Industrial Schools in Scotland, 1832–1872' published in *Scottish Economic and Social History*, I put forward the line of argument elaborated in the present volume: in the 1840s significant new approaches to the treatment of juvenile offenders were pioneered in Scotland which contributed to national legislation; thereafter, national factors replaced local considerations in determining the form taken by the schools; a dual system of reformatory and industrial schools developed which applied to both England and Scotland; after 1872 the development of the Scottish schools in a sense came full circle, with the revival of the day industrial schools.[10]

Some years later, Linda Mahood's *Policing Gender, Class and Family: Britain, 1850–1914* (1995) traced the development of juvenile justice from the first half of the nineteenth century, which she designates as the 'prevention' era, up to the 'protective' era of the early decades of the twentieth century, which saw a move beyond reformatory treatment and 'involved the assertion of new powers of state intervention in parent/child relationships'.[11] Mahood deals mainly with the later nineteenth and early twentieth century and does not aim to examine in detail how individual institutions of the 1840s and 50s were set up or how these evolved in the light of legislation. Moreover, as the title of the book suggests, juvenile crime is only one aspect of a broader study which encompasses numerous other aspects of social policy relating to children and families.

Similarly, the focus of Lynn Abrams' *The Orphan Country: Children of Scotland's Broken Homes from 1845 to the Present Day* (1998) is not on the juvenile delinquent but on children affected by family breakdown, particularly in the post-Second World War era when many children were 'separated from their parents on a mass scale'[12] and placed in children's homes. The book highlights aspects of continuity with nineteenth-century practice, such as the Scottish preference for 'boarding out' children under the poor laws, but the author specifically states that 'children admitted to reformatories and industrial schools … are only mentioned in passing…'[13]

More generally, recent years have seen a growing interest in research into numerous aspects of nineteenth century Scottish social history, with such works as J.F. McCaffrey's *Scotland in the Nineteenth Century* (1998), W.W. Knox's *Industrial Nation: Work, Culture and Society in Scotland 1800-Present* (1999), T.M. Devine's *The Scottish Nation, 1700–2007* (2012) and David G. Barrie and Susan Broomhall's *Police Courts in Nineteenth-Century Scotland* (2014), the latter being of particular relevance in the present context. This two-volume study shows how important police courts became in the nineteenth century, processing vast numbers of offenders accused of minor crimes and in so doing making a considerable impact on social behaviour and cultural ideas.

★

In addition to outlining legislative developments relating to the treatment of juvenile delinquency between 1812 and 1872, *Opening Schools and Closing Prisons* aims to look at the 'social welfare' dimension of the subject in depth. The social conditions which gave rise to juvenile crime are examined and reformatory and industrial schools are placed in a wider historical context, covering not only the legal dimension but also other relevant areas such as educational provision and the administration of poor relief. This in turn entails a greater emphasis on the ecclesiastical background, as traditionally the Church of Scotland played a central role in these matters. At the Disruption of 1843[14] over a third of the ministers left to form the Free Church, making existing arrangements for education and welfare even more unsuited to an urban and industrial society. Significantly, most of the key figures in the industrial school movement also played an important role in the Free Church.

A further aspect of the approach followed here is that much of the detailed discussion centres on how individual schools evolved to meet local needs. A major theme of this analysis is that most of these establishments originated from within the existing framework of penal practice, poor relief and educational provision; it is argued that the distinctive features of Scottish institutions can largely be explained by reference to this background and to the differing local circumstances of the three main cities, Edinburgh, Glasgow and Aberdeen. This interpretation has particular resonance today, at a time when there is a growing awareness of a separate Scottish identity in many areas of public policy.

A considerable amount of contemporary source material exists which allows the story to be told in depth. As they sought public donations, most individual schools issued annual reports and held meetings which were often reported in local newspapers. Government inquiries amassed a large amount of evidence from witnesses, while inspectors of prisons and certified schools wrote detailed reports of their visits. A century and a half later, it is still possible, through an examination of these documents, to gain some understanding of the temptations faced by children living in poverty in the mid-nineteenth century, their experience of appearing in police courts and the kind of regime they followed when sent to prison or reformatory school. Similarly, surviving correspondence and biographical material sheds light on the values and experiences which inspired philanthropic reformers like Watson and Guthrie to devote their lives to improving the lot of such children. Behind the criminal statistics, legal processes and Acts of Parliament lies a fascinating human story.

My interest in the history of the treatment of juvenile crime dates back to the late 1970s when I studied nineteenth-century history at Glasgow University under the late Geoffrey Finlayson. I subsequently carried out research on 'The Treatment of Destitute and Delinquent Children in Scotland, 1812–1872' for the degree of D.Phil at Balliol College, Oxford, where I was supervised by John Prest. This preface provides the opportunity to record – albeit belatedly – my sincere thanks to both of these scholars for their help and encouragement. I would also like to express my gratitude to Dr. W.W. Knox of St. Andrews University and Emeritus Professor W. Ian P. Hazlett of Glasgow University for their interest in this project.

Notes

1 www.gov.uk/government/speeches/prison-reform-prime-ministers-speech (first published 8 February 2016; accessed 18 March 2016).
2 *Glasgow Herald*, 1 May 1818.
3 Thomas Beggs, *Juvenile Delinquency and Reformatory Institutions: A Lecture delivered to the members of the Leeds Mechanics' Institution* (London, 1857), p. 6.
4 Samuel Smiles, *Self-Help* (London, 1903), p. 366.
5 J. Carlebach, *Caring for Children in Trouble* (London, 1970), p. 180.
6 David J. Rothman, *The Discovery of the Asylum* (Boston and Toronto, 1971), p. xviii.
7 Michel Foucault, *Discipline and Punish* (London, 1977), p. 308.
8 David Garland, *Punishment and Welfare* (Aldershot, 1985), p. 5.
9 Ibid., p. 8.
10 *Scottish Economic and Social History*, 1988, Volume 8, Issue 1, pp. 40–55.
11 Linda Mahood, *Policing Gender, Class and Family: Britain 1850–1914* (London, 1995), p. 40. A lawyer's perspective on the subject of juvenile justice in nineteenth-century Scotland can be found in Christine Kelly's *Criminalisation of Children, 1840–1910* (Glasgow University, PhD thesis, 2012), which covers the period from Sheriff Watson's experiments in Aberdeen in the 1840s to the 1908 Children Act. The author argues that, in spite of the philanthropic motivation of the early reformers, criminalisation of children 'on an immense scale' had occurred by the beginning of the twentieth century. By the 1880s the statutory system in Scotland had evolved into a 'net widening diversionary mechanism under which thousands of children were subjected to prolonged detention in penal establishments' (p. 2). Although she notes that the 'pre-statutory system of Scottish day industrial schools … in many ways had been a genuinely crime preventive, social welfare initiative' (p. 2), this aspect is not the main focus of her discussion, the stated intention being 'to address matters from the legal angle' (p. 19).

12 Lynn Abrams, *The Orphan Country: Children of Scotland's Broken Homes from 1845 to the Present Day* (Edinburgh, 1998), p. vii.
13 Ibid., p. 30.
14 See www.scotland.org.uk/history/disruption for a chronology of the events leading up to the Disruption and a summary of the issues involved.

1 Punishment, reformation and prevention

Changing attitudes to juvenile crime in mid-nineteenth century Britain

Sometime during the 1840s, the Rev. Thomas Guthrie of Edinburgh witnessed the following episode:

> I was in Hanover Street, when a vinegar-looking old lady was toddling along, with a huge umbrella in her hand. A little urchin came up who had no cap on his head, but plenty of brains within ... I saw him fix upon that venerable old lady to be operated on. He approached her with a most pitiful look and whine. Her response was a snarl and poke of her umbrella. He saw there was no chance of getting at her purse through her philanthropy, so he thought to get at it through her selfishness. In an instant he rolled up the sleeve of a tattered jacket to the elbow of his yellow skinny arm, and running up displayed it, crying out to her, 'Just out o' the Infirmary, ma'am, with typhus!' It was a *ruse* got up for the occasion; but the acting was perfect — the effect sudden, electric ... Diving her hand to the very bottom of her pocket, she took out a shilling, thrust it into his palm, and hobbled away, glad to get the wind between the little rogue and her nobility![1]

That encounter could equally well have taken place in the streets of London, Glasgow, Birmingham or any other British city. While not without its humorous side, it illustrates a problem that was becoming of serious concern to both the authorities and the general public in the mid-nineteenth century: the perceived rise in the number of predatory children involved in vagrancy, begging and petty criminality and the lack of effective means of dealing with them. In Guthrie's vivid image, 'the streets swarmed with boys and girls whose trade was begging, and whose end was the jail. They rose every morning from the lower districts like a cloud of mosquitoes from a marsh, to disperse themselves over the city...'[2]

In the absence of reliable statistics from the early part of the century, it would be difficult to state categorically that a dramatic increase in juvenile crime had occurred, but there is no doubt that, from about 1840 onwards, contemporaries were convinced that a large proportion of crime was committed by the younger generation.[3] Mid-century observers pointed out that while one-tenth of the population of England and Wales was aged between fifteen and twenty, this age group committed nearly a quarter of the crime.[4] 'In Newcastle', reported Joseph Kay,

'Juvenile Crime is increasing FOUR times as fast as the Population, and in thirteen years has <u>doubled</u> its amount'[5] – the capitalisation and underlining only serving to emphasise the author's feeling of desperation.

While such alarming figures were regularly quoted, most commentators took an anecdotal rather than an analytical approach, citing specific cases rather than discussing statistics. This is understandable as the phenomenon which Professor Sir Brian Harrison called 'the pursuit of precision in modern social investigation' had barely commenced in the 1840s: detailed collection and examination of statistical returns was a feature of the second rather than the first half of the century. Equally, writers felt it unnecessary to prove that juvenile crime was on the increase, as this was a belief that was almost universally accepted. Urging the immediate opening of an institution for young offenders in Glasgow in 1838, a correspondent of the *Glasgow Herald* considered it sufficient to state that 'we all know that juvenile delinquency exists in this city to an alarming extent'.[6] The relative absence of attempts to prove the rise in juvenile crime through analysis of figures, and the fact that no writer attempted to argue that it was on the decline, are in themselves indirect evidence that delinquency was widespread and, by implication, increasing.

The extent of juvenile crime being considered self-evident by contemporaries, discussion centred instead on (i) the factors causing it, (ii) the ineffectiveness of existing approaches and (iii) what should be done to tackle the problem. This chapter will examine these issues from a UK-wide perspective in order to provide a context for the rest of the book which focuses in detail on Scotland's contribution to the debate.

Causes of juvenile delinquency

The 1840s and 1850s were the critical decades in the formation of a new approach to juvenile crime. The background to this was the widespread investigation of social abuses by Parliamentary Select Committees and Royal Commissions which had already led to reforms such as the 1833 Factory Act and the 1834 Poor Law Amendment Act. It must be remembered, too, that at the time, 'adopting the device of investigation prior to legislation'[7] was in itself something a novelty.

The subject of juvenile crime was thoroughly examined by two Select Committees: the first, in 1847, examined 'the Execution of the Criminal Law, especially respecting Juvenile Offenders and Transportation' and the second, in 1852 and again in 1852–1853, reported on 'Criminal and Destitute Children'.[8] Taken together, these reports reveal much about the attitudes towards delinquency which developed in the middle of the century. The extent of agreement is remarkable: from the testimony of witnesses as far apart geographically as Alexander Thomson of Banchory, Aberdeenshire and G.L. Chesterton of Coldbath Fields House of Correction, London, or as far opposed ideologically as Sir Joshua Jebb, Surveyor-General of Prisons and the social reformer Mary Carpenter, it is clear that a new consensus was emerging in which children who committed petty offences were viewed as the victims of circumstances beyond their control.

Certainly, temptations lurked everywhere in the Victorian city. The practice of displaying goods outside shops made it easy for a child to steal, and there were many seemingly respectable businessmen who encouraged young thieves by receiving stolen goods. In parts of London, these individuals hung about the streets, ready to take any stolen item 'easily carried, easily sold' from a child in return for a few pennies which would then be spent on gingerbread or cakes. When asked a leading question by the 1847 Committee – 'Do [young offenders] appear to be persons set on by Receivers of Stolen Goods, or by other Thieves?' – Lieutenant Tracy, Governor of Tothill Fields House of Correction, readily concurred: 'That appears most distinctly; they are the Dupes and Victims of others who reward them.'[9]

The 1837 Report of the Prison Inspectors for the Northern and Eastern District gives a particularly incisive analysis of the multiplicity of causes behind the growth of juvenile crime in Liverpool, showing how just about every social and economic trend of the time had some bearing on the problem. The report highlighted

> the fluctuating variety and vicissitudes of the population of a great maritime town; the continual ingress of poor Irish; the absence of factory employment or other work for children; the number of destitute orphans, from the deadly visitation of cholera and fever; the temptation afforded to want and idleness by the comparatively unguarded and careless exposure of valuable property in the markets, stores, and about the docks; the excitements to criminal pursuits induced by the low shows and theatres, and the little attention paid to [children's] condition by a community deeply engaged in the absorbing transactions of commercial enterprise.'[10]

Some of these have a familiar ring to modern ears. Current concerns about the effects of computer games on young minds, for instance, had their mid-Victorian equivalent in fears over the malign influence of 'low shows and theatres'. Caroline Francis Cornwallis (1786–1858), a champion of the poor and under-privileged, gives a fascinating account of this forgotten side of popular culture in her 1851 book *The Philosophy of Ragged Schools* in which she describes how 'boys and girls of the very lowest description' flocked to establishments known as 'penny gaffs' to watch 'scenes of grossness, crime, and blood, all represented with a revolting coarseness'. A typical production was 'The Red-Nosed Monster' or 'The Tyrant of the Mountain', with a cast of characters that included 'The Assassin', 'The Ruffian of the Hut' and 'The Villain of the Valley'. As an encore, the youngsters were treated to a performance of 'the Blood Stained Handkerchief' or 'The Murder in the Cottage'. Cornwallis quotes one young offender who admits that 'the first beginning of my bad conduct was seeing a play acted at the theatre ... the play was about a highwayman so we thought we would try to do as he did', while another precocious young thief explains that 'I noticed them picking one another's pockets on the stage. It gave me a great insight into how to do it.'[11]

If theatres planted ideas in the young criminal's mind, they also provided ideal opportunities to put them into practice. One (presumably reformed) offender, identified only by his initials – 'M.C., alias W.R.' – gave the following account of his first steps on the road to ruin:

> I first met with bad companions at the Sanspareil[12] ... We used to put our hands over the rails when the people were going down stairs, and take off shawls, hats or anything else; the people that had lost them could not get back, the crowd was so strong. If the hat was a good one, we used to put our own inside and put it on our heads; we also used to creep under the seats; strangers would have their pockets hanging down, (men or women). We used to cut them off sometimes. I have found bottles with liquor in them, copper, oranges and other things; in the women's we sometimes found purses. My father has often said those cursed places have been my ruin.'[13]

At least 'M.C.' had a father who, albeit retrospectively, offered some kind of moral guidance. Others were less fortunate. A common response to the first question usually put to witnesses who appeared before the Select Committees – 'what in your opinion are the main causes of juvenile crime?' – was to blame negligent parents. John Adams, Serjeant at Law, of London, believed delinquent children were not 'naturally worse than other Children; but that their offences spring from the Want of proper moral and religious Education, and in the Want of proper Friends to attend to them'.[14] John MacGregor of the Ragged School Union talked of children 'sliding into gaol [from] their mother's lap'[15] while Guthrie said that 'if there was a white slave-market in Edinburgh, they would sell their children for drink'.[16] In the same vein, the prison chaplain at Glasgow observed that

> it is not an uncommon thing for such people, instead of training up their children in the way they should go, to send them out to the streets day after day, in rags and starvation, to shift for themselves ... with the strict orders not to return ... without bringing in something along with them, come how it may, either by begging or stealing.[17]

Such practices led Thomas Beggs, in a lecture to the Leeds' Mechanics Institute in 1857, to conclude that 'the great corrective for the evil of juvenile delinquency is to be found, and found only, in the corrected habits of the parents...'.[18] Some looked at the problem the other way round, arguing that such parents were beyond hope; the priority should instead be to prevent their offspring growing into adult criminals and, in time, becoming the parents of the next generation of criminal children. Sir Joshua Jebb considered it to be 'of Importance to deal specifically with Juveniles, as it is striking at the Root of Crime'.[19]

Deprived of any meaningful support at home, young offenders could easily be led astray by their peers – a factor frequently mentioned to show how it was virtually impossible for a child to return to the straight and narrow once he had embarked on a criminal career. The prison inspectors' reports quote numerous case histories to illustrate what happened to young offenders on release from confinement, often going into a surprising amount of circumstantial detail. Take the story of 'A.N.', for example. Sent to the General Prison in Perth at the age of fifteen, he was released on 6 January 1846 with the intention of obtaining employment after serving a two-year sentence. He travelled to Edinburgh, where he met 'two fellows' and treated them 'to a gill and some porter, which cost him 7d', after which at two he caught the train for Glasgow, where he arrived about four. He had only reached the length of the High Street when he fell in with three former associates who, 'finding that he was just returned from Perth and flush of money, were very friendly, and adjourned with him to a neighbouring public-house'. Whatever money he had not spent on drink was taken from him so that by eight o'clock he was 'perfectly drunk', had lost his waistcoat and found himself without a farthing of the £1 3s. 10d. with which he had left prison. Over the next couple of days he drifted from one lodging 'of the vilest description' to another until the 10th, when he was arrested for pickpocketing. By the 13th – a week after his release – he was back in the prison at Perth.[20]

Figure 1.1 'Oliver amazed at the Dodger's mode of going to work': one of George Cruikshank's illustrations for Charles Dickens' *Oliver Twist*

Source: 'The Victorian Web' www.victorianweb.org/art/illustration/cruikshank/ot6.html (accessed 25 April 2016)

The prison inspectors often showed genuine understanding of the plight of boys of this type:

> A good few of these unfortunate youths have gone from us with the express determination of doing well. They have begged for employment, they have tried to enlist, they have sought to get to sea, and have been disappointed in all. When brought back for a new crime you cannot reason with them effectually ... They reply with too much truth, 'What can I do? I have tried everything, and nobody will give me work; I cannot starve, and must steal.'[21]

It is not surprising, then, that to contemporaries there appeared to exist a separate and self-perpetuating criminal class. As one social investigator, Thomas Plint, put it,

> May it not be said of the class that it is *in* the community, but neither *of* it, nor *from* it? Is it not the fact that a large majority of the class is so by descent, and stands as completely isolated from the other classes, in blood, in sympathies, in its domestic and social organisation...?[22]

The advantages to society of breaking this vicious circle were obvious: dealing with offenders when they were children would save the expense of dealing with them when they were adults. Thomas Beggs calculated from income tax returns that out of a population of eighteen million in England and Wales, fewer than half a million had an income of over £100 a year, yet every convict cost the state, on average, £100–£150 per annum, giving a total cost of not less than two million pounds.[23]

Thus, a new understanding was emerging in mid-nineteenth century Britain of the complex variety of factors contributing to the phenomenon of juvenile delinquency. Those who investigated the subject all arrived at a similar conclusion: the problem could not be dealt with in isolation from the other social ills that contributed to it. The plethora of books and pamphlets written about juvenile delinquency and the exhaustive deliberations of the Select Committees are not so much investigations of the children themselves as reports on a range of deep-seated social evils. As a result, many social reformers concerned about the plight of the young, such as Lord Shaftesbury, were equally active in campaigning for improvements in other areas such as housing and health. 'Moral and religious Instruction, sanitary Regulations, everything which tends to raise the Tone of the lower orders, to give them a pleasure in social Duties, which increases their self-respect, their knowledge, etc. is most valuable', considered John Adams.[24]

While the importance of the bigger social and economic picture was increasingly acknowledged, those professionally involved with young offenders constantly highlighted a more immediate and specific issue. Existing legal and penal procedures were not just failing to provide a solution; they were in fact making things worse.

Juvenile offenders and the law in the early nineteenth century

There is a sense in which no such thing as juvenile delinquency existed in pre-industrial Britain. Juveniles did, of course, appear before the courts, but they were not dealt with as a separate category from other offenders.

This has led to much criticism of the early nineteenth-century penal code. The anti-capital punishment campaigner Arthur Koestler (1905–1983) typified a popular misconception when he wrote in his *Reflections on Hanging* that 'hanging was regarded by the Bloody Code as a cure-all for every offence, from stealing a handkerchief upward'.[25] The operation of such laws was, however, mitigated in practice: B.E.F. Knell's study of criminal statistics has shown that only one offender under the age of fourteen was executed in the period 1801–1836.[26] Nevertheless, perhaps the most important point is not so much that a child was hanged in the nineteenth century, but that the law said a child could be hanged – that is, no legal distinction was made between offenders on the grounds of age. Although Knell found only one case of a child being executed, his study of the Criminal Register, the Newgate Calendar of Prisoners and the Old Bailey Session Papers revealed that 103 children were sentenced to death, the usual procedure being to commute the sentence to transportation.[27] In theory, the legal position was that up to the age of seven there was a presumption that the child was *doli incapax* (that is, unable to form the intention to commit a crime) while in cases of children under fourteen the onus was on the prosecution to prove that the accused had the ability to distinguish between right and wrong. In practice, however, as Jeannie Duckworth notes in her book *Fagin's Children*, 'In most cases the fact that the offence was committed suggested that the perpetrator possessed a guilty mind and therefore punishment was justified'.[28]

The Bristol Sunday School teacher and social reformer Mary Carpenter (1807–1877) drew attention to the inconsistency of the law in holding juveniles criminally culpable: a person under the age of twenty-one could not marry, make legally binding agreements, or become an apprentice without his father's signature, yet

> No sooner does the child *prove to society* his utter incapability to govern himself wisely and well, by falling into crime, than he is deemed worthy, even if of the age of 6 or 7, to be placed on the footing of a man.[29]

The corollary was that the child had to go through the same lengthy legal process as the adult offender, and this had an important effect on the number of juveniles who were tried in the period before 1847. For example, at this time prosecutions had to be pursued privately in England – it was the responsibility of the wronged party to prosecute the culprit.[30] The consequences of this are discussed by David Philips in his study of crime in the Black Country, and he quotes a passage from the Second Report of the Select Committee on Public Prosecutors (1865) which sums up the defects of the law in this respect:

> The duty of prosecution is usually irksome, inconvenient, and burthensome; the injured party would often rather forego the prosecution than incur the expense of time, labour, and money. The entrusting the conduct of the prosecution to a private individual opens a wide door to bribery, collusion and illegal compromise...[31]

One of the earliest organisations to investigate the treatment of juvenile delinquents, the Society for the Improvement of Prison Discipline and the Reformation of Juvenile Offenders (founded in London in 1818), pointed out in its first report that the criticisms which could be made of the system of private prosecution were particularly applicable to juvenile offenders, and drew attention to the additional problem that the severity of punishments often increased reluctance to prosecute youngsters.[32]

Even magistrates prepared to take the age of an offender into consideration were hampered by the lack of appropriate sanctions available to them. Some, such as Matthew Davenport Hill and John Adams, experimented with dismissing young offenders instead of imprisoning them, but Adams discovered that of 278 juveniles convicted at the Middlesex Sessions

> it was not found possible to remit more than four or five to the care of masters or relations; so few were the instances in which these unhappy children had any connections, or at least any from whom they could be expected to derive benefit.[33]

Charles Pearson, an experienced lawyer who had been City Solicitor since 1839, told the 1847 Select Committee, 'Knowing not what to do with them, the Magistrates, frequently from compassionate Motives, send them to Gaol' – a practice, he added, that suited certain types of parents as 'a Means of getting rid of their Obligations'.[34]

Hence, the pattern was that many delinquents ended up being imprisoned for trivial offences for short periods. In 1851 fifty-five children under the age of fourteen were sent to the Westminster House of Correction for stealing fruit, or some article under the value of sixpence, and 136 for stealing items valued between sixpence and four shillings, all of them being sentenced to terms of imprisonment of under two months.[35] Captain W.J. Williams, Prison Inspector for the Northern and Eastern District, said that in 1850 2,070 boys were sent to prison for periods of fourteen days, 2,146 for between fourteen days and a month and 2,024 for between one and two months, 'which constitutes the great bulk of juvenile delinquency'.[36] Charles Pearson claimed that 'It is of frequent Occurrence to send Children to Prison for such offences as flying Kites in a public Road'.[37]

Some of the Select Committee members were well aware that there was a class dimension to this. When one reactionary witness, Captain Donatus O'Brien, spoke in favour of every child who broke the law being sent to some kind of penal establishment, Richard Monckton Milnes pertinently asked, 'Would you carry that principle to this extent, that you would have a parent of the middle or upper classes of society bring his child up before a magistrate for stealing an apple when he was six years old?'[38] Similarly, when Adam Black, the Lord Provost of Edinburgh, visited the city's gaol in August 1846 and met two boys of ten or twelve years of age who had been locked up for pulling some beans from a field, he remarked that this was 'an offence of which, when I was a boy, I was more than once guilty; and if the same judgment had been meted out to me, I might have been ruined for life'.[39]

Brief spells of incarceration were unlikely to contribute anything to a delinquent's reformation: they were too short for anything in the way of education or rehabilitation to be achieved, but long enough to remove a child's fear of prison. In the opinion of the Rev. Thomas Carter, Chaplain of Liverpool Gaol, children were frightened of the prospect of going to gaol, but once they had been there they lost this fear. 'Gaol', he said, '… has a deterring effect only as long as boys keep out of it'.[40] The result was that children would, as one of them told Captain W.J. Williams, 'rather Ten thousand Times be in a Prison than in a Poor-house…'[41]

Frequently children who were released found their home environment less comfortable and secure than that to which they had become accustomed in prison. Captain Williams said that it was not uncommon for a child released from gaol one morning to be returned there the next, while Edwin Chadwick, the poor law and public health reformer, blamed the humanitarian improvements in prison conditions instigated by Howard and Fry for making prisons so comfortable as to attract inmates to them. The chaplain of 'the gaol palace at Reading' claimed that 'Many of our juvenile culprits have never feasted upon such luxurious abundance before they entered prison'.[42] All this, of course, could be evidence of the poverty of their normal living standards, rather than of the luxury of the prisons. One must, however, accept the point made by John Smith, Governor of Edinburgh Gaol, that repeated incarceration of juveniles for short periods 'inures them to Imprisonment by slow Degrees, and thoroughly accustoms them to the Punishment till it becomes no Punishment at all'.[43]

A number of prisons did attempt to provide some kind of industrial training and elementary education. At London's Millbank penitentiary, for example, children were given two and three-quarter hours of schooling per day and engaged in some productive work. But more often they received an education into crime rather than away from it. After a period in prison mixing with hardened criminals whose escapades could appear heroic in the eyes of a child, the young offender was

> 'thenceforward marked by the Police as one who has been in Prison; he is a suspected Character; he is driven to associate habitually with those worse than himself, and his Ruin consequently becomes certain'.[44]

Thus, the treatment meted out to children by the law was increasingly viewed as one of the causes of juvenile crime. The Rev. John Clay, chaplain of Preston House of Correction, sensed the irony of the situation:

> Ignorance, idleness and parental neglect are no doubt greatly instrumental in creating such proneness to crime in young persons; but all these are little in

comparison with the mischief done ... under the present system of discipline, in the very place intended for their correction.[45]

It is not surprising, then, that demand for change was at its strongest within legal and penal circles for, as John Adams said, the magistrate 'cannot do right from the state of the law'.[46]

The first attempt to meet this demand was the *Act for the more speedy Trial and Punishment of Juvenile Offenders*, which received royal assent in July 1847 [10 & 11 Vict. c.82]. Many witnesses to the Select Committee had urged an extension of the powers of summary jurisdiction, arguing that if the power of dismissing or punishing a delinquent was vested in an inferior court such as a police magistrate's, the necessity for a full trial by jury and the consequent evil of children spending long periods in gaol awaiting trial would be eliminated. This power was already available under Scottish Law and the experience of its operation north of the border played a significant role in shaping the 1847 legislation.[47] Under the terms of the new Act, an offender under the age of fourteen convicted of larceny could now be committed by two justices or a magistrate to three months' imprisonment, accompanied by a fine or whipping as required. The jurisdiction was extended to children under sixteen in 1850 and to adults by the Criminal Justice Act of 1855.

The main significance of the 1847 Act, as Margaret May has pointed out, is that it made the first distinction in law between juvenile and adult offenders.[48] Henceforth, juvenile delinquency officially existed. Nevertheless, the extension of summary jurisdiction did no more than facilitate the administration of existing measures, and although the legal status of juveniles was altered, the need for more effective methods of treatment remained. In fact, by leading to an increased number of convictions, and therefore more short imprisonments, the summary jurisdiction Act made the provision of alternative places of detention all the more urgent. Thus, when a second Select Committee to investigate 'Criminal and Destitute Children' was appointed by the House of Commons in 1852 on the motion of C. B. Adderley (1814–1905), Conservative member for Staffordshire North, the need for more far-reaching reform was recognised.

Proposals for change

At first sight, the early attempts to tackle the juvenile problem appear to stem from two separate sources: on the one hand, demands were made by 'official' figures involved in the penal process from the police force, prison system and courts, while on the other, privately run houses of refuge were set up at an 'unofficial' level by philanthropic individuals and societies. There is, however, no dichotomy here, as the same people tended to be involved in both. The words of David Power, Recorder of Ipswich, to the 1852 Select Committee would have been endorsed by practically any concerned magistrate in England or Scotland:

The very fact of the recorder of a town, whose duty it is to commit young prisoners to gaol, feeling it also part of his duty to get an institution established by which he could do away with the ill effects arising from the sentence he is compelled by law to pronounce, argues very strongly against the expediency or justice of the present system.[49]

A pattern replicated in many cities was that magistrates and their associates, frustrated by the inadequacy of existing means of disposing of young offenders, took steps in co-operation with like-minded people to set up small-scale ventures, generally for boys released from prison, providing education and industrial work in preparation for employment. Such experiments soon showed that little could be achieved without legal powers to commit and detain the children, the result being more organised pressure for legislation, and the development of a 'movement' at a national rather than a local level.

There was consequently a close connection between the existing system and the various proposals for alternative approaches. When Jeremy Bentham designed a building called the Panopticon for use as either a prison or a school, he neatly symbolised the continuity which existed between the gaol and the reformatory.[50] Though an opposition was to grow up between these two institutions, the origins of the reformatory lie within the prison system. As they were particularly aware of the side-effects of the existing approach, it was predominantly 'Recorders of Cities and Boroughs, Judges of local Jurisdiction, Magistrates, Governors and Chaplains of Gaols and Penitentiaries, Prison Inspectors, and others having the Care of Convicts'[51] who put forward suggestions for alternative ways of dealing with young offenders. What was to become the fundamental principle of the training provided in a reformatory school – the combination of industrial work and education – had been a feature of the separate system of prison discipline, whose creed was that every prisoner should be 'furnished with suitable labour and employment; and with the means of moral and religious instruction'.[52] Often reformers were doing little more than urging the extension of this system to the treatment of young offenders in separate institutions outside prison instead of in separate cells inside it. As Matthew Davenport Hill put it in 1854,

> 'That the treatment of children must differ from the treatment of men is obvious ... But as regards the propriety of applying the same principles of punishment to each class, no vital distinction between the two can be established.'[53]

This connection between the prison system and the treatment of young offenders was preserved throughout the century, for while the prison element gradually diminished, it never wholly disappeared, a spell in prison being required before admission to a reformatory until as late as 1899. Just as the convicts of the period in Millbank or Pentonville served time in separate confinement with hard labour before going on to a period of employment on public works, so juveniles had to spend at least fourteen days in a prison before proceeding to reformatory school.

The link that existed between new and existing approaches can be seen in the earliest reformatory societies and institutions. The Society for Investigating the

Causes of the Alarming Increase of Juvenile Delinquency in the Metropolis, founded in 1815 by the Quaker Peter Bedford, not only visited London prisons to collect data but was also managed by a committee which included many of the most prominent prison reformers of the day, such as James Mill, the younger Samuel Hoare and Fowell Buxton, who, with Sir James Mackintosh, had led the movement for penal reform.[54] Three years later, Bedford and his associates formed the Society for the Improvement of Prison Discipline and for the Reformation of Juvenile Offenders to continue the investigations of the first society in greater depth. According to Leon Radzinowicz, this was as a result of the publication of Fowell Buxton's 'An Inquiry whether Crime and Misery are produced or prevented, by our present System of Prison Discipline'[55] – a clear example of how the movement to reform young delinquents was an aspect of the general question of penal reform. Similarly, the Philanthropic Society (founded 1788) saw itself as working in harmony with the existing penal process. Although it pioneered a system less restrictive than imprisonment under the separate system – operating initially in houses in the Hackney district of London, each supervised by a workman who taught his trade to the boys under his care – the Society emphasised that 'A remedy is wanting, that shall aid and co-operate with the law',[56] one of the main ways in which this was done being the admission of children on the recommendation of the justices before whom they appeared.

The continuity between old and new approaches is similarly evidenced by the views of prison governors and chaplains, many of whom, while favouring reformatory schools, also believed that much could still be achieved within the prisons. Within his first year of observing young thieves under separate confinement at Preston Gaol, the Rev. John Clay was writing in favour of reformatories. But Clay envisaged a system in which reformatory schooling would follow, rather than supersede, imprisonment; 'the cell is invaluable as preparation for the school', he said.[57] He did not minimise the evils of imprisonment discussed earlier, but argued that these evils could be eliminated and imprisonment made to work. The separate system, as long as it was accompanied by intellectual, moral and religious and industrial education, was in his view sufficient to reform a juvenile; only those with whom the prison had failed should be sent to a reformatory school. Clay considered it to be important that admission to a reformatory school should always be preceded by a spell in prison, so that it could be impressed upon the offender that he had done wrong and deserved punishment.

The process is again exemplified in the first government establishment run solely for juvenile prisoners – Parkhurst Prison on the Isle of Wight, set up in 1835. The founding of Parkhurst can be regarded as an extension of the separate system: instead of classifying juveniles separately within existing prisons, a separate institution was opened – but it was still very much a prison. The first report on Parkhurst said that it aimed to provide 'a judicious course of moral, religious and industrial training; but the means adopted for this purpose should not be of such a nature as to counteract the wholesome restraints of corrective discipline'.[58] There was to be nothing which would appear to 'weaken the terror of the law or to lessen in the minds of the juvenile population at large, or their parents, the dread of being committed to prison'.[59] Parkhurst, moreover, never claimed to provide a complete system of reformation: it was designed as a preparation for transportation, and an idea of the extent to which the punitive element was present in this preparation can be gained from remarks of the Governor, Captain Hall, in his evidence to the 1847 Select Committee, when he described the system operated in the prison:

> In the first instance [the offender] is placed in a separate Cell, where he is not allowed to communicate with any other Prisoner, but is visited by the Chaplain, the Schoolmaster, and the Instructor in Knitting and Tailoring, as well as by me; he goes to School and to Chapel, and is allowed there to be in company with other Prisoners, but he is not allowed to speak to them; and after a few Months he is passed into the general Ward, where he is allowed to go to some Trade, and to School in company with other Prisoners, to walk about in the Yard, and while there to converse with other Prisoners, under the Eye of the Warder, who would check any Irregularity or Impropriety of Conduct.[60]

In some respects, Parkhurst provides an example of the transition from prison to reformatory: it was like a prison in its regime and in much of its training, but like a reformatory in its recognition of the principle that juveniles required to be treated separately.

However, while this evolution was taking place, a different approach to reformatories was emerging, outside the prison system. The crucial development in this respect came during the period between the two Select Committees, and its extent can best be judged by a comparison of the recommendations of the two reports. On the subject of the place of detention of juvenile offenders, the 1852–3 Committee goes further than its predecessor. What is tentatively suggested by the first Committee is strongly urged by the second:

> 1847: 'The Committee are disposed to recommend the Adoption, by way of Trial, of … reformatory Asylums…'[61]
> 1853: … penal reformatory establishments ought to be founded and supported entirely at the public cost…'[62]

The prison chaplains, governors and magistrates who gave evidence in 1847 appeared again in 1852–1853, but there were also people who had gained expertise in managing schools for delinquent and destitute children, such as Dr. Guthrie, Alexander Thomson of the Aberdeen Industrial Schools and John MacGregor of the Ragged School Union. Thus, by the time of the second inquiry a greater variety of voluntary institutions existed and the Committee was able to investigate how well they were working.

These developments introduced two main new factors to the debate. First, legal powers and financial grants were now seen as indispensable. The Philanthropic Society and other similar experiments like the Hackney Wick Asylum in London and the Reformatory at Stretton-on-Dunsmore, Warwickshire, found that they could achieve little without the power of legal detention, as inmates could not be prevented from running away.[63] Of these three institutions, only the Philanthropic Society managed to raise sufficient funds to survive; Hackney Wick closed in 1841 and Stretton in 1854 because of lack of money. On the basis of such experience, the passage of legislation was considered necessary as a preliminary to tackling the real problem of reforming the inmates themselves.

Secondly, the movement for a fresh approach to delinquency had now developed beyond the prison system. The Rev. Joseph Kingsmill (himself a prison chaplain) struck the keynote of this new phase when he wrote that 'Our times have more need of an Ashley than a Howard',[64] by which he meant that wider social reform was required rather than improvements in prison conditions.

The most prominent individual in bringing about this change in opinion was Mary Carpenter, who organised a reformatory movement based not on her experience of the prison system, but on her philanthropic interest in the education of destitute children. Through her Sunday School teaching amongst the poor she became aware of the extent of the problem, and, influenced by the industrial schools of Aberdeen, opened her own ragged school in 1846 in Lewin's Mead, Bristol. It was here that she first learned about the effects of incarceration on those of her pupils who had been in prison, which led her to study the subject of delinquency in greater depth.

Her approach was based on the belief that when children are 'treated with respect, with true Christian politeness ... they will give a ready response'.[65] This approach, she felt, could not be pursued in prisons, which demanded 'absolute submission'.[66] Consequently, she proposed reformatory schools as an alternative rather than an adjunct to prisons for convicted delinquents, and preventive industrial schools for destitute and beggar children, to which they should be sent by the magistrate, being fed and educated during the day but returning home at night in order to preserve the family connection she thought vital.

Her ideas made a great impact at the time. The influence of her books, and the publicity gained by the conferences she organised from 1851 onwards with her ally M.D. Hill, did much to bring the problem of delinquency to public attention. It was also as a result of the first conference that the Reformatory and Refuge Union was founded as a central body to promote the reformatory concept and as a means of contact between the schools.[67] The fact that 'Convicted children were assured of an education more than fifteen years before children whose crime was merely to be poor'[68] is to a considerable extent due to the initiative of Mary Carpenter.

Thus, the major debate with regard to the treatment of juvenile offenders was not whether they should be deterred or reformed, for the principle of reformatory education and industrial training was widely accepted inside and outside the prison system; rather, the arguments were about how to put this principle into practice. Whereas the Rev. John Clay, for example, said that the reformatory should be the last resort for those with whom gaol had failed, M.D. Hill argued precisely the opposite and considered that gaol should only be used where the reformatory had failed. There was agreement on reformatory methods but not on reformatory institutions. All agreed that a juvenile offender must be punished and reformed; but some thought the two tasks had to be undertaken in separate institutions while others thought they could be carried out simultaneously.

In 1854, those who favoured a period of imprisonment before a child was admitted to a reformatory carried the day. C.B. Adderley, who had moved for the appointment of a second Select Committee, introduced the bill which became law as the Youthful Offenders Act [17 & 18 Vict., c. 86]. Applying to both Scotland and England, the Act concerned all reformatory schools which had been established by voluntary contributions and certified by a government inspector appointed for the purpose. It gave magistrates the power to send any offender under the age of sixteen to one of those schools, with the consent of the managers, for a period of two to five years, following a prison sentence of at least fourteen days. The parent or guardian was to contribute up to five shillings a week, the rest being paid by the Treasury. By the time of the first inspector's report, 1858, there were forty certified schools in England, containing 1,609 boys and 257 girls, and seven in Scotland, containing 773 boys and girls.[69]

In spite of the previous imprisonment clause to which Mary Carpenter and her supporters objected, the official sanctioning of the reformatory and industrial school system marked a crucial change in emphasis: the Act was the first legislative step in a process which would eventually take the treatment of juvenile delinquency out of the penal system.

The wider context

The consideration of juvenile delinquents by the 1852–3 Select Committee alongside destitute children – rather than with criminal adults, as had been the case in 1847 – is indicative of the new assumption that the delinquent was a particular type of destitute child, rather than a particular type of criminal. As the problem of delinquent children began to merge with the wider one of poor children in general, so the agencies for treating young offenders became realigned with those for the relief of impoverished and vagrant children and the provision of education to those most in need of it. Hence, the development of schools for offenders inevitably overlaps with other agencies and institutions and there is a sense in which the 'new' approach to delinquency was not radically innovative: industrial training had long been part of the poor law system and the education of street urchins had been attempted by various charitable agencies such as ragged schools. It is here that the greatest divergences between English and Scottish practice can be found, and subsequent chapters will examine these in detail. The closing section of this chapter takes a more general look at aspects of poor relief and educational provision which relate to the treatment of delinquents.

The 1834 Poor Law Amendment Act had not been in operation for long before the Poor Law Commissioners recognised that one of its key principles – that 'children should follow their parents'[70] – required modification. The plight of children in workhouses was soon being depicted in terms comparable to that of delinquent children in prisons. Samuel Phillips Day's strictures on the workhouses sound very similar to his remarks on prisons:

> 'Children should not be permitted to inhale the pernicious atmosphere of the workhouse, and hold unreserved intercourse with the able-bodied pauper ... The stigma of being workhouse-bred is in itself a lasting reproach.'[71]

Others went further, and complained that such children were more likely to end up in prisons: the Fourth Annual Report of the Poor Law Commissioners asserted that

> a large proportion of [Criminals] have passed their infancy and youth in the workhouse, and can trace the formation of the habits which have led them to the commission of crime to the entire want of training in these institutions.[72]

Consequently, demands that pauper children should be dealt with outside workhouses paralleled the movement to remove the treatment of juveniles from prisons. Two Poor Law Inspectors, J.P. Kay and E. Carleton Tufnell, repeatedly proposed in their annual reports that groups of neighbouring unions should combine to set up district schools which could provide a better education, with trained teachers, separate from the workhouse. This was finally embodied in permissive legislation in 1844 and 1855, and its extension further urged by the Newcastle Commission on the Education of the Poor in 1861. Later, in the 1870s, the Scottish system of boarding children out was favoured, leading to the introduction of 'cottage homes' by men such as Dr. Barnardo.[73]

The educational emphasis in the poor law system and in the treatment of young offenders was an aspect of the growing belief in the efficacy of educating the poor in general. As the value of compulsory education was by no means universally accepted in England 150 years ago, its proponents had to justify it in terms of its advantages to society. From the 1800s to the 1860s the particular emphases altered according to the needs of the moment, but the same theme ran through them all: widespread education produced social stability. For example, at the time of the agitation for parliamentary reform in 1831, it was argued that

> It is not to be denied that a manufacturing population is particularly inflammable, and apt to be misled; and the only way to secure the labourers, as well as the other classes, from the ruinous consequences that are sure to arise from their supporting any unsound or impracticable principle, is to instruct them in their real interest.[74]

Again, in the aftermath of the 1848 revolution in Europe, education for the poor was recommended because 'The insurrections and slaughters which have deluged with blood almost every great city in Europe, have formed a fearful comment on the mistakes and neglects of governments'.[75]

In the 1850s, in keeping with the mood of the Great Exhibition of 1851, the benefits to industry of education were stressed, while the extension of the franchise to the working classes in 1867 further stimulated demands for education, as in Robert Lowe's well-known comment that 'we must educate our masters'.

Just as the education of young offenders was urged by virtue of its benefits to society, so, too, universal schooling was proposed in terms of its social gains. It is here that the two movements connect, for one of the social benefits most frequently put forward in favour of universal education was its supposed efficacy in preventing crime. If reformatory schools stopped juvenile criminals from becoming adult criminals, then national schools would surely stop children from becoming juvenile criminals. National education was the reformatory system taken a step further back. The almost inevitable progression from reformatory to general education was perceived by one contemporary commentator:

> in taking up the subject of juvenile delinquency as we are now doing, in my humble opinion, we are taking too narrow, too limited a view of a portion of a very large subject ... The Reformatory Schools will no doubt work well, and effect a great deal of good; but ... if a national and universal system of education were adopted, the Reformatory Schools, as such would not be required...[76]

In this way, concern with juvenile crime led to support for the education of potential as well as actual delinquents, and it is not surprising that, almost without exception, those who promoted the establishment of reformatory schools also believed that in the long run the only real solution would be the provision of educational facilities for all. The 1851 conference organised by M.D. Hill and Mary Carpenter resolved that 'in all cases prevention was better than cure'. The idea was perhaps most graphically expressed by a correspondent of the Howard Association for Penal Reform, who advised the authorities: 'rail your precipices at the *top*, and don't content yourself with providing ambulances for the poor mangled remains at the bottom.'[77]

Education was held to be the 'rail' which would prevent children falling into the abyss of crime. As Jo Manton puts it in her biography of Mary Carpenter, 'for every Victorian ill there was a Victorian panacea'.[78] E.E. Antrobus states that out of 1481 boys and 194 girls under the age of seventeen committed to Westminster Prison in 1851, 728 of the boys and 152 of the girls could neither read nor write.[79] As R.M. Rolfe told the 1847 Committee, 'The Union of a total Want of Instruction with criminal Conduct is too general to be merely accidental...'.[80]

If ignorance caused crime, the obverse side of the coin was that the removal of ignorance would diminish crime. To many contemporaries the matter was perfectly simple: ignorance and crime were directly linked as cause and effect, and schooling and lack of crime would be also. As Victor Hugo said, he who opens a school closes a prison.

The Prison Inspector Frederic Hill, in his book on crime, claimed that literacy in itself was a safeguard against crime:

> To what an extent the simple power of reading fluently is often a protection from habits of crime, may be judged of from the fact that a home missionary in Edinburgh, in whom I had full confidence ... told me that in all his visits

to the poor he never met with a single person who was at the same time addicted to crime and in the habit of reading.[81]

However, not everyone involved in the treatment of delinquents viewed this type of education as a panacea. Many supporters of education as a preventive of crime stressed that it was a particular kind of education that was required. The Rev. J. Kingsmill, for instance, believed that an education which did not go beyond imparting literacy would be harmful, since 'increased intellectual power implies no change whatever of character; and if it stand alone, only qualifies for a higher degree of villainy'.[82] Education of this sort, wrote one judge in a reply to a questionnaire circulated by the 1847 Select Committee, 'will alter the Nature of Crimes more than the relative Number of Criminals.'[83] Even Mary Carpenter was aware of the limitations of a merely intellectual schooling for the class of children most likely to fall into crime. Addressing a conference on education held in London in 1857, she said that 'moral and religious training, the inculcation of virtuous habits, and a love of labour' were the necessities. 'To these, intellectual instruction may indeed be subsidiary, but it is the means, not the end.'[84]

Where, then, should such children be educated? Much had been done by the charitably run ragged schools. These were an offshoot of the late-eighteenth-century Sunday School movement and the first is usually attributed to John Pounds (1766–1839), a shoemaker from Portsmouth who began a small school for ragged children, teaching them reading, writing and arithmetic and giving them industrial training in the form of cooking for girls and shoemaking for boys. The subsequent development of such voluntary schools in England owed much to the influence of Scottish pioneers like Sheriff Watson of Aberdeen and Dr. Guthrie of Edinburgh. In 1844 the Ragged School Union was formed by William Locke, and by 1852 there were one hundred schools with 13,000 pupils. These were not residential, but provided meals and the rudiments of education, together with religious and industrial training.

Mary Carpenter approved of these schools in principle: the voluntary services of the middle classes in them had made them aware of the plight of the destitute. She noted, however, that the ragged schools were open to certain abuses, such as lack of discipline. What she envisaged was a system of industrial schools, without the drawbacks of the voluntary ragged schools – she wished to see legislative and financial backing and trained teachers, providing an education basically similar to the kind being provided for delinquents in the reformatories. Thus one is led to a final connection between the education of young offenders and poor children. In England legislation for reformatory schools preceded legislation for industrial schools by three years, and it began to be asked: why should a child have to 'qualify' for such an education by committing a crime? The difficulty had been anticipated in 1847 by the Lord Chief Justice, Lord Denman (1779–1854). He agreed that it was necessary to inculcate the principles of religion and morality, but added: 'I greatly dread the Effect of giving [delinquents] Benefits and Privileges which they never could have hoped for but from the Commission of Crimes.'[85]

This commonly voiced criticism was perhaps most effectively refuted by

Jelinger C. Symons, one of the Inspectors of Union workhouse schools. If it did turn out that delinquents were being treated more advantageously than other children,

> ... it would be through the defects in other schools, and defects in the education of the poor; and supposing that to result, it would perhaps apply a very useful stimulus to our national and general efforts for the improvement of the education of the poor at large, so that no such superiority in the penal school education should continue.[86]

As later chapters will demonstrate, this difficulty did not occur in the same form in Scotland, as preventive industrial schools were set up and given legislative sanction in 1854, three years before similar provision was extended to England. It was the opinion of the inspector, Rev. Sydney Turner (1814–1879), that through the expansion of industrial schools which aimed at prevention rather than cure, 'ere long many of our reformatories [might be] almost dispensed with'.[87] Subsequent developments went some way to satisfy his wish. In 1865 there were sixty-five reformatories and fifty industrial schools in Britain; in 1875 there were over 15,000 children industrial schools, whereas the number in reformatories remained static at around 5–6,000.[88] With more children being dealt with before they became offenders, fewer reformatories were required, a process continued by the Education Act of 1870 which widened further the role of education in preventing delinquency by providing elementary schooling for all. When, in 1870, the industrial schools – which dealt with the bulk of juvenile delinquency – were transferred from the Home Office to the control of the newly instituted School Boards, the treatment of minor juvenile offences well-nigh ceased to be a penal matter.

Although it was not until the 1870s that the treatment of minor juvenile transgressions became integrated with the educational system, theorists had already envisaged, twenty years earlier, the possibility of preventing delinquency not just through education but through a co-ordinated attack on the social deprivation which was seen as its major cause. This was but one instance of what is generally known as the Benthamite belief that the material conditions of the poor determined their moral state. Mr. Sergeant Gaselee, a witness to the 1857 Select Committee, believed that

> much may be expected from a general System of Education; but unless coupled with great Improvements in our whole social System, and a more uniform Regard to the spiritual and temporal Wants of the great Body of the Population, I do not anticipate any great Prevention of the Prevalence of Crimes.[89]

Joseph Kingsmill's aphorism sums up the conviction that an improved environment would lead to less crime and more social stability: 'Sanatory reform is moral reform.'[90]

In the 1970s A.P. Donajgrodzki argued in *Social Control in Nineteenth Century*

Britain that 'social order is the produce not only of law, but of a much wider set of phenomena'.[91] In this sense, 'Teachers, clergymen, poor law officials and distributors of charity were to some extent policemen'.[92] As will be clear from the foregoing discussion, the concept of social control is particularly applicable to the treatment of juvenile delinquency in view of the complex inter-relationship between its causes and treatment. Even in 1845, Frederic Hill was drawing attention to the many causes of crime

> which are beyond the reach of prison discipline, such as the want of a better education, the want [in Scotland] of a better poor law, and the causes which produce the present frequent and violent changes in trade and commerce.[93]

While few would question the theory today, in practice joined-up thinking in social service provision remains as difficult to achieve as ever.

Thus, the history of the treatment of juvenile delinquency in the nineteenth century is the history of the widening context in which it came to be viewed. From being a legal and penal concern it evolved into a question of social welfare, and the emphasis moved quickly from reformation to prevention. While the reformatory movement of the 1850s had grown out of the recognition of juvenile crime as a problem separate from adult crime, by the 1870s the treatment of delinquency was becoming absorbed in the general question of educating the poor. Instead of being schooled in a prison as he might have been in the 1840s, the juvenile delinquent of the next generation found himself imprisoned in a school.

Notes

1. *Autobiography of Thomas Guthrie, D.D., and Memoir by his sons*, Rev. David K. Guthrie and Charles J. Guthrie, M.A. (London, 1877), p. 460.
2. Ibid.
3. The term 'juvenile delinquency' as used in the present volume refers to the commission of minor crimes, usually petty thefts, in urban areas by boys and girls under the age of sixteen, although some statistical sources are referred to which make the division between juveniles and adults at the age of seventeen.
4. E.g. Joseph Adshead, *On Juvenile Criminals, Reformatories, and the Means of Rendering the Perishing and Dangerous Classes serviceable to the State* (Manchester, 1856), p. 9; Thomas Beggs, *Juvenile Delinquency and Reformatory Institutions* (London, 1857), p. 5.
5. Joseph Kay, *The Condition and Education of Poor Children in English and in German Towns* (London, 1853), p. 12.
6. *Glasgow Herald*, 19 February 1838.
7. H.M. Clokie and J.W. Robinson, *Royal Commissions of Inquiry* (Stanford, 1937), p. 113.
8. Second Report from the Select Committee of the House of Lords appointed to inquire into the Execution of the Criminal Law, especially respecting Juvenile Offenders and Transportation (PP 1847 VII 534); Report from the Select Committee on Criminal and Destitute Juveniles (PP 1852 VII 515); Report from the Select Committee on Criminal and Destitute Children (PP 1852-3 XXIII 674). In footnotes, these will be referred to hereafter as SC 1847, SC 1852 and SC 1852-3 respectively.
9. SC 1847, para. 1774.
10. Second Report of the Inspectors of Prisons of Great Britain, II Northern and Eastern District, 1837, p. 85-6.

11 C. F. Cornwallis, *The Philosophy of Ragged Schools* (Small Books on Great Subjects, No. XVIII, London, 1851), pp. 30–32.
12 A theatre in Liverpool. R.J. Broadbent, in *Annals of the Liverpool Stage* (New York and London, 1908), p. 216, states that 'The patrons of this theatre were drawn from the poorest classes, yet so prosperous was the house that the number of copper coins taken at the door … was truly prodigious'.
13 Sixth Report of the Inspectors of Prisons of Great Britain, II Northern and Eastern District, 1841, p. 125.
14 SC 1847, para. 101.
15 John Macgregor, *Shoe Blacks and Broomers* (London, 1853), p. 10.
16 SC 1852-53, para. 579.
17 Eleventh Report of the Inspector of Prisons of Great Britain, IV Scotland, Northumberland, and Durham, 1846, p. 3.
18 Beggs, op. cit., p. 32.
19 SC 1847, para. 2100.
20 Eleventh Report of the Inspector of Prisons of Great Britain, IV Scotland, Northumberland, and Durham, 1846, p. 29.
21 Eighth Report of the Inspector of Prisons of Great Britain, IV Scotland, Northumberland, and Durham, 1843, p. 23.
22 Thomas Plint, *Crime in England* (London, 1851), p. 153.
23 Beggs, op. cit., p. 6.
24 SC 1847, p. 36.
25 Arthur Koestler, *Reflections on Hanging* (London, 1956), p. 22.
26 B.E.F. Knell, 'Capital Punishment: Its Administration in Relation to Juvenile Offenders in the Nineteenth Century and its Possible Administration in the Eighteenth', *British Journal of Criminology* V (1965), pp. 198–207.
27 Ibid., p. 202.
28 Jeannie Duckworth, *Fagin's Children: Criminal Children in Victorian England* (London, 2002), p. 41.
29 Mary Carpenter, *Reformatory Schools for the Children of the Perishing and Dangerous Classes, and for Juvenile Offenders* (London, 1851), p. 286.
30 For example, in 1836 84.7 per cent of prosecutions at the Staffordshire and Worcestershire Quarter Sessions were brought by the victim or his employee: David Philips, *Crime and Authority in Victorian England* (London, 1977), p. 101.
31 Op. cit., p. 118.
32 Leon Radzinowicz, *A History of English Criminal Law and Its Administration from 1750*, Vol. I (London, 1948), p. 597.
33 S.P. Day, *Juvenile Crime; Its Causes, Character, and Cure* (London, 1858), p. 18.
34 SC 1847, para. 2926.
35 E. E. Antrobus, *The Prison and the School* (London, 1853), p. 49.
36 SC 1852, para. 198.
37 Ibid.
38 SC 1852-3, para. 895.
39 Quoted in F. Hill, *Crime, Its Amount, Causes, and Remedies* (London, 1853), p. 157.
40 SC 1852-3, para. 1429.
41 SC 1847, para. 2705.
42 Day, op. cit., p. 263.
43 SC 1847, para. 3680.
44 SC 1847, para. 3760.
45 SC 1852, para. 1618.
46 SC 1852, para. 1900.
47 There had been numerous attempts to bring about this reform in England over the previous twenty-five years. Limited summary jurisdiction was available under the terms of some local statutes, such as at Liverpool. See evidence of E. Rushton, Stipendiary

Magistrate, SC 1847, para. 1549 ff.
48 M. May, 'Innocence and Experience: The Evolution of the Concept of Juvenile Delinquency in the mid-Nineteenth Century', *Victorian Studies,* XVII (September 1973), p. 14.
49 SC 1852, para. 1114.
50 See Michael Ignatieff, *A Just Measure of Pain* (London, 1978), a study of the development of penitentiaries in the 1750–1850 period.
51 SC 1847, p. 3. Of the thirty-six witnesses questioned on juvenile delinquency, thirteen were magistrates, recorders or other members of the legal profession; seven were prison chaplains; eight were prison governors; and three were prison inspectors.
52 Third Report of the General Board of Directors of Prisons in Scotland, PP 1842 XXII (371), p. 6.
53 M.D. Hill, *Suggestions for the Repression of Crime* (London, 1857), p. 337.
54 Ivy Pinchbeck and Margaret Hewitt, *Children in English Society* Vol. II (London, 1973), p. 433.
55 Radzinowicz, op. cit., p. 534.
56 An Account of the Philanthropic Society, Instituted September 1788 [Bodleian Library, Oxford].
57 Rev. W.L. Clay, *The Prison Chaplain: a Memoir of the Rev. John Clay, B.D.* (London, 1861), p. 371.
58 Quoted in J. Carlebach, *Caring for Children in Trouble* (London, 1970), p. 26.
59 Ibid., p. 26.
60 SC 1847, para. 2191.
61 SC 1847, p. 6.
62 SC 1852-3, p. iii.
63 For details of these early institutions, see Pinchbeck and Hewitt, op. cit., Chapter XVI.
64 Joseph Kingsmill, *Chapters on Prisons and Prisoners* (London, 1857), p. 422.
65 Carpenter, op. cit., p. 83.
66 SC 1852, para. 862.
67 See Pinchbeck and Hewitt, op. cit., p. 479 ff.
68 Jo Manton, *Mary Carpenter and the Children of the Streets* (London, 1976), p. 123.
69 First Report, Reformatory and Industrial Schools, PP 1857-8, XXIX (2426), pp. 5 and 40–41. Hereafter, these reports will be referred to in footnotes by the abbreviation RIS.
70 That is, children should be treated in the same way as adults (Pinchbeck and Hewitt, op. cit., p. 500).
71 Day, op. cit., p. 235.
72 Quoted by Pinchbeck and Hewitt, op. cit., p. 501.
73 See Lynn Abrams, *The Orphan Country* (Edinburgh, 1998).
74 *Quarterly Journal of Education,* I (1831), p. 214.
75 Cornwallis, op. cit., p. 104.
76 Quoted in W. Knighton, *Training in Streets and Schools* (London, 1855), pp. 71–72.
77 The Howard Association Annual Report, October 1880, p. 10.
78 Manton, op. cit., p. 182.
79 Antrobus, op. cit., p. 14.
80 SC 1847, Appendix, p. 56.
81 Frederic Hill, *Crime: Its Amount, Causes, and Remedies* (London, 1853), p. 40. Frederic Hill, who lived between 1803 and 1896, was the brother of Matthew and of Rowland of Penny Post fame.
82 Rev. Joseph Kingsmill, *On the Present Aspect of Serious Crime in England, and the Means used for its Punishment and Repression by Government* (London, N.D.), p. 24.
83 Evidence of W. Erle, SC 1847, Appendix, p. 15.
84 Mary Carpenter, 'Juvenile Delinquency, in its Relation to the Educational Movement', in Alfred Hill (ed.), *Essays upon Educational Subjects Read at the Educational Conference of June 1857* (London, 1857), p. 329.

85 SC 1847, Appendix, p. 3.
86 SC 1852, para. 2481.
87 Third report, RIS, PP 1860 XXXV (2688), p. 19.
88 Gordon Rose, *Schools for Young Offenders* (London, 1967), p. 7.
89 SC 1847, Appendix, p. 39.
90 Joseph Kingsmill, *Chapters on Prisons and Prisoners* (London, 1852), p. 429.
91 A. P. Donajgrodzki (ed.), Social *Control in Nineteenth Century Britain* (London, 1977), p. 10.
92 Ibid., p. 54.
93 Tenth Report of the Inspector of Prisons of Great Britain, IV Scotland, Northumberland, and Durham, 1845, p. vii.

2 'The lamentable extent of youthful depravity'
The Tron Riot of 1812

The 1840s and 1850s were the key decades in which juvenile delinquency began to be seen as a separate phenomenon and new approaches to the problem emerged. But there was nothing new about the commission of crimes by juveniles. The issue erupted in a particularly dramatic way in Edinburgh in the Tron Riot of 1812,[1] and this provides a convenient starting point for an examination of developing attitudes to juvenile crime in nineteenth century Scotland. The authorities' reaction to the event could be interpreted as a final attempt to respond in terms of repression and punishment, paving the way for the transformation in approach that was to emerge soon afterwards.

Sir Walter Scott famously observed that in Scotland

> Each age has deemed the new-born year
> The fittest time for festal cheer.[2]

In Edinburgh, the nineteenth-century equivalent of today's Hogmanay street party used to take place around the clock tower of the Tron Church in High Street, at the junction of the North and South bridges. There was a good deal of celebration and frivolity among the crowds welcoming in the New Year, particularly among the young. Generally this amounted to no more than 'harmless but noisy mirth'. However, on the last day of 1811, gangs of 'young thieves, pickpockets and idle apprentice boys' used the festivities as an opportunity to surround and rob the more prosperous-looking members of the crowd.[3]

It was a cleverly planned operation. As a preliminary, the watchmen on duty were driven from their positions, and one officer was murdered. Such outrages, declared the Town Council the next morning, were 'hitherto unexampled' in Edinburgh.[4] So, too, were the ways in which the authorities and inhabitants reacted. The ringleaders were punished with great severity and the alarm that spread among the citizens can be judged from the flood of pamphlets that appeared in the wake of the riot. As a result, the police force was strengthened and its administration put on a new footing.

Before 1760 it was possible to walk from one end of Edinburgh to the other in ten minutes. The entire population, rich and poor alike, was crammed into the area between the Castle and Holyrood Abbey. In 1767, however, the city's boundaries

Figure 2.1 New Year's Eve at the Tron Church

Source: *Cassell's Old and New Edinburgh,* Volume 2, London, Paris and New York, N.D. The spire shown in the picture was erected in 1828

were extended and the construction of the elegant Georgian New Town commenced. The wealthier inhabitants thus abandoned to the lower classes the labyrinth of lanes and wynds which surrounded Scotland's historic political, legal and ecclesiastical buildings. The New Town grew in size and style; the Old Town grew only in population. In the nineteenth century a minister of the Tron Church, Rev. Dr. James MacGregor, described his overcrowded parish as a dense block of buildings intersected by lanes so narrow that the tall houses almost touched each other, leaving a mere chink through which the heavens were seen. It would have been difficult to find anywhere an equal amount of filth, ignorance and crime within an area equally small.[5]

It was in these streets that a group of boys known as the 'Keellie Gang' frequented the tenement closes, picking fights and intimidating the residents until they gave them money or whisky. John Kidd, an inmate of the Tolbooth Prison, who presumably lived in the vicinity, testified at the trial of three members of the gang that for weeks before the riot they had been evolving a plan – in conjunction with gangs from the Canongate and Grassmarket areas – to 'give the police a licking' and to rob the New Year's Eve crowd.[6]

On Hogmanay it was the custom of the wealthier classes from the New Town to return to the Old Town across the North Bridge to welcome in the New Year. Although religious festivities like Christmas were shunned as smacking of Popery, the supposedly Calvinist people of Scotland nevertheless vented their spirits in the celebration of the New Year. Under the influence of drink and the generally festive atmosphere, social distinctions were forgotten as everyone joined to welcome in the New Year. 'To such an extent did this custom prevail in Edinburgh … that the principal streets were more thronged between twelve and one in the morning than they usually were at midday', says *Chambers' Book of Days*.[7] Immediately after midnight on 1 January 1812, the 'first footing' began: the crowds dispersed to visit and take gifts to their friends for the first time in the New Year. There was consequently no shortage of victims on the streets for the gangs. From about 11 p.m. on 31 December, the members of the Keellie Gang armed themselves with wooden sticks, hid in closes and, at pre-arranged signals, pounced on passers-by, surrounding them and threatening them until they gave up their valuables.

Each victim had a similar experience to relate. George Edmondstone, a clerk in the office of the *Edinburgh Evening Courant* newspaper, was passing Fleshmarket Close in the High Street at about 11.30 p.m. when a number of youths attacked him with sticks and attempted to steal his watch. William Jolly, a divinity student, was surrounded by two or three dozen boys on the South Bridge between twelve and one, and had his purse stolen. John Buchan Brodie was knocked down by a group of youths at Milne's Square on the North Bridge. In spite of his cries for the police, he was held down and his pockets were rifled. The most serious incident, however, took place when one of the watchmen on duty, Dugald Campbell – notorious for being hard on young offenders – was chased by a mob near the Stamp Office Close. He was felled by the blows of sticks and left dying while the mob headed in the direction of the crowd at the Tron Church.

A number of youths were arrested on the spot during the night, and the authorities lost no time in making known their intention to 'follow up the inquiry in the most rigorous manner'.[8] On 3 January a notice appeared in the newspapers, offering a reward of 100 guineas [about £7,581 in today's values] for information leading to the arrest of the principal offenders. Another 100-guinea reward was offered the next day, following the announcement that Dugald Campbell had died of his wounds. By 15 January three of those involved had been named, and a further fifty guineas was offered for the arrest of James Johnstone (who was never caught), George Napier and Alexander Macdonald. The leaders had all been apprehended by the 27th: John Skelton, an apprentice gunsmith; Hugh Macdonald, aged eighteen, a shoemaker; Neil Sutherland, aged eighteen, an apprentice painter; and Hugh McIntosh, aged sixteen, a journeyman shoemaker. The latter two had been discovered in Glasgow, where they had fled with two trunks containing stolen goods, and a notice appeared in the press advising those who had been robbed of watches to enquire at the Council Chambers, where much of the stolen property had been assembled. What was particularly worrying, though, was the extent of the ringleaders' influence on the younger generation. A total of sixty-eight arrests were made, mostly of young males between the ages of twelve and twenty.

The trials that followed demonstrated the determination of the magistrates and Town Council to make an example of those who had engineered the riot. For instance, on 5 and 6 March John Skelton was tried at the High Court of Justiciary, found guilty of attempting to rob three people of their watches and sentenced to death as a result, although it was admitted that the evidence was circumstantial. Several witnesses claimed to have seen him in the vicinity of some of the attacks, but none was able to implicate him directly. Thomas McGibbon, a painter, remembered seeing him at the corner of the North Bridge, but could only say that 'he appeared concerned in the riots'. Walter Alexander, an apprentice shoemaker, 'did not see Skelton in the riots, although, he thinks, he heard his name called in the High Street … between twelve and one o'clock'. Walter Robertson, a stoneware merchant, was walking down High Street when he was stopped and held up against a wall, where he was robbed of his watch and wallet containing over £34. He thought there were between forty and fifty boys in the mob, 'headed by three rather taller than the rest, of a size with the prisoner, but he could not recognise any of them'. Again, the opinions of the witnesses differed as to whether or not Skelton was armed with a stick. He was apprehended by a policeman and taken to the police office, where he was found to have a number of stolen items in his possession. He claimed, however, to have picked them up from the street, having seen them being dropped by a boy who was being pursued. It was admitted that 'in general the prisoner's declarations were remarkably clear and candid as to the proceedings of the rioters', and Mr. James Gordon was able to put forward a convincing defence: Skelton, he said, had not been proved to have been present at any of the robberies. Moreover,

> although the articles mentioned in the indictment had been found upon him, yet he had accounted for his possession of them in a possible, nay, probable, was, and that, so long as that possibility, or probability, of innocence did exist, he contended, it was their duty to lean to the side of mercy.[9]

Evidence of Skelton's good character was then presented. For the past three years he had been apprenticed to a Mr. James Innes, who testified to his integrity, while a fellow apprentice, Harry Gray, related how, when collecting accounts for his employers, Skelton had been given a £5 note instead of £1 by a customer. When he discovered the error, he returned the note to the owner and was given a shilling reward, which he shared with the witness.

Nevertheless, the Solicitor-General, David Monypenny, argued in his address to the jury that there was sufficient evidence to convict Skelton:

> In reviewing the proof, he admitted that there was no direct evidence that the prisoner did assault or knock down any person; that it was not necessary, nor at all times possible, in transactions of this nature to procure such proof; but that he was guilty, actor, or art and part,[10] in the robberies and outrages of that night, was established by a train of circumstances beyond the possibility of doubt.[11]

The jury was unanimous in finding him guilty and he was sentenced to death by the Lord Justice Clerk David Boyle, although, in view of his former good character, this was commuted to transportation for life.

The other ringleaders were not so fortunate. Macdonald, Sutherland and McIntosh were found guilty of having planned the riot, and of carrying out a total of ten attacks; in addition, McIntosh, the youngest of the three, was charged with involvement in the murder of Dugald Campbell. All three were hanged on 22 April. The handling of their trial illustrates some of the attitudes to the causes of juvenile delinquency which were current at the time, and demonstrates how their case was exploited for the purpose of deterring potential young offenders.

Although all three pleaded not guilty, there were convincing testimonies to their involvement in the ten robberies in the area of the North and South Bridges and of their theft of gold watches, seals, penknives, purses and money. One James Black witnessed McIntosh hitting Campbell with a stick, and saw Macdonald kick him as they left him lying on the street, saying 'he's well out of the way'. James Burges, who was out for two or three hours that night, saw McIntosh several times in the vicinity, 'knocking down gentlemen'. Other witnesses saw the three offenders at different times during the night, setting upon and robbing passers-by who were making first-foot visits to their friends.

Throughout these trials the objective of the authorities was simple and clear-cut: to deter others by making an example of the riot's ringleaders. This can be seen from the way in which some of the minor offenders were treated. At the trial of Robert Gunn and Alex Macdonald, who pleaded guilty to the six robberies with which they were charged, the Solicitor-General described the prisoners as 'not the leaders, but the led, in the late disgraceful outrages', and 'as he trusted enough had been done on the way of example', he sentenced them to transportation for life.[12] Similarly, George Napier and John Grotto, who each pleaded guilty to one robbery, were sentenced to fourteen years' transportation.

The dramatic spectacle of the hanging was designed to impress further upon the youth of Edinburgh the fate that awaited the delinquent. A contemporary report emphasised that 'The execution of these young men being intended as a dreadful example, to be remembered for years to come, everything was studiously contrived to impart, if possible, additional solemnity to a scene in itself sufficiently awful'.[13]

The gibbet was erected opposite the Stamp Office Close, where Dugald Campbell had been murdered. Four hundred of the Perthshire militia lined the route from the Tolbooth Prison to the scene of the execution. The streets, windows and even roofs were crowded with spectators. The procession left the prison at 2.40 p.m., each of the boys reading their Bibles on the way. After three-quarters of an hour of devotions, they were hanged at 3.30 p.m. The bodies remained on the gibbet until 9 p.m., when Sutherland and Macdonald were taken for burial in Greyfriars churchyard, while the body of McIntosh, as a final humiliation, was taken for anatomical dissection – a severe sentence for one so young. It is a measure of how heinous McIntosh's offence was deemed to be that he shared this fate with William Hare, the infamous murderer who, fifteen years later, was himself dissected after he had delivered the bodies of perhaps as many as thirty victims to Dr. Knox for that very purpose.

It was common at the time for the visual impact of an execution to be reinforced by the printed word. For example, in the account of a hanging at Dorchester in Thomas Hardy's short story, 'The Withered Arm', a newsvendor is already hawking copies of the hanged man's 'last dying speech and confession' while the crowds are still gathered at the gallows. Similarly, in Edinburgh in 1812 the Rev. William Innes (1770–1855), a Baptist minister who had visited the three condemned in prison, published a rather romanticised account of their lives under the title of *Notes of Conversations with Hugh Macdonald, Neil Sutherland and Hugh McIntosh,* in which he spelt out the moral lessons to be drawn from the episode, attributing the boys' downfall to idleness, bad company and Sabbath-breaking.[14] In addition, the ministers who had attended the boys at their execution, the Revs. Thomas Fleming, John Campbell and Andrew Thomson, issued their 'Narrative of some Interesting Particulars' concerning the case. This account was written to show how the youths had been converted before they were executed, and was designed to provide an example to others of their class.

> They expressed thankfulness to God for having arrested them in the career of iniquity; and they considered the awful situation into which they were brought, as having been blessed for the good of their precious souls. As their minds opened to the reception of evangelical truth, they imbibed it with avidity, and yielded to its influence.[15]

If we are to believe the narratives, the children, like the judges who condemned them, saw themselves as providing an example to warn others: at the scene of the execution Macdonald is credited with saying that 'in this great multitude there are many wicked people; O that our fate may be blessed for bringing them to repentance and glory!'[16]

The Tron Riot was inevitably followed by considerable debate about the issues raised by the event, and discussion of steps that should be taken to prevent a recurrence. An anonymous pamphlet entitled 'An Appeal to the Public ... arising from Recent Alarming Events' argued that making an example of the chief offenders would only be partially effective. It might occasionally prevent the commission of crimes from a mere fortuitous recollection, but while the root of the evil remains, whether in the distribution of justice, or in the inclination of offenders, it will shoot in every direction, where not restrained by legal power.[17]

As yet, the solution was not seen in terms of a different method of dealing with young offenders or, indeed, in a re-examination of the factors which made them offend in the first place. The immediate consequence was a demand for a strengthening of the local police force. The authorities themselves had not been slow to realise this, for the day after the riot a meeting of the Lord Provost and magistrates passed two important resolutions: first, that the present system of police was totally inadequate; second, that a new bill containing 'a powerful system of police' should be brought into Parliament without delay.

Even this was not sufficient for some. A pamphlet by 'a member of one of the City Corporations', entitled 'An Address to the Inhabitants of Edinburgh, on the Necessity of Immediately following up the Measure recommended by the Magistrates, for the Purpose of forming an interim additional System of Police', argued that the situation in Edinburgh was so bad that people were frightened to go out at night. The writer proposed that, while the police system was in the process of revision, 'it was the duty of every man, without exception from 18 to 56, to offer his personal service in patrolling the streets'.[18]

The Edinburgh Police Act of 1812 was therefore a direct outcome of the Tron Riot. One weakness of the old system had been the number of separate police establishments, each having its own officers acting independently of the rest. A second was the cumbersome administrative system, under which lighting, cleansing and watching were the responsibility of different bodies. These anomalies were ironed out by the 1812 Act: the Sheriff was put in charge of the police system, so that all offences committed outside the city boundaries were dealt with by him alone, while the magistrates handled those within the city. All police functions, previously under the control of the old and corrupt, self-perpetuating Town Council, were transferred to a single Board of Commissioners; the inefficient City Guard was reduced, and power to employ watchmen was given to a new board, a fund being set aside to reward particularly diligent officers, in order that the streets might be more efficiently policed.[19]

The Tron Riot, then, revealed to the civil authorities that its police system had failed to maintain law and order. But it also demonstrated to the ecclesiastical authorities that their attempts to spread Christian education and improve public morality were inadequate. Some members of the community now argued that less energy should be devoted to catching young delinquents and more to preventing children becoming delinquents in the first place. For instance, the author of a pamphlet called *A Blow at the Root!* argued, as his title suggests, that reforming the police force would not reach the source of criminal activity. His pamphlet took the form of a series of searching questions: did the clergy pay sufficient attention to visiting their parishioners? Did they teach the catechism to the young? Was drink too readily available? Were licences to sell it granted indiscriminately? Were the upper classes setting an example to the lower?[20]

Although as recently as 1800 the institution of Sunday Schools had been opposed as potentially radical by members of the anti-Evangelical Moderate party[21] within the Church of Scotland, in 1812 the established clergy were quick to realise the seriousness of the moral condition of the populace and looked to Sunday Schools as a means of remedying the situation. A Committee was appointed, one of its members being the Rev. Dr. Fleming who had attended the three youths at their hanging. It was proposed to establish Sabbath Schools in every parish, but once their work got underway it was hampered by many children's inability to read. In spite of Scotland's proud tradition of parochial education, illiteracy was widespread in the burghs, and the country was fast becoming what the Rev. George Lewis in 1834 called 'a half-educated nation'.[22] In April 1813, therefore, a day school was opened as an auxiliary to the Sunday Schools – the Edinburgh Sessional School, so called because the governing body of each congregation, the Kirk Session, was allowed to send five of its Sunday School children there free of charge, and a further ten at a fee of sixpence per month. By 1828 over 500 children were attending.

Like the 1812 Police Act, then, the Sessional School was a response to the problem of juvenile crime dramatically highlighted by the Tron Riot. As the history of the school written by the Headmaster, John Wood, points out, it was because the Tron Riot had 'disclosed the lamentable extent of youthful depravity' in the city that the clergy had taken steps to provide for 'the Education, and particularly the Religious Education of the poor'.[23] With its avowed intention of diminishing juvenile delinquency, in some ways the school anticipated the direction the treatment of young offenders was to take in the following decades with the development of reformatory and industrial schools.

In 1812, however, all this lay in the future. While the Tron Riot marked a turning point in the recognition of the extent of the juvenile problem, it did not lead to a revolutionary new approach. Even the opening of the Sessional School could be interpreted as being more in the tradition of seventeenth-century Scottish parochial education than a forerunner of mid-nineteenth century industrial schools. The aim was to provide religious and moral instruction rather than to counteract social disadvantages by offering meals and industrial training.

Similarly, there was as yet no move towards viewing children as belonging to a separate category from adult offenders. No allowance was made for the youth of the culprits and the traditional view of the age of responsibility under the law was upheld. David Hume, in his *Commentaries on the Law of Scotland Respecting Crimes*, summed up the principle as follows: children over the age of seven were liable to punishment as criminals, and 'in fixing the measure of punishment to be inflicted on a pupil, the Court are not, and cannot be confined to dispense it, according to years and days'.[24]

The perpetrators of the Tron Riot, far from being seen as victims of social circumstances, were portrayed by the authorities as hardened criminals. It was considered of paramount importance to make an example of the ringleaders in order to deter others. One of the High Court judges, Lord Gillies, summed up the prevailing attitude:

The awful warning which had been given by these trials, where four had been condemned to be hanged, two transported for life, and two for fourteen years, would not be lost on the youth of this city, but be the means of making them abhor such conduct as had been recently perpetrated here.[25]

In a recent re-examination of the significance of the riot in relation to previous outbursts of mob violence, W.W. Knox has described the approach adopted by the authorities as a 'discourse of otherness' which portrayed the culprits as alien, wicked and therefore 'disconnected from the communities in which they were raised and lived'.[26] The ringleaders were executed, he argues, 'in order to lodge a lasting and powerful image in the collective psyche of the might and power of the state and of the dangers inherent in challenging it'.[27]

Thus, while the Tron Riot revealed that existing agencies for dealing with crime were deficient, the event was followed by the reinforcement of old methods, rather than their replacement by new ones. In many ways the popular interest in the trial and executions had more in common with the curiosity created by the Burke and Hare murders in 1828 than with the public sympathy for destitute children that social reformers like Guthrie were to arouse so successfully in the 1840s. At the same time, the events of New Year's Eve 1811 dramatically demonstrated the existence of a social malaise that was to preoccupy the authorities for many decades thereafter. As Knox concludes, 'The dangerous classes were born and bourgeois society could not afford to look the other way'.[28]

Notes

1. This chapter is based on my article on the Tron Riot published in *History Today*, May 1980, Vol. 30, No. 5, pp. 41–45. The material has been included by kind permission of the publisher, Andy Patterson (www.historytoday.com).
2. Sir Walter Scott, *Marmion*, Introduction to Canto VI.
3. Unless otherwise stated, details of the Tron Riot in this chapter come from a pamphlet entitled *Substance of the Trials for Rioting in Edinburgh* (Leith, 1812). The full title reads 'Substance of the Trials of John Skelton, Neil Sutherland, Hugh MacDonald, Hugh Macintosh, George Napier, John Grotto, Robert Gunn, and Alex. Macdonald, alias White, before the High Court of Justiciary, for Committing Murder and Robbery, on the streets of Edinburgh, on the 31st December, 1811, and 1st January, 1812'.
4. *The Edinburgh Star*, 3 January 1812.
5. Rev. D. Butler, M.A., *The Tron Kirk of Edinburgh* (Edinburgh and London, 1906), p. 350.
6. *Substance of the Trials*, p. 33.
7. R. Chambers, *The Book of Days* (Two Volumes, London and Edinburgh, 1888), Vol. I, p. 29.
8. *The Edinburgh Star*, 3 January, 1812.
9. *Substance of the Trials*, p. 21.
10. That is, aiding or abetting the commission of a crime.
11. *Substance of the Trials*, p. 21.
12. *Edinburgh Annual Register for 1812* (Edinburgh, 1814), p. 52.
13. *The Scots Magazine*, Vol. 74, February 1812, p. 395.
14. Notes of Conversations with Hugh McDonald, Neil Sutherland, and Hugh McIntosh, who were executed at Edinburgh, on the 22nd of April 1812, by William Innes, Minister of the Gospel' (Third edition, Edinburgh, 1812).

15 'Narrative of some interesting particulars respecting Hugh McDonald, Neil Sutherland and Hugh McIntosh; who were executed at Edinburgh, on the 22nd April; with some Remarks by the Ministers who attended them' (Edinburgh, 1812), p. 5.
16 'Narrative of some interesting particulars', p. 7.
17 'An Appeal to the Public; comprehending General Observations on a Peculiar System of Policy existing in Public Opinion, and among Inferior Officers of the Public Peace in Large Cities; arising from Recent Alarming Events by a Friend to Order' (Edinburgh, 1812), p. 17.
18 'An Address to the Inhabitants of Edinburgh, on the Necessity of Immediately following up the Measure recommended by the Magistrates, for the Purpose of forming an interim additional System of Police' by a Member of one of the City Corporations (Edinburgh, 1812), p. 11.
19 For a detailed study of the development of policing in Edinburgh in this period, see John McGowan, *A New Civic Order: the Contribution of the City of Edinburgh Police, 1805–1812* (Musselburgh, 2013).
20 'A Blow at the Root! Being Queries relating to the Police of the City of Edinburgh: Addressed to the Citizens by a Fellow Citizen' (Edinburgh, 1812).
21 From the mid-eighteenth century onwards, the Church of Scotland was dominated by the Moderates. In *The Church of Scotland: a Short History* (Edinburgh, n.d.), Professor G.D. Henderson sums up the main characteristics of this party as follows: 'They loved the ancient classics and modern literature more than works on Dogma. They laid stress on Toleration and Broadmindedness rather than on Conviction. They were very much afraid of uncovering the soul or exposing religious feelings… Their sermons were said to be cold morality rather than warm gospel' (p. 115).
22 See Chapter 7, page 106.
23 John Wood, 'Account of the Edinburgh Sessional School, and the other Parochial Institutions for Education established in that city in the year 1812; with strictures on Education in General; (Edinburgh, 1828), pp. 19–20.
24 David Hume, *Commentaries on the Law of Scotland Respecting Crimes* (Edinburgh, 1819), Vol. I, p. 35.
25 *Substance of the Trials*, p. 52.
26 W.W. Knox, 'The Attack of the "Half-Formed Persons": the 1811–2 Tron Riot in Edinburgh Revisited', *The Scottish Historical Review*, Vol. XCI, No. 232, October 2012, p. 292.
27 Ibid., p. 308.
28 Ibid., p. 310.

3 Stirrings for change
Developments in Edinburgh, 1812–1846

Four years after the Tron Riot, the General Commissioners of Police in Edinburgh congratulated themselves on 1 January that

> in the course of the preceding night, being the last of the year (a night which will long be remembered for proceedings of a very different nature) not one instance had occurred of a person being taken into custody for riotous or improper conduct of any kind.[1]

If the Commissioners took that as an indication that crime in the city was under control, they were to be sadly disillusioned. Profound social changes were taking place that would create major new challenges for the city over the ensuing decades. Writing in 1847, the public health investigator Dr. James Stark looked back over the previous thirty years and remarked that 'since 1818 the lower classes of Edinburgh have undergone a gradual but increasing physical and moral deterioration'.[2] Up until about 1825 large numbers of Irish labourers were attracted to Edinburgh by the plentiful supply of work on such ventures as the Union Canal. As the Irish moved into the Old Town, the better class of tradesmen and skilled workers moved out. There was hardly a native Scot left in the Cowgate or West Port areas, claimed Stark, and the area gained the nickname 'little Ireland'.[3] Conditions were further worsened by the economic crisis of 1825 when speculation failures led to unemployment and reductions in wages. Over twenty years later, Stark could write that 'trade, building, everything has languished in Edinburgh since that period, while the destitution, misery, and numbers of these lower classes have increased...'[4]

By the 1830s the Old Town had degenerated into an overcrowded slum. In 1842 Dr. W.P. Alison, the poor law reformer, estimated that 18 per cent of the population of Edinburgh lived on charity,[5] and even in the late 1870s Robert Louis Stevenson, looking down at the Cowgate from the South Bridge, was struck by the fact that 'Social inequality is nowhere more ostentatious than at Edinburgh ... Sometimes ... there is not so much as a blade of grass between the rich and the poor'.[6]

Consequently, the geographical limits of the homes and haunts of the poor, the drunken and the criminal could be precisely defined:

the lowest [class] consisting of the labourers, porters, carters, scavengers, paupers & c., may be said to be confined to the Old Town, including the High Street, Canongate, Cowgate, Grassmarket, West Port, Potterrow, Crosscauseway, Pleasance, and all the narrow closes, lanes and courts therewith connected.[7]

The Very Rev. Dr. James MacGregor, minister of the Tron Kirk in the 1860s, described his parish, which was situated in this area, as 'one of the blackest spots on earth',[8] with a population so dense that in 1865 it was calculated there were 646 people to the acre in parts.

Not surprisingly, much of the crime committed in Edinburgh was concentrated in this section of the city. In the mid-1840s John Smith, Governor of the Edinburgh prison, stated that over 60 per cent of the prisoners lived in the streets of the Old Town listed above.[9] The general distress which characterised the years following the end of the Napoleonic wars resulted in rising crime rates. There were six times as many commitments to Edinburgh Bridewell in 1819 as in 1812 while, with the influx of Irish immigrants in 1818 who did not have any claim on poor relief in Scottish parishes, crime again increased: in the year ending January 1819, 5,807 cases were tried at the police court, compared with 2,820 the previous year.[10] Bridewell returns indicate the presence of five times as many juvenile prisoners in 1822 as in 1812 (481 compared to 76).

During the 1820s there was a trend towards dealing with these young offenders by prison sentences of short duration. Juveniles convicted of small offences such as petty thefts would initially be brought before the police court set up by a series of local Acts in 1805–1822, which was able – conducting its proceedings in a summary form, without written evidence – to impose sentences of up to sixty days' imprisonment. In 1826 an amending Act permitted the police judges, when they considered an offence too trivial to merit imprisonment in Bridewell, to send the offender to cells in the police office for up to three days. In the past few years extensive research has been carried out on Scottish nineteenth-century police courts by David G. Barrie and Susan Broomhall, who conclude their analysis of the Edinburgh records by saying 'these figures show that the police court was dealing with proportionately more cases of non-adult apprehension and conviction over time in relation to the higher courts'.[11]

The *Reports of the Interesting Proceedings in the Police Court* contain much fascinating anecdotal evidence of how this system worked in practice. It is worth giving a few of these stories verbatim as, even allowing for journalistic exaggeration, there are few period sources which reveal the human side of both judges and judged so effectively.

Take, for example, the story of the 'six by twelve inch thief'. On 24 March 1829 'five little fellows, from seven to nine or ten years of age' appeared before Bailie Robert Ritchie. The youngsters were convicted of stealing

> seven bottles of small beer from a grocer. One of the youngest effected the theft by squeezing himself into an aperture only six and ¾ inches by twelve inches,

which serves as a window to the grocer's cellar. The other boys stood around to receive the bottles as they were handed out; and they were all, except the actual thief, concerned in selling them. A noise being heard in the cellar, the master of the shop went there and caught the young thief by the feet as he was making his exit through the confined space by which he had entered the premises. The parents (of very decent appearance) of four of the children attended in Court. The judge exhorted them to look strictly after them on their return to their protection, as they had entered upon a career which must bring ruin upon themselves and disgrace upon their families, if persisted in. He sentenced the whole of the prisoners to three days confinement in the Police office, and each to give caution in 40 shillings for his future good behaviour.[12]

But magistrates were well aware that sending children of such a young age to prison would achieve little. Peter White and John Riley, two boys of about ten and eleven years of age, were charged with taking coals from the premises of a Mr McKay, Hat Manufacturer of Candlemaker Row,

> whose property of various kinds, in the yard belonging to his premises, has recently suffered sundry depredations by juvenile delinquents. As this was not the boys' first offence, the magistrate told them: 'I fear we must give both of you a more severe punishment than you have had before, which has had no effect on you. Thirty days of solitary confinement, and bread and water, may possibly save you from destruction.' At this point an elderly woman intervened, stating that the boy White (who had wept during the whole proceedings) was 'no very richt in his mind.' He was looked after by a 'puir widow ... a decent respectable woman ... who has keepit the laddie ever sin' he was an infant, when his mother ... ran awa' and left him.'... Riley's mother also now stepped forward to the bar, and with many tears stated that she had hoped his last appearance there would have been a warning to her boy as long as he lived. The broken-hearted mother added that her husband had deserted her, and that she had no means of subsistence but from making carpet shoes, at which she employed her son as well as herself.

The magistrate responded: 'Well: as he has not taken warning from the past, it will be necessary, perhaps, to give him thirty days in Bridewell'. Mrs White then pleaded: '(in an agony of grief, at sight of which her helpless son wept passionately) – my Lord, dinna send my puir boy to Bridewell. Nane belonging to him have ever come to the likes o' that ... Ony thing but Bridewell. I can bear onything but Bridewell!'

Clearly her words had some effect.

> The worthy Bailie compassionately told the wretched woman that his chief object in sending her son to Bridewell was to preserve him from the vicious association to which he might be exposed elsewhere. After consulting with the Captain of Police, however, the Magistrate said, that for the sake of Mrs

White's feelings as a mother, which he respected and pitied, he would again try the effect of leniency. He should therefore confine her son for ten days in the lock-up house. As for Riley, in consideration of the alleged state of his mind, – of his decent and apparently contrite behaviour, – and of the charitable widow who had so long maintained him, he should for the present allow him to go at large; and he (the Magistrate) would recommend that the widow should have some assistance.[13]

For all its tendency to dramatise, the account does convey the undoubted desire of the magistrate to do his best for the child, though we will never know whether Mrs. White was a concerned parent or simply an accomplished actress – or, indeed, whether young Peter ever learnt his lesson. From what is known about the conditions in Edinburgh's jails in this period, it seems likely that his experience of confinement would merely further his education in crime. A Report on the Prisons of Edinburgh by the Prison Discipline Society of Scotland, published in 1835, reveals that in the lock-up house attached to Calton Jail, there were seven rooms into which up to fifty prisoners would be crammed, without any sort of classification. Similarly, the police prison, with fifty-five rooms, was described as a 'fertile nursery of crime'.[14] Both these institutions lacked a work room or airing yard, and offered no instruction of any kind other than a visit from a missionary on Sundays.

The police court records not only reveal the shortcomings of existing procedures; they also give hints about how the authorities felt the system could be improved. The account of the case of 'A Young Female Thief' who appeared before Bailie Ritchie on 16 March 1829 is particularly enlightening in this respect:

> Euphemia Haxton, a little girl scarcely 11 years of age, was charged with having stolen from Mr. Anderson, Castle Street, some silver spoons, – boxes, – stockings, – a silk spencer, – a quantity of lace, – lace caps, and a number of other articles. Ann Donaldson was charged with resetting the same.

After hearing the sad tale of Euphemia's background – her parents having abandoned her, she stayed for a time with her grandmother, then another woman, and finally Ann Donaldson –

> the Bailie said that this was one of those cases in which a Magistrate must always feel perplexed as to what sort of punishment to inflict. The prisoner might yet … become a useful member of society; but if she was sent to Bridewell, or the lock-up house, she would be certain to come out worse than she had gone in.

This showed the positive necessity for the existence of

> Houses of Refuge, to which persons like the prisoner – young and open to advice – might be beneficially conveyed. He, therefore, under every consideration, though it best to confine her for three days in the Police Office, to be

fed on bread and water; and 'after the expiry of that time,' added the benevolent Magistrate, 'I shall ascertain what can be done to prevent her from falling into the hands of vicious and depraved characters.'[15]

In the accounts of cases such as these, contradictory attitudes can be discerned on the parts of individual magistrates. The 'worthy Bailie' dealing with Peter White considered a spell in Bridewell would be to the boy's benefit, whereas his colleague felt that sending Euphemia Haxton there would expose her to harmful influences. And this, in fact, was a further aspect of the problem. Writing in the 1840s, Sheriff Andrew Jameson complained about

> the faulty constitution of the Police Courts, in which a number of unprofessional magistrates sit, who change every month, and who, differing in opinion in regard to the objects of penal discipline, pronounce every variety of sentence. The consequence is, that the punishment being uncertain and variable, as well as inadequate, the evils of short imprisonments are increased: they become a subject of mockery among the criminals themselves.[16]

Nevertheless, the police magistrates of the 1820s were among the first to appreciate the need for a more suitable place to send young offenders, and it is noticeable that the earliest initiatives for the establishment of some kind of reformatory institution in Edinburgh were taken through official channels, rather than being promoted by charitable individuals. As early as 1819 a special committee was appointed, which met in the Council-Chamber on 26 January 'to inquire into the expediency of establishing a house of refuge for delinquents in this city'.[17] An institution that would act as a kind of halfway house was envisaged, catering for between 50 and 100 boys who had been released from Bridewell with the intention of providing them with some kind of industrial training to ease their transition to the outside world and help them find employment. Nothing was done until 1822[18] when one of the Police Commissioners – a Mr. R.B. Blyth, described as a metal merchant – revived the idea and another committee was appointed which, after outlining a scheme similar to that of 1819, recommended that 'Ideally they would have an institution of this kind in the precincts of the Bridewell...'[19]

This time, steps were taken to put the plan into effect. Unwilling to go ahead without charitable funding, the Commissioners arranged a public meeting on 23 October at which it was resolved to establish an institution for thirty boys. However, the venture failed to arouse public interest, partly because it coincided with widespread fires in the city which made a more urgent demand on the contributions of the benevolent.[20] The nearest approach to a refuge in these years was a small house opened at Dalry by a wealthy patron, Lady Carnegie, and supervised on her behalf by Mr. Myles Fletcher, an advocate and police commissioner. This held eight to ten children who were given food and lodging on release from Bridewell and trained as shoemakers. The small scale of the institution, however, made running costs very high – over £23 a head – and desertions were frequent, admission being voluntary. Consequently, the refuge was never expanded.[21]

Another factor which held back progress towards a juvenile refuge was that at about this time attempts were made to restore the Bridewell to its proper reformatory function, and this distracted attention from the juvenile question. An 1827 report on the Bridewell concluded that 'in place of proving a House of Correction [it] had actually proved a school of Vice'. Blame was laid on the Bridewell Commissioners, appointed by the Town Council, and a demand for an elective element arose among what Professor L.J. Saunders terms the 'enlightened and propertied' class of 'lawyers and business men' who were becoming more politically aware at this time.[22] This was only achieved in 1828, after much dispute and various parliamentary deliberations.

The importance of this dispute to the question of a reformatory institution was pointed out by John Wigham, one of the staunchest supporters of the idea, who argued at a Police Commissioners' meeting in 1827 that prison reform was a necessary preliminary to the separate treatment of juveniles – 'I ... anxiously look forward to Bridewell being reformed in the hope, that it will answer, in a more certain and complete manner, the purpose intended by those who wish for a house of refuge'[23] – by which he meant that young offenders would be given longer sentences in Bridewell during which they would be trained in a trade.

Wigham's remarks prefigure the development which was to take place over the next few years, leading to the demise of the idea of a separate juvenile institution in Edinburgh until revived, in a different form, in the 1850s. When in 1832 a general-purpose House of Refuge for the Destitute, young and old, was opened, some of the aims of those who had promoted a juvenile institution were met. The background to the establishment of this Refuge was a cholera epidemic which broke out in the overcrowded tenements of the Old Town, putting an intolerable strain on the existing charitable institutions – the infirmary and charity workhouse – already hard-pressed by vagrancy and unemployment. The Refuge was an ambitious attempt to deal with the problems of disease, poverty and crime under one roof. Members of the public were encouraged not to give money to beggars, but to direct both their contributions and the importunate to the Refuge, which was funded mainly by benevolent donations.

'Destitution is the claim' for admission, stated the first Annual Report, 'and delinquency will neither be a qualification nor a bar...'.[24] Once admitted, inmates were subjected to a routine which was to become increasingly common in nineteenth-century institutions: they were set to work, trained to greater cleanliness and industry and given moral and religious instruction. Trades such as shoemaking, carpentry and weaving were taught, and cooking and washing was done by the inmates. Of particular interest was the emphasis on the care of children, who made up almost half of the total number of inmates (around 500), as it was believed that 'it is chiefly in the case of the children, that the good effects of the care bestowed on the instruction and discipline of the House may be expected to be permanent and satisfactory'.[25]

Although its emphasis was on destitute rather than convicted delinquent children, this Refuge clearly fulfilled some of the functions of the juvenile institution which had been contemplated by the Police Commissioners. As a result, the

Commissioners actively supported it: boys recently entered into a career of crime were found places there by the police, and an annual grant of £100 was made to the funds.

After the foundation of the general House of Refuge, the Police Commissioners no longer took the initiative with regard to a juvenile institution. However, they continued to encourage others who did and, by a clause in the Edinburgh Police Act of 1832,[26] provided for the financial support of any house of refuge for young offenders which might be set up privately, up to a limit of £400 annually. There was, moreover, provision for a degree of involvement in the running of the institution: the Sheriff of the County, the Lord Provost of the City and the Lord Dean of Guild, plus three others elected by the Commissioners, were to manage the institution jointly with twelve managers elected by subscribers.

The passing of the Police Act containing this clause coincided with an attempt on the part of Archibald Thomson, one of the Resident Commissioners of Police,[27] and John Wigham[28] to organise support for such an institution as was envisaged in the Act, and in September 1832 Wigham notified the Commissioners of his intention to claim the grant. Again a public meeting was held but the Lord Advocate, Sir William Rae, put an end to the scheme by refusing to approve it on the grounds that putting children under restraint would be an interference with the liberty of the subject.[29]

The Commissioners, however, came to the aid of the small house at Dalry, which was in danger of closing by 1838. Its directors applied for help, expressing their willingness to 'surrender the Establishment entirely to the control of the Police Board' to ensure that it would operate on a more secure basis.[30] The Commissioners were unwilling to go as far as this, and contented themselves with granting £100 and electing representatives as directors under the terms of the statute.

A similar policy was followed with regards to other child-care institutions. In 1832 another small privately run refuge was set up: the Dean Bank Institution for Female Juvenile Delinquents in Stockbridge. Some lady members of the visiting committee for Edinburgh gaol established by Elizabeth Fry opened the home in order to train as domestic servants about twenty 'Young Females from about ten to fifteen years of age, who, without being habitual offenders have already fallen into crime, or, ... are in great danger of doing so...'.[31] By 1844 Frederic Hill noted in his prison report that neither of the institution's twin sources of revenue – subscriptions and the proceeds of laundry and needlework – was sufficient.[32] Hence the Secretary, Mrs. Sophia Bonar, applied for a grant from the police funds in 1834 which was paid annually, subject to a favourable report by Sheriff Speirs, until 1856, when the Police Board ceased to exist.

By the beginning of the 1840s, in spite of much discussion, little action had been taken on reformatories for juvenile offenders. The idea of a publicly managed institution had proceeded no further than the planning stage, and the extent of the city's reformatory facilities was two privately run houses which were struggling to muster enough support even for their very limited objectives.

Why then did the early interest in juvenile delinquency not result in the foundation of a reformatory institution in Edinburgh on a large scale? Three factors go some way towards explaining this situation.

Firstly, the Police Commissioners, the major public body with an interest in the subject of juvenile delinquency, had their attention distracted by the more pressing question of the election of Bridewell Commissioners during 1827–1828, which became a focal point for those interested in social as well as political reform in Edinburgh.

Secondly, the establishment of a General House of Refuge for the Destitute more or less put an end to the Police Commissioners' attempts to set up an institution specifically for juveniles, while the all-inclusive nature of the Refuge must have made the public less willing to contribute to the support of institutions dealing with specific social problems. Lack of public interest was mentioned in connection with both Dalry and Dean Bank, while *The Scotsman* attributed the failure of the 1825 attempt to the same reason.

Thirdly, an examination of the available evidence points to a temporary drop in the amount of juvenile delinquency, which may well have made it difficult to arouse enthusiasm for a new way of dealing with young offenders. For instance, the number of juveniles under the age of seventeen committed to Bridewell declined from 381 in 1822 to 87 in 1829. While such figures must be offset against the fact that more juveniles were sent to the police office gaol opened in 1824, the comments of the police superintendents reinforce the impression that crime was diminishing. 'Within the last two months, there has been a most sensible diminution of crime within the city and its suburbs', reported *The Scotsman* on 19 March 1824. By February 1828 the Police Commissioners felt justified in reducing the amount of money allocated to the prisons because of the decline in commitments from the police courts; one year later the Quarterly Report of the Superintendent of Police stated that crime had 'considerably decreased', and no mention was made of juvenile delinquency.[33]

Nevertheless, progress was made in certain areas in the 1820s and 1830s which was to be of value in the following decade. The idea of reformatory institutions had at least been put into circulation in Edinburgh, so that by the time of Thomas Guthrie's 1847 *Plea for Ragged Schools* the local authorities were aware of the issues involved. Furthermore, a tradition of co-operation between official and philanthropic circles had been established, and although no local authority reformatory was set up, its protagonists incorporated a clause in the 1832 Police Act enabling the Commissioners to aid private institutions. Thus Edinburgh became the first city in Scotland to make legislative provision for a house of refuge for juveniles, although the last to have such an institution.

A great deal of interest in juvenile delinquency was generated in official circles in Edinburgh in these years. In fact, there appears to have been more discussion of reformatory institutions in the capital than in any other Scottish, and possibly British, city between 1819 and 1830. This discussion, moreover, took place in circles which had the power to take action, as much of Scotland's legal and professional expertise was concentrated in Edinburgh. Even so, public sympathy was not yet engaged to a sufficient extent to ensure the backing of any scheme sponsored by the local authorities. In addition to this, the close connection between the suggested reformatories and prison reform, combined with the fact that the General House of Refuge for the Destitute was viewed as an instrument for diminishing the juvenile problem to some degree, would suggest that as yet not all reformers viewed juvenile delinquency as a distinct problem requiring separate treatment from adult crime, which was to be the characteristic demand of the reformatory school movement later on. In short, juvenile crime in Edinburgh between 1812 and 1846 remained predominantly a 'penal' concern.

Notes

1. Edinburgh Police, Minute Book, General Commissioners, Vol. II, p. 167.
2. James Stark, M.D., *Inquiry into some points of the Sanatory State of Edinburgh* (Edinburgh, 1847), p. 12.
3. Ibid., p. 12.
4. Ibid., p. 13.
5. Anon., *The Poor of Edinburgh; or, Recollections of the Canongate in 1842* (London, 1842), p. 25.
6. Quoted in David Daiches, *Edinburgh* (London, 1978), p. 225.
7. Stark, op. cit., p. 4.
8. Rev. D. Butler, *The Tron Kirk of Edinburgh* (Edinburgh and London, 1906), p. 350.
9. Quoted in Thomas Guthrie, *A Plea on Behalf of Drunkards and Against Drunkenness* (Edinburgh, 1851), p. 24.
10. Edinburgh Police, Minute Book, General Commissioners, Vol. VI, p. 377.
11. David G. Barrie and Susan Broomhall, *Police Courts in Nineteenth-Century Scotland*, Vol. 2 (Farnham, 2014), p. 91.
12. 'Reports of the Interesting Proceedings in the Police Court', 24 March 1829.
13. Ibid., 7 February 1829.
14. 'Address by the Committee of Directors of the Society for the Improvement of Prison Discipline in Scotland' (Edinburgh, 1835), p. 80.
15. Reports of the Interesting Proceedings in the Police Court', 16 March 1829.
16. Rev. Thomas Guthrie, *A Second Plea for Ragged Schools* (Edinburgh, 1849), Appendix, p. 56.
17. Report of the Committee Appointed by a Meeting held in the Council-Chamber on January 26th 1819, 'to inquire into the expediency of establishing a house of refuge for delinquents in this city', p. 2.
18. Edinburgh Police, Minute Book, General Commissioners, Vol. V, p. 53.
19. Report of a Committee of General and Resident Commissioners of Police, Respecting the Practicability of establishing a House of Refuge in Edinburgh for Male Juvenile Delinquents (Edinburgh, 1824), p. 1.
20. *The Scotsman*, 26 November 1825.
21. *The Scotsman*, 3 May 1828.
22. L.J. Saunders, *Scottish Democracy, 1815–40* (Edinburgh and London, 1950), p. 95.
23. *The Scotsman*, 21 March 1827.
24. House of Refuge for the Destitute, and Asylum for their Children (December 1832), p. 8.
25. Second Report by the Committee of the House of Refuge for the Destitute (July 1834), p. 5.
26. 2 Geo. IV. C. 86.
27. That is, resident or having business premises in the ward which elected him under the terms of the 1822 Police Act.

28 Wigham, a Quaker, described himself as a 'manufacturer'; in about 1832, he gave up business to concentrate on his interest in social reform which, in addition to a juvenile refuge, included membership of the General Prison Board of Scotland.
29 *The Scotsman*, 27 December 1858.
30 Edinburgh Police, Minute Book, General Commissioners, Vol. IX, p. 14.
31 Report of the Dean Bank Institution, Edinburgh, for 1841–44.
32 Ninth Report, Report of the Inspector of Prisons of Great Britain, IV Scotland, Northumberland, and Durham, 1844, p. 5.
33 Edinburgh Police, Minute Book, General Commissioners, Vol. VI, pp. 137–8.

4 'An intermediate step'
The Glasgow House of Refuge, 1838–1854

In 1846, *Chambers' Edinburgh Journal* expressed regret that the Scottish capital was 'always behind in movements for social advancement'.[1] By contrast, Edinburgh's rival in the West, Glasgow, could record three significant achievements as far as the treatment of juvenile delinquency was concerned. Firstly, it was the only Scottish city to make an influential contribution to the development of reformatory institutions in the form of the House of Refuge, opened in 1838. Secondly, Glasgow was the only city in Britain to have its own local Act of Parliament for the purpose of dealing with juvenile crime, passed in 1841.[2] Thirdly, by opening an industrial school in 1847 to prevent vulnerable children falling into crime, Glasgow became the first city in Scotland to have both a reformatory institution and an industrial school, anticipating the post-1854 pattern.

Economic and social background

Nineteenth-century Glasgow offers a clear illustration of the connection between socio-economic conditions and crime. As one historian has put it,

> The unenviable pre-eminence of Glasgow in the social problems of the period is to be attributed to that rapid development of industry there which brought about a diminution in the relative proportion of the wealthier and middle class and made Charles Baird, the lawyer who wrote the survey of the condition of Glasgow for Edwin Chadwick's Sanitary Inquiry, state that 'at least four-fifths of the population of the city of Glasgow and suburbs consist of the working classes and their families'.[3]

From about 1830 onwards the Clyde Valley was increasingly dominated by heavy industry – iron, steel, mining and shipbuilding. Between 1830 and 1849, for example, the production of iron increased by over ten times.[4] The result was a dramatic influx of workers seeking employment, the population of the city increasing by 360 per cent in the first forty years of the century. The census total in 1831 was 202,426; in 1861 it was 403,142. Much of this increase was a result of Irish immigration: in 1841, when 4.8 per cent of the population of Scotland was Irish-born, the figure was 16 per cent in Glasgow.

However, housing accommodation did not increase proportionately. Dr. Sutherland of the General Board of Health commented in the 1860s that 'for years a population of many thousands has been annually added to Glasgow by immigration, without a single house being built to receive them'.[5] It was the combination of these factors that led Chadwick to conclude that 'the condition of the population in Glasgow was the worst of any we had seen in any part of Great Britain'.[6]

These years were also characterised by a steady increase in crime. Commitments to Glasgow Bridewell between August 1838 and August 1839 were 2,097, compared to 1,389 in 1825–1826,[7] and the increase continued annually until about 1850. Contemporaries accounted for this growth by reference to the fact that a large section of Glasgow's population was at the mercy of economic vicissitudes. Commenting on the rise in commitments to prison during part of 1838, the prisons inspector Frederic Hill pointed to the 'bad state of trade and the high price of food', reflected in the fact that the average cost of keeping each prisoner was almost double that of 1834.[8] At the time of his 1842 visit he noted that 258 prisoners in Bridewell attributed their fall into crime to inability to find employment.[9] Similarly, the rise in crime in 1847–1848 may be explained by the combined effects of a trade depression which threw many out of work and a wave of Irish immigration, resulting in rioting and looting in the city centre. The number of prisoners on the day of Hill's visit in 1847 was 533, compared to a daily average of 420 in the previous year.[10]

A growing proportion of this increase in crime was committed by those under the age of seventeen, of whom there were nearly twice as many in Bridewell in 1838–1839 compared to 1825–1826 (409 to 211). This increase, too, was attributed to social and economic conditions. Criticising the lack of poor relief in Scotland for able-bodied persons unable to find employment, William Brebner, Governor of the Glasgow Bridewell, added that 'the consequence is, that many persons, and even children of 12 or 14 years of age, are almost driven into crime when trade is bad…'[11] Similarly, in 1846 Councillor Andrew Liddell, an advocate of industrial schools, complained of the lack of education in the city and noted that

> In very many cases it can be traced to the parents keeping the children at home for the produce of their labour. Except during periods of stagnation of trade, work can be had in factories and other places for even very young children.[12]

The formation of a local system of treating juvenile delinquency

In Glasgow, as elsewhere, attempts to reclaim juvenile offenders originated from the exertions of both philanthropists and prison officials. The earliest charitable scheme aimed at dealing with juvenile delinquents appears to have been operated by the Glasgow Society for the Encouragement of Penitents, founded in 1815 by the Rev. Stevenson Macgill (1765–1840), predecessor of Rev. Thomas Chalmers in the Tron Parish. Its principal object was the reclamation of prostitutes, for which purpose a

Magdalene Asylum was opened in 1816, but the Society also attempted, on a much smaller scale, to apprentice out boys released from Bridewell. Although in the first year of its existence it was only able to claim success in one instance, the Society gained an insight into some of the problems of reforming delinquents.[13] Finding that success was frustrated by the lack of powers of detention or by 'foolish and unprincipled relations' who seduced youths back to their old ways, the Society recommended, as early as September 1815, 'a Public Establishment for the Tuition and Reformation of Boys who have been convicted of crimes, properly arranged and supported by the authority of law...'[14]

Interest in the reformation of young offenders was equally strong within the penal system, the result being a close connection between the city's Bridewell and proposals for a House of Refuge. In his prison inspection reports Frederic Hill takes the Bridewell as the standard against which he judges other prisons. In 1836 he describes it as 'incomparably the best-conducted Prison in Scotland'[15] because 'the two great principles of separation and constant employment are here carried into effect'.[16] Much of the credit for this is due to William Brebner, governor from about 1815 until his death in 1845. Nevertheless, Hill considered the Bridewell was not as successful as it might have been. Although housed in modern premises built in 1824 on the radiating principle with separate cells, its accommodation did not suffice for the ever-growing number of prisoners.

As many of these prisoners were juveniles, it is not surprising that Brebner was one of the first to draw attention to the problem of young offenders in a letter to the Lord Provost in 1829. As Governor, he strongly believed that 'It is of the utmost importance that, before [young offenders] leave prison, they should, as far as possible, be divested of their former bad habits and propensities, and new and better principles be ingrafted in their stead'.[17]

Hence, 'boys, in being committed to Bridewell, are kept constantly at work; and when the term of imprisonment will admit, they are taught some useful trade',[18] this regime being reinforced by separation from other prisoners, instruction in reading and writing and religious education. Frederic Hill endorses the success of this procedure in his official reports, but the problem was that the terms of imprisonment were too short for anything to be achieved. Lord Provost James Ewing clearly agreed, as he wrote in the Bridewell visitors' book in 1826 that 'the existing system is bad ... not from any want of virtue in the medicine, but from its having been given in too slight a dose'.[19]

These shortcomings determined the sphere of operation of the House of Refuge which Brebner proposed. Unlike some pioneering institutions, such as Redhill in Surrey, it did not at first aim to provide a comprehensive system of reformation within its walls. It was not designed to replace, but rather to supplement, the prison system, as 'It would furnish an intermediate step between coercive confinement and unrestrained intercourse with the world'.[20]

The emphases of Brebner's plan were therefore slightly different from those of others proposing similar schemes. While others viewed imprisonment as preceding the task of reformation, or even as a hindrance to it, the prison sentence was an integral part of Brebner's schemes. Some reformers, like Mary Carpenter, repudiated completely the imprisonment of juveniles, and drew a contrast between prisons and reformatories; others, like Rev. John Clay, Chaplain of Preston House of Correction, favoured a spell in prison prior to admission to a reformatory. Whereas Clay proposed that a juvenile should be punished in prison and then reformed in a reformatory, Brebner envisaged reformation as taking place in prison, the House of Refuge being for boys coming out of prison who had been reformed but whose environment would make it difficult for them to find an honest livelihood – in other words, a Refuge to ease the transition of discharged juvenile prisoners to the outside world, rather than a reformatory institution as such. Instead of an institution from which reformed children would be released, Brebner planned an institution into which reformed children would be admitted: 'It would confirm voluntarily, a system of reform, which the House of Correction may have commenced compulsorily. It would give time for ripening, in sheltering security, any seeds of good which may have been implanted.'[21]

While the resulting institution was not in fact restricted to discharged prisoners, it retained this vital element of Brebner's scheme – voluntary admission. This was to be a particular feature of Glasgow's local system of dealing with delinquents, although it proved to be a complicating factor in the years after 1854, when the system had to operate in conjunction with the national one. Thus, the original conception of the House of Refuge, and the form it was to take, must be explained by reference to the strengths and weaknesses of existing local facilities for dealing with juvenile delinquents in Bridewell.

Municipal support was a decisive factor in putting the plan into practice. In October 1832 a Town Council Committee was appointed to discuss extending the gaol and establishing a Refuge. It reported in favour of the latter, and the Lord Provost, James Ewing, convened a public meeting to consider the subject. That sufficient public support existed is evident from the fact that Ewing had received a 'numerously signed requisition' urging that such a meeting be held. As a consequence of this meeting, the Glasgow Society for Repressing Juvenile Delinquency was formed, and £1,500 was subscribed on the spot, the City contributing a further £500.

The composition of the first Board of Directors reveals something about the variety of interests which came together to promote the institution: William Brebner's presence on the Board symbolises the link between Refuge and Bridewell; Hugh Tennent (1780–1864), a prominent industrialist and city magistrate, reminds us of the contribution of the legal and philanthropic interest to the institution; the linen merchant John Leadbetter (1788–1865) and Andrew Liddell, members of the Town Council and later poor law officials, would have emphasised the 'refuge' rather than the 'reformatory' side of the institution, their interest being in destitute children, while the presence on the board of David Stow (1793–1864), founder of the 'training system' of education, reveals the connection between the Refuge and contemporary educational developments in the city.[22]

The main features of the system to be pursued in the Refuge were outlined in the constitution framed in 1837. As Brebner had proposed, the institution was designed for 'young delinquents who showed hopes of improvement, to settle the impressions which penal confinement had produced'. To this class were added those who had committed a first offence, who could thereby escape the stigma of having been in prison. 'A complete system of education ... is to be adopted – the strength, age, genius and inclinations of the boys are in all cases to be considered before putting them to any trade...'[23]

This ambitious project finally began its operations in February 1838 in purpose-built premises situated in ten acres of ground off Duke Street. By the time of the first annual meeting there were 164 inmates and Brebner observed that since the Refuge had been opened there had been about a hundred fewer juvenile prisoners in Bridewell.[24]

In an address delivered some years later, the then Governor of the Boys' Refuge, the Rev. A. K. McCallum, gave an insight into what life was like for the inmates. 'Idleness', he declared, 'is the bane of our juvenile population and almost invariably leads to crime'.[25] Certainly, the daily routine of the Refuge made sure that the young offender was never idle. The day began at 5.30 a.m., summer and winter; from 6 until 8 a.m. the boys worked at their trades – tailoring, shoemaking, weaving, farming or carpentry; at 8 a.m. there was worship, breakfast and drill; between 9 a.m. and 2 p.m. half the inmates went to school while the other half continued their industrial work; at 2 p.m. dinner was served, followed by a short playtime; from 3 until 7 p.m. it was back to classes or industrial training, with supper, worship, play and reading from 7 until bed at 9 p.m. 'Every duty has its appointed time and place', boasted McCallum, 'while the spirit of religion is expected to pervade the whole'.[26]

The next step was to provide a similar institution for girls and in 1838 Brebner addressed a letter on the subject to the Lord Provost, as he had done nine years earlier for the boys' house. Again, a public meeting was held and a 'House of Refuge for Juvenile Female Delinquents' opened in 1840 in the premises of the Magdalene Asylum, whose Directors had been among the first to show interest in dealing with delinquency in the city. The girls' house was a refuge of a more general nature than the boys', catering for both criminal and destitute children, for a time making little distinction between the original inmates of the Magdalene Asylum and the Refuge cases. The routine followed was similar to that of the boys' house, though life was not altogether grim: there was even 'an excellent playground, with swings and other means of amusement' where 'the children are encouraged to play heartily'.[27]

In spite of initial public support, the Houses of Refuge faced financial problems from the moment they opened. In fact, the opening of the Boys' House had to be delayed since there was insufficient money to furnish it,[28] and after the first year of operation debts amounted to nearly £2,000. In justification, it was argued that earnings from industrial work would necessarily be small at first, since the initial outlay on machinery and materials was included in the expenditure, and trades like tailoring, shoemaking and nail-making required a number of months' experience before proficiency was attained. But the Directors cannot be entirely exonerated from responsibility for the financial situation. While most institutions of this kind had modest beginnings, Glasgow's was from the outset one of the largest in the country and it might have been more prudent to start in a smaller way at first. The Directors, moreover, were criticised for extravagant spending. One contemporary social investigator ridiculed the 'outrageous and unnecessary' expenditure on the 'imposing appearance' of the building, which was 'surmounted with an elegant dome'.[29]

At any rate, by December 1839 the debt had increased to £5,971, and more drastic measures had to be considered. The Directors stated in May of the following year that, as voluntary subscriptions did not cover their running costs, they had decided to apply for an assessment.[30] While the Town Council unanimously agreed to this on account of the 'great public usefulness'[31] of the institution, the inhabitants of Glasgow were less enthusiastic. On 9 November 1840, a public meeting was convened in the Town Hall,

> for the purpose of considering the propriety of applying to Parliament for a Bill to place the House of Refuge, for juvenile delinquents, on a secure basis, by an assessment – not exceeding a penny per pound on the rental or annual value of property within the bounds of the Parliamentary district.[32]

This was to be levied 'on the same principle as the Poor Rate Bill' and 'collected by the existing machinery'.[33]

However, many citizens resented the fact that wealthy manufacturers and merchants who lived outside the city boundary were not contributing their fair share, as the assessment was levied only on their business premises within the city. A correspondent of the *Glasgow Argus* suggested that, as the inhabitants were already burdened with rates for prisons and the poor, the wealthy ought to give the Refuge donations out of the savings they had made.[34] The *Argus* was also critical of local government 'jobbing' and wastage and looked for 'securities that the House of Refuge is not to be transformed into another huge job, whereby the people are to be taxed for the benefit of a few interested parties'.[35] What eventually prevented the motion in favour of an assessment being carried at the public meeting was a large group of Chartists in the audience who turned the occasion into a call for universal suffrage, demanding that no new tax should be imposed on the people 'until they were enabled effectually to control the expenditure of their money through the medium of their representatives'.[36] Thus, as happened in the dispute over the election of the Edinburgh Bridewell commissioners in 1828, local politics intruded into the question of the treatment of juvenile crime.

Nor did the press give the proposed assessment any warmer reception. Already it is possible to detect dissatisfaction with any attempt to deal with delinquency purely on a local or regional basis, and the possibility of a national system was raised. The inadequacies of the Scottish poor law, claimed the *Argus*, drove the country population to look for work in the towns:

> At this very moment we have reasons for thinking that crimes are actually committed as a means of qualifying for the House of Refuge; and the source of attraction will be increased in a degree which it is impossible to calculate,

so soon as it is known that Glasgow has a large establishment, supported by taxation, for the reception of juvenile delinquents, and that it is the only institution of the kind existing in Scotland.[37]

Nevertheless, the Directors disregarded the unpopularity of the measure and it reached the statute book in June 1841 as 'An Act for repressing Juvenile Delinquency in the City of Glasgow' [4 & 5 Vict. c. 36, 1841]. The significance of the Act was twofold: it was the only one of its kind to apply to a specific area and it confirmed the different character of the Glasgow institutions in comparison with other reformatory experiments throughout the country.

Designed to put the system on a secure footing, the Act dealt with administration, the admission of inmates and finance. The running of the Houses of Refuge was vested in a Board of Commissioners made up of seven *ex officiis* members, the Provosts of Glasgow and neighbouring burghs and the Sheriff of the County of Lanark; a further forty-five members (reduced to twenty-seven in 1850) were nominated annually by the Magistrates of the Town Council of Glasgow, Calton, Anderston and Gorbals. There was no stipulation in the Act that a child had to serve a prison sentence before being admitted; the Board could receive 'such young Persons as they shall think fit, and as shall request to be received into the same...'.[38] That did not mean the Refuge was open to applications from all and sundry. The children eligible to apply were either those at present in Bridewell, those who were recommended for admission by the magistrate before whom they appeared or those whose parents asked for admission because they could not control them. If a child under the age of twelve agreed to become an inmate, the case against him or her would be dismissed, thus saving the child from the stigma of being a convicted criminal.[39] In the first year of the Act's operation, ninety-six boys were admitted under the terms of this clause. Occasionally, there were children who preferred weeks in prison to years in the Refuge,[40] but the published statistics suggest that such cases were rare, as there was always continued pressure on places. An 1851 admissions register[41] for the Boys' House survives which illustrates the variety of ways a boy could end up in the Refuge (see Table 4.1).

One typical case is recorded in Archibald Broun's *Reports of Cases before the High Court and Circuit Courts of Justiciary in Scotland*. In September 1845 three girls were brought before Lords Moncrieff and Cockburn charged with breaking into a house in Sauchiehall Street and stealing gold jewellery. Mary Ann O'Brien, 'by Habite and Repute a Common thief', was sentenced to ten years' transportation

Table 4.1 Admissions to Boys' House of Refuge, 1851

Total admissions in 1851:	67
Sent from police court charged with theft:	41
Admitted on application of parent or guardian	18
Sent by parochial boards:	5
Admitted voluntarily:	3

but her accomplices, Agnes Wallace and Janet McNaught, asked to be admitted to the House of Refuge. The proceedings against them were discharged on condition that one remained in the Refuge for three, and the other for five, years.[42]

As far as finance is concerned, though, the Act did not entirely fulfil expectations. The Board of Commissioners had hoped the estimated £2,000 per annum to be raised by the assessment would be sufficient to ensure a stable income. In this, however, they were doubly disappointed: the assessment not only failed to produce as much as anticipated but also led to a reduction in charitable contributions, the subscribers assuming the proceeds of the assessment would obviate the need for their support − a pattern which would be repeated in practically every industrial and reformatory institution after the national legislation of 1854.

Consequently, the field of operation had to be restricted. By 1843 there were only ninety-six boys in a building which could hold well over 300.[43] The problems of the Refuge began to be reflected in criminal statistics: the Superintendent of Police, Henry Miller, attributed the increase in the number of young offenders to 1,510 in 1842 to 'the difficulty of procuring employment' and 'the impossibility of getting such young persons into the House of Refuge from the want of sufficient funds for the support of that institution'.[44]

Notwithstanding these difficulties, Glasgow had developed its facilities for dealing with delinquents further than most other places by the mid-1840s: the Juvenile Delinquency Act allowed magistrates to send children to the Refuge, a power for which the rest of the United Kingdom had to wait until 1854, and the assessment, though inadequate, was at least an acceptance of the principle that provision for delinquents was a public service and should not be dependent on charity.

The House of Refuge had not been operating for long before it began to be asked, as Superintendent Miller put it in a letter to Lord Provost Henry Dunlop in October 1840, whether it was not 'at least as proper to save a destitute child from the certainty of becoming a criminal as to shelter him after he has earned the privilege by the actual commission of crime'.[45] Andrew Liddell, a member of the Board of Commissioners of the Refuge, corresponded with Sheriff Watson of Aberdeen and, influenced by developments there, outlined the arguments in favour of preventive education in his 'Letter on Industrial Schools' in 1846. The time was particularly propitious for his move in view of the passage of the new Scottish Poor Law Act the previous year. Liddell believed this Act could be used to provide authority for setting up industrial schools, and representatives of Glasgow's four parochial boards (City, Barony, Govan and Gorbals) met with officials of the House of Refuge, the Night Asylum for the Houseless[46] and other similar institutions to consider the subject. The response from the parochial boards was lukewarm, with only the City board − of whose committee Liddell was chairman − being prepared to take active steps to set up an industrial school, but the Directors of the Night Asylum expressed willingness to allow part of their premises to be used for the purpose. The Board of Supervision, set up by the 1845 Act to be a central advisory body on poor law matters, agreed that money from the poor rates could lawfully be applied to the support of such a school. From the beginning, then, the establishment of industrial schools in Glasgow was part of the city's system of poor relief.

52 'An intermediate step'

In the customary mid-Victorian way, a public meeting took place in March 1847 which resulted in the formation of the Glasgow Industrial School Society with the support of 'fifty of the most influential merchants and bankers in Glasgow'.[47] The offer of accommodation from the Night Asylum was taken up and in July 1847 a day school was opened, with children who had no homes to return to being boarded out in the same way as poor law children at the time. Liddell successfully argued that this cost the parochial board less than boarding out a child in the countryside and on this basis the City board made an agreement with the Industrial School Society to pay an allowance of one shilling and sixpence for each child it sent there.[48] Figures have not survived for the early years of the school, but in 1858 income for poor law sources amounted to £1,220, about half of the school's total income.[49]

Glasgow was therefore the first Scottish city to have both a dedicated institution for convicted offenders and an industrial school for destitute children, anticipating the arrangements that developed nationally after the legislation of 1854.

Figure 4.1 The Glasgow House of Refuge (one of Allan & Ferguson's views of Glasgow, published in 1843 and reproduced in *Sketch of the History of Glasgow* by James Pagan in 1847). Pagan describes the building, designed by John Bryce, as 'a good example of plain Roman architecture'.

One of the conclusions drawn from the city's experience at a local level was that provision on a wider scale was necessary. Even in 1840 the *Glasgow Argus* had criticised the local Juvenile Delinquency Act as being 'a partial measure ... which is to affect one locality alone, and not applicable to the whole country'.[50] In May 1842 it was stated at a meeting of the Commissioners of Supply for the County of Ayr that 'the Glasgow House of Refuge was open for the reclaiming of youth *from all parts of the country*'.[51] At that time there were three boys in it from Ayr, although Ayr contributed nothing for their support. Why, asked the *Argus*, should the inhabitants of Glasgow, already burdened with excessive taxation, pay for the maintenance of boys from other areas? After 1845, this grievance was further aggravated by contrast with the industrial school which, because it worked in conjunction with the poor law authorities, could hand over children from outside the city to the appropriate poor law board to deal with. Liddell had estimated in his 'Letter on Industrial Schools' that about 25 per cent of all paupers in Glasgow could be disposed of by being returned to their places of settlement. Here, then, was another reason for the Refuge to be linked with some national system, rather than operating independently.

Once again, though, financial necessity was the decisive factor. There was much local opposition when the Commissioners of the Refuge proposed raising the assessment from one penny in the pound to twopence[52] and in January 1844 Brebner and Miller, in a document containing 'observations and suggestions concerning Glasgow Prisons, Crime, Etc.' for the consideration of the Lord Advocate, concluded with respect to the Houses of Refuge that 'The expense of maintaining, or the benefits to be derived from, such institutions, should not be confined to particular localities – for the evil being a national one, so also should be the remedy'.[53]

Those involved in the Refuge therefore started looking towards government, like their English counterparts. At a council meeting in February 1852 Bailie James Playfair brought forward a motion concerning the Boys' and Girls' Houses, proposing that 'this Council do memorialise her Majesty's Government for the means of extending these establishments, or for the adoption of other reformatory measures in connection with them'.[54] By this stage the idea of a further local assessment had been abandoned and responsibility was placed on the shoulders of the state rather than the local ratepayers. As Playfair said,

> were this establishment not in existence the Government would have not only a larger number of criminals to support, but also a larger number to transport, thus it is manifest that a very considerable saving of money is effected to the country.[55]

Similarly, the Juvenile Delinquency Commissioners hoped that national legislation would improve existing arrangements for the committal and detention of inmates. Playfair, representing the Boys' House, and James D. Bryce, representing the Girls', dealt with this in some detail in their evidence to the 1852–3 Select Committee. Under the 1841 Act, charges against a child could be dropped if he or she agreed to go the Refuge. The magistrate thus had in effect the power to send a child to the Refuge should the child agree, or to commit him to prison for sixty days. After sixty days, however, there was no power of detention over children in the Refuge. Playfair and Bruce emphasised that they did not want magistrates to have the power to *sentence* to the Refuge, because they thought that 'it would be looked upon more in the light of a prison'[56] by the children. Instead, if the magistrate had power to sentence children to prison for one or two years, the Commissioners could tell a child who attempted to leave that they would send him back to the magistrate who would commit him to prison. By this means, they considered that greater powers of detention could be gained without the voluntary character of the House being sacrificed.

Thus, while supporting national legislation and state funding for reformatory institutions, the Glasgow Refuge Commissioners had significantly different expectations from those who drew up the Youthful Offenders Act of 1854. As had been urged by the Select Committee, this sought to give magistrates power to commit children to reformatory schools for a period of up to five years, after a compulsory two-week prison sentence. But the Glasgow Houses of Refuge had evolved their own admissions procedure and wished to retain the provisions of the 1841 local Act. Whereas the 1854 Act aimed to encourage private efforts at establishing reformatories by providing financial support and legal powers, the Commissioners of the Glasgow Houses of Refuge looked to the legislation for assistance in extending a local system that was already in operation. They were soon to discover that such assistance came with strings attached.

Notes

1 *Chambers' Edinburgh Journal*, New Series, No. 130, June 27, 1846, p. 409.
2 In 1854 a local Industrial School Act for Middlesex was passed (17 & 18 Vict. c. 169) but this is too late to be considered as a pioneering effort, as it coincides with the national Acts. Moreover, the Middlesex Act was given up in 1864 so that the school could be certified under the national Act whereas the Glasgow Act continued to operate, in conjunction with the Reformatory Schools Act, after 1854.
3 Stewart Mechie, *The Church and Scottish Social Development 1780–1870* (London, 1960), p. 28.
4 John Strang, LL.D., *The Progress of Glasgow, in Population, Wealth, Manufactures, & c.* (Glasgow, 1850), pp. 11–12.
5 Quoted in Thomas Ferguson, *The Dawn of Scottish Social Welfare* (London, etc., 1948), p. 58.
6 Ibid., p. 19.
7 Figures compiled from 'Glasgow Bridewell – Minutes and Accounts of Commissioners' (Glasgow City Archives).
8 Third Report of the Inspector of Prisons of Great Britain, IV Scotland, Northumberland, and Durham, 1837–8, p. 103.
9 Eighth Report of the Inspector of Prisons of Great Britain, IV Scotland, Northumberland, and Durham, 1843, p. 27.
10 Twelfth Report of the Inspector of Prisons of Great Britain, IV Scotland, Northumberland, and Durham, 1847, p. 101.
11 Seventh Report of the Inspector of Prisons of Great Britain, IV Scotland, Northumberland, and Durham, 1842, p. 67.

12 *Glasgow Courier*, 1 October 1846.
13 'Report of the Proceedings of the General Meeting of subscribers to the Glasgow Society for the Encouragement of Penitents' (Glasgow, 1815), p. 8.
14 Ibid., p. 8.
15 [First] Report of the Inspector of Prisons of Great Britain, IV Scotland, Northumberland, and Durham, 1836, p. 4.
16 Ibid., p. 53.
17 William Brebner, 'Letter to the Lord Provost, on the Expediency of a House of Refuge for Juvenile Offenders' (Glasgow, 1829), p. 7.
18 Ibid., p. 7.
19 Ibid., p. 25.
20 Ibid., p. 11.
21 Ibid., p. 11.
22 Details taken from the report of the meeting in the *Glasgow Herald*, 1 November 1833. David Stow was a philanthropic merchant whose interest in education stemmed from his Sunday School work. Having discovered that one day's teaching per week could not counteract the influences on children during the other six, he formed the Glasgow Infant School Society in 1826 to pursue his object of moral training. His biographer writes that 'Mr. Stow, looking to the inner life or moral history, sought there evidences of improvement' (Rev. William Fraser, *Memoir of David Stow, founder of the Training System of Education* (London, 1868), p. 92). In many ways Stow was ahead of his time: he believed in the need to educate the whole person; he repudiated corporal punishment and competitiveness; he recognised the value of the playground and attempted to harness what would now be called 'peer pressure' as a positive means of counteracting harmful influences. In a letter to the *North British Daily Mail* on 27 September 1855 the Governor of the Boys' Refuge, Rev. A.K. McCallum, pointed out that Stow's emphasis on intellectual, moral and physical training was not unique, being part of the Refuge's system also, but we may surmise that the debt of the latter to Stow's theories was greater than McCallum cared to admit.
23 *Glasgow Argus*, 5 October 1837.
24 *Glasgow Herald*, 1 February 1839.
25 Rev. A.K. McCallum, 'Juvenile Delinquency – Its Principal Causes and Proposed Cure, as adopted in the Glasgow Reformatory Schools', *Journal of the Statistical Society of London*, XVIII (1855), p. 359.
26 'Report of the Glasgow Reformatory Institution, Boys' House of Refuge, Duke Street (Glasgow, 1856), p. 16.
27 SC 1852-3, para. 4525.
28 *Glasgow Herald*, 9 February 1838.
29 J. Smith, M.A., *The Grievances of the Working Classes; and the Pauperism and Crime of Glasgow* (Glasgow, 1846), pp. 52–54.
30 *Glasgow Herald*, 1 May 1840.
31 Glasgow City Archives, Council Act Book, Vol. 57, p. 364.
32 *Glasgow Argus*, 9 November 1840.
33 *Constitutional*, 11 November 1840.
34 *Glasgow Argus*, 12 November 1840.
35 *Glasgow Argus*, 9 November 1840.
36 *Glasgow Argus*, 9 November 1840.
37 *Glasgow Argus*, 19 November 1840.
38 Clause XIX.
39 Clause XX.
40 A case of this type is reported in the *Glasgow Courier*, 10 February 1844.
41 Glasgow University Library, Special Collections Department.
42 Archibald Broun, *Reports of Cases before the High Court and Circuit Courts of Justiciary in Scotland, during the Years 1844 and 1845* (Vol. II, Edinburgh, 1846), p. 499.

43 *Glasgow Herald*, 7 August 1843.
44 *Glasgow Herald*, 27 January 1843.
45 Letter from Henry Miller to the Lord Provost, Hon. Henry Dunlop, in the *Glasgow Argus*, 19 October 1840.
46 The Night Asylum, in the foundation of which Liddell had taken a prominent part, had been opened in 1838 to provide food and shelter for the homeless. In 1839 its Directors had attempted to provide schooling in the institution, but it proved impossible to deal with large numbers of children in badly ventilated rooms. No doubt this accounts for their willingness to house the industrial school in their new premises, opened in 1847. For details, see John Goodwin, *History of the Glasgow Night Asylum for the Houseless, from Origin till Jubilee* (Glasgow, 1887).
47 *Glasgow Courier*, 4 March 1847. Many of these people had also been influential in setting up the House of Refuge: Liddell, Leadbetter, Tennent, J.D. Bryce of the Girls' Refuge, etc.
48 *Glasgow Courier*, 3 June 1848.
49 *Glasgow Herald*, 29 January 1858.
50 *Glasgow Argus*, 19 November 1840.
51 *Glasgow Argus*, 19 May 1842.
52 *Glasgow Herald*, 7 August 1843.
53 *Glasgow Courier*, 30 January 1844.
54 *Glasgow Herald*, 26 February 1852.
55 *Glasgow Herald*, 12 April 1852.
56 SC 1852-3, Para. 4447.

5 Prevention is better than cure
The Aberdeen industrial schools, 1841–1854

Whereas Glasgow tackled juvenile delinquency by providing for offenders released from prison, Aberdeen approached the problem from a different angle by focusing on children who had not yet fallen into crime. An explanation can be found in an examination of local economic variations and of the different types of agencies for the poor and needy which already existed in these cities. However, the role of remarkable individuals in influencing the course of events should not be underestimated and this is particularly true of Aberdeen, where credit for developing the concept of day industrial feeding schools is largely due to two prominent figures, Sheriff William Watson (1796–1887) and Alexander Thomson of Banchory (1798–1868).

Economic and social background

Aberdeen is perhaps not the most obvious place for a new approach to juvenile delinquency to emerge. It was much smaller than Glasgow or Edinburgh and the growth of its population was less dramatic in the first half of the century: between 1811 and 1851, for example, the population of Glasgow increased by three and a half times, whereas that of Aberdeen doubled.[1] Only 2 per cent of this increase was attributable to Irish immigration, compared to 18 per cent in Glasgow. It has also been suggested that industrial change in Aberdeen was largely based on traditional activities such as cotton manufacture, distilling, fishing and port facilities which 'produced less social disruption in Aberdeen than in other Scottish cities'.[2] On the other hand, A.A. McLaren, in his study of *Religion and Social Class* in Aberdeen in the 1840s, argues that

> Over a few decades Aberdeen changed from being an entrepôt for the export of hosiery and textile goods produced in the rural hinterland to an urban centre whose economy was largely based on the manufacture of textiles on a factory system.[3]

This view tends to be substantiated by the information contained in the *New Statistical Account of Scotland*, published in 1845. Approximately 14,000 people were employed in factories in the city in mills producing cotton, flax and wool, and in iron, paper and rope-making, with perhaps another 2,000 working in the stone industry for which Aberdeen is famous. 'On opposite sides of the River Don', writes McLaren, 'stood the largest linen factory and perhaps the biggest cotton factory in the United Kingdom'.[4] Simply stated, the replacement of old crafts and agricultural occupations by new work in factories caused a dislocation of country life, leading to agricultural workers coming to the city in search of employment.

One manifestation of this which became a cause for concern in the late 1830s was the growing number of vagrants to be found in both the city and the county. Gangs of beggars were reported to be roaming the countryside, demanding food and money, and as a rural police force was not established until 1845 it was claimed that 'the law could not be carried into effect in the counties of Aberdeen and Banff'.[5] Between April 1840 and April 1841, 2,459 vagrants were reported in the county.

Such problems were a foretaste of the social distress which was to characterise Aberdeen throughout the decade. In common with the rest of Scotland, the city did not escape the effects of the general depression of the 'hungry forties'. The closure of a woollen mill in the parish of Old Machar[6] in 1840 deprived 300 workers of their jobs, and in the winter of 1841–1842 an 'unemployed labourers' fund' had to be set up to provide food and work such as stone-breaking and road repairs. In 1842–1843 there was 'a great outcry of want of employment'[7] and a further crisis occurred in the mills in 1845, followed by a potato blight in 1846 which led to high food prices which continued into 1847. Prices fell between 1847 and 1850 but rose again over the next five years, during which vagrancy once more increased, being affected also by a change in the poor relief regulations whereby able-bodied women with only one child were refused relief.

'The Children's Sheriff' and 'the simple country gentleman': William Watson and Alexander Thomson of Banchory

In spite of the growing amount of distress, there was no great interest in social reform in Aberdeen in the early 1840s. Many of the members of the Society of Advocates were high Tories who believed the poor were quite adequately provided for. Dr. Alison, the poor law reformer, was called a 'bigot, an enthusiast and a man of little experience' and even Alexander Thomson, a great supporter of industrial schools, thought that 'the poor were in the spirit of the Gospel liberally supplied by voluntary charity'.[8]

But there was one prominent member of the legal profession in the city who took a stand against such opinions: Sheriff William Watson. Born in April 1796, the son of a Lanarkshire sheep-farmer, Watson had been educated at Edinburgh University and served his legal apprenticeship with Andrew Storie, Clerk to the Signet. He passed his examination and secured a commission as Writer to the Signet at the age of twenty-four but worked as principal clerk in Storie's office as he had neither the capital nor connections to set up his own business. Largely through Storie's recommendation, he was offered the post of Sheriff-Substitute of Aberdeenshire in March 1829, a position he held for thirty-seven years.

Prevention is better than cure 59

Figure 5.1 Sheriff William Watson

Source: *Sheriff Watson of Aberdeen: the Story of his Life, and his Work for the Young* by Marion Angus, Aberdeen, 1913

One of his earliest recorded impressions of Aberdeen was his dismay at the prevalence of drunkenness. After observing the previous night's New Year celebrations, he wrote in his diary on 1 January 1831: 'How many headaches and empty pockets will there be to-morrow? – probably 5,000 out of the 55,000.'[9]

Like other legal figures such as Andrew Jameson of Edinburgh or M.D. Hill in Birmingham, Watson's interest in the reformation of criminals arose out of his encounters with offenders in his official capacity in the courtroom. His granddaughter and biographer Marion Angus tells how he was soon known for his

> great facility in eliciting the truth ... One story is recalled of a witness who had been primed beforehand as to what to say and whose long statement...was listened to patiently by the Sheriff... 'Now, my good woman,' he then said quietly, 'will you look at me, and tell me if this story is true.' Silence in the court for the space of half a minute, and then in a burst of candour, possibly of relief – 'Not a single word o't, my Lord. It's a' a lee, fae beginning to end.'[10]

The year of Watson's arrival in Aberdeen saw a rise in recorded crime thanks to the 1829 Police Act which, by creating a number of new offences, immediately resulted in a dramatic rise in prison commitments. 'Every day called upon to punish crime', says Marion Angus, 'it was impossible for one of his warm and emotional nature to do so without pity for and consideration of the condition of the criminal'.[11] As was the case with Wilberforce and Shaftesbury, this concern was motivated above all by his evangelical faith, and he strongly believed that not only society, but he personally, had a responsibility to the criminal and destitute. On the last day of 1839 he wrote in his diary:

> What have I done for my fellow-men?
> Nothing!
> Nothing!
> Nothing!
> What can I do?
> What does He will that I do?
> That I love Him with all my strength and might – and my neighbour as myself.
> How can I love the Father and not the child?
> I must live no longer for myself but for His little ones.
> Faith without works is dead.[12]

Described as a 'liberal' in politics, he nevertheless felt that as Sheriff he should keep aloof from party politics, and accordingly sought to promote the cause of social reform through involvement in local boards and charities rather than through political or parliamentary channels. Watson's importance in the history of the treatment of poverty and crime in Aberdeen can scarcely be exaggerated: his time in office spans the most important years in the development of new approaches to social problems and he was involved in all the local administrative bodies connected with police, prisons and poor law as well as playing an active part in most of the city's charitable institutions. Watson's life is thus a unifying force in the social history of Aberdeen in the period.

The Sheriff evidently had strong ideas about the efficacy of various philanthropic efforts. He supported the setting up of a House of Refuge for the destitute which opened in 1836, thanks to the generosity of Dr. George Watt, who had lost his son from cholera. On the other hand, it is recorded that, while he was impressed by meeting the prison reformer Elizabeth Fry, he did not consider that her Ladies' Visiting Society would achieve much for prisoners and he suggested to one of its local members, Miss Elizabeth Ogilvie, that more good would be done by preventing girls becoming prisoners than by attempting to reform them afterwards. Watson's initial proposals for more targeted help for children were at first met with 'much opposition and few promises of help',[13] but he pressed on regardless and opened his industrial school on 1 October 1841.

On the first day, one of those waiting anxiously with Watson was his most influential supporter, Alexander Thomson of Banchory House. While posterity has, rightly, recognised the Sheriff as the founder of the industrial school system which soon spread across Scotland and beyond, Thomson's name has lapsed into obscurity. Part of the reason, as Rev. Professor George Smeaton notes at the start of his biography of Thomson, may be that his life was one 'with little in it of the imposing, and nothing of stirring incident'.[14] That did not prevent Smeaton filling a total of 548 pages, leaning heavily on lengthy extracts from Thomson's diaries and correspondence. Reviewing this volume – which appeared only a year after the death of its subject – *The Spectator* reckoned that 'the memoir will not be widely read' as Thomson 'belonged to a school fast passing away; but it will be long before his name perishes out of the country…'[15] Today, little is heard of either.

In one of his more succinct passages, Smeaton describes the book as

> the record of a man who was, by the circumstances of his fortune, enabled to set apart a large portion of his time to the cultivation of his mind and, prompted by Divine grace, to consecrate his position and talents to the glory of God and the good of others…[16]

This effectively summarised three of the most significant features of Thomson's character: his insatiable thirst for knowledge, his religious devotion and his passionate desire for social improvement.

Figure 5.2 Alexander Thomson
Source: *Memoir of Alexander Thomson of Banchory* by Rev. George Smeaton, Edinburgh, 1869

Thomson was born at his family's country estate at Banchory House, near the mouth of the River Dee, in June 1798. Appropriately enough for one who was to take a keen interest in the ecclesiastical controversies of his day, he could trace his genealogy back to John Knox, and an antique watch said to have belonged to the great Scottish reformer was one of the family's proudest possessions. Brought up as an only child, Thomson lost his father at the age of eight and soon showed signs of academic brilliance. He was sent to the Grammar School of Aberdeen and at the age of seventeen began keeping a diary which he continued for the rest of his life. His studies at Aberdeen University were followed by reading for the Bar at the University of Edinburgh in 1816, though he never practised, deciding, with his customary sense of duty, that devoting himself to managing the family estate was 'his true calling'. Signs of his latent social concern were seen when he resolved on coming of age to be 'a humble but sincere Christian ... allotting my income so as to be always able to assist my tenants in hard times, and securing a due share to the wants of the poor'.[17] At the same time, by pursuing measures such as extensive tree planting and allowing crofters on his land to work on reclaiming wasteland, he vastly increased the value of the estate.

Yet Thomson's main love in life was scholarship. He embarked on a number of extensive tours throughout Europe, meticulously recording visits to universities, libraries and archaeological sites. Of one visit to Paris, he wrote that 'To me the most tempting places were the book-stands'.[18] At home he worked on Egyptian papyri, and systematically pursued studies in languages, geology, history and many other fields, publishing papers on everything from the tenets of Roman Catholicism to the cultivation of chicory and flax in Belgium.

Like Watson, Thomson held many prominent roles in Aberdeen, including convener of a committee appointed to organise a rural police force and chairman of the County Prison Board. His biographer notes that

> his long connexion with the Prison Board of Aberdeen (from 1840 to 1862), and the legal studies of his youth requiring, as it were, some practical outlet for activity, led him to mature his views on the whole subject of criminal law and penal servitude.[19]

Thomson also shared Watson's religious outlook. Around 1830 he had a conversion experience which gave him a new set of priorities, and he became involved with the evangelical party within the Church of Scotland, supporting the work of church extension and erecting a new church at Portleith near his estate. Again like Watson, he was conscious of his personal responsibility to help improve society. His diary entry for his fifty-seventh birthday reads: 'Far past the prime of life. How little done! O God, for more grace and more activity in thy service.'[20]

In spite of such feelings of inadequacy, by then he had thrown 'the whole weight of his influence'[21] behind Watson's industrial school experiment which he helped to publicise through two books, *Industrial Schools; their Origin, Rise, and Progress, in Aberdeen* (1847) and *Social Evils, their Causes and their Cure* (1852). Thomson was gratified to learn that Sir Joshua Jebb, Surveyor-General of Prisons, had reproduced a large section of *Social Evils* and circulated it in a report sent to all members of the Houses of Parliament. Thomson further promoted the work of industrial schools through lectures in connection with the Social Science Association and by supporting the campaign for legislation in the 1850s. His biographer is no doubt correct in observing that, if he had chosen to follow a parliamentary career, 'he might perhaps have filled a larger place in the public eye'.[22] On the other hand, that remark might well be balanced against the words of the novelist William Makepeace Thackeray who, after visiting the Aberdeen industrial schools, told Watson: 'You are doing more good than all the members of Parliament in Great Britain.'[23]

In common with the majority of evangelicals, both Watson and Thomson joined the Free Church at the Disruption in 1843, a movement which was particularly strong in Aberdeen, where the ministers of every church in the city left the Establishment. As A.A. McLaren has shown in his study of religion and society in the city in these years, many of the middle-class and professional men of the Free Church brought as much energy to bear on social problems as they brought to the formation and extension of their new denomination, and the Aberdeen industrial schools were the most remarkable example of this.

Origins of the industrial schools experiment

In his book *Chapters on Ragged and Industrial Schools*, Sheriff Watson makes a significant observation about the eclectic nature of the Aberdeen system: 'There is no one feature … which is not to be found in some other school, or poorhouse, or hospital. But there is no other institution where the different parts are so combined into one whole.'[24]

His comment is one of the clearest contemporary statements of a theme which runs through the present volume: that new developments in the prevention and treatment of juvenile crime were shaped by the need to supplement rather than replace the work of other institutions, whether these were inside or outside the penal system. The remainder of this chapter will show how Watson used existing local provision for the poor and destitute to produce his own distinctive method of preventing children falling into crime.

In the eighteenth century, Aberdeen was one of the few Scottish towns with a poorhouse, founded in 1739 'to promote religion, suppress vice, propagate industry and virtue, and be a general benefit to society'.[25] By 1828 a separate Boys' Hospital had been opened, followed by a similar institution for girls, but admission to these was restricted to those who had a claim on the parish. The Town Council of Aberdeen was also active in taking steps to suppress vagrancy: it was resolved in 1824 that all vagrants not able to give an account of themselves should be apprehended and that the Commissioners of Police should 'give the use of their lock-up Cells, any time they may be wanted'.[26] Provision for this was embodied in a clause in the local Police Act of 1829 which, although inoperative, was to be made use of later in connection with the industrial schools.

These activities of the local authorities were supplemented by private benevolence when a House of Refuge was opened in 1836, thanks to Dr. George Watt's

£1,000 donation. The intention behind Watt's benefaction was primarily to provide for homeless children, but the Town Council felt that something wider was required and extended the facilities to include adults. Even so, children constituted a large proportion of the inmates: during the first seven months of its existence, 90 of the 161 admissions to the Refuge were under the age of fourteen. The object of the training they received was both preventive and reformatory: the juveniles were described either as 'penitent delinquents', in whose case 'the discipline begun in Jail or Bridewell would be continued', or orphans who 'as yet had committed no crime, but who derive a precarious subsistence by begging'.[27]

The year 1840 marked the beginning of a period of economic hardship and the development of new and more organised social services to deal with it. The establishment of a Prison Board, the Aberdeenshire Rural Police, the industrial schools, the Poor Law Board – in each of which Sheriff Watson was involved – all date from the early years of the decade. Moreover, the existence of these agencies meant that poverty, vagrancy and crime could now be more accurately quantified through admissions registers, criminal returns and similar statistics. It is not only the existence of, but also the awareness of the existence of, social distress which makes the 1840s such a decisive decade in the formation of new attitudes and approaches to crime and poverty.

All of this forms the background to Watson's experiment with a new type of school. His decision to focus on preventing rather than curing delinquency is understandable as Aberdeen's problem was primarily one of juvenile vagrancy rather than juvenile crime. Bridewell returns from the 1830s show no consistent increase in the number of adult or juvenile commitments for crime.[28] On the other hand, both adult and juvenile vagrancy was high: between 1841 and 1845, well over 2,000 vagrants were annually reported to be in Aberdeenshire; in 1840 the rural police reported 328 children begging in the county, while the city police found over 280 begging and thieving in their area.[29] As it was widely held that juvenile vagrancy was the prelude to crime, Watson and Thomson felt that providing industrial schools would forestall the inevitable rise in criminality.

Though accounts of the schools were to talk of an 'Aberdeen system' based on a distinctive ideology, this only developed gradually in the light of experience. The examination of the individual schools which follows shows that Watson's methodology was based on an empirical approach, and the Aberdeen 'system' was in fact worked out retrospectively. As Thomson put it, 'Selecting from other schemes whatever was beneficial to the class whose welfare he sought to promote, and carefully avoiding whatever he felt would exercise a hurtful influence, he gradually worked out the plan which has proved so successful'.[30]

Industrial school in Chronicle Lane (1841)

Watson's practical, step-by-step approach can be seen from the origins of his first school – described by Marion Angus as 'the wee, small school in Chronicle Lane' – opened in October 1841. A dingy loft above a blacksmith's shop was hired and, with the co-operation of the police, half a dozen children, 'the most ragged and pestilent beggars of their acquaintance',[31] were rounded up. They were told that if they came to school they would receive daily meals, but that henceforth no street begging would be tolerated by the police. There was no certainty that the children who had attended on the first day would return on the second, and even the opening of the school merited only a brief paragraph in the local press. This low-key start is explained by the fact that the school was commenced not as a new venture but 'by way of experiment in connection with the House of Refuge'.[32] Edward Reid, the Superintendent of the Refuge, was also in charge of the industrial school, and he made use of some of the inmates of the Refuge in supervising the children. Homeless youngsters attending the school were lodged at the Refuge, while boys who were already inmates there were taught and given industrial training at the school, in exchange for which the industrial school pupils were fed at the Refuge. These arrangements also help to explain one of the central features of Watson's system: his insistence that industrial school children should not be detained in the school in dormitories. This was partly based on the conviction – which he held for the rest of his life – that allowing children to return to their parents at night not only maintained the family tie but might also result in some of the lessons they had learned regarding conduct, industry and hygiene being transferred to their home environments. However, it is also true to say that because the House of Refuge took in necessitous cases, a dormitory attached to the school was superfluous from a practical as well as an ideological point of view.

Over the next ten years the work of the original school was supplemented by others, and by the end of the 1850s these had all been consolidated into a complex of inter-related institutions designed to prevent juvenile delinquency.

Girls' School of Industry (1843)

According to Marion Angus, the Girls' School, like the Dean Bank Institution in Edinburgh, originated as a result of the work of a ladies' prison visiting committee set up by Elizabeth Fry. On Watson's suggestion, some ladies on the committee organised a public meeting to consider a girls' industrial school based on the model of the Chronicle Lane experiment. This opened on 5 June 1843 at Longacre and although there were only three children at first, the roll increased to twenty-six by the end of the year.

In the tense religious atmosphere in the years after the Disruption, the Girls' School fell victim to sectarian rivalry. It was dominated by members of the Free Church, who comprised eighteen of the twenty-four ladies on the committee, and disagreements came to a head in December 1846. The Free Church majority refused to allow the pupils to attend the East Parish (i.e. Established) Church where the minister, the Rev. Simon Macintosh (1815–1853), one of the city's most popular preachers, had agreed to preach and take a collection on behalf of the school. Inevitably, this led to a proposal at the next annual meeting that the school should be placed 'on a more liberal and catholic footing', a committee composed equally of Free Church, Established Church and dissenting members being suggested.[33] Watson, a member of the Free West Church, took the side of the existing committee – 'I am here to defend the ladies' – but the Rev. Dr. James Forsyth (1797–1879) of the West Parish Church attributed the decline in subscriptions which the school had suffered to 'public knowledge that it had become a sectarian institution', while the *Aberdeen Herald* noted that there was only one person on the platform at the meeting who was not a minister or member of the Free Church.[34] The outcome was a split which had echoes of the Disruption in the church four years earlier. Taking all but three of the children, but leaving the property and funds, the Free Church ladies seceded to carry on a school in temporary accommodation in Charlotte Street, after which they moved to premises in Skene Street purchased with £700 raised by Watson's supporters. The school assumed the name of Sheriff Watson's Female School of Industry, reflecting his approval of its principles. Meanwhile, the original school – left, as it had commenced, with three girls – reconstituted its committee and re-opened in July 1847 in Shaw's Court, Gallowgate, as the Aberdeen Female School of Industry.

Unedifying though this episode may have been from the point of view of Christian ecumenism, it did produce two schools for girls instead of one, the staff of both having had experience in running an industrial school. One school may have split but the number of girls provided for was doubled. In December 1846 there were sixty-eight girls on the roll of the School of Industry; two years later there were seventy, plus a further sixty-seven in the Free Church school. There are obvious similarities with the dispute in Edinburgh over the education of Roman Catholic children which resulted in the setting up of the United Industrial School. However, while these differences of opinion were accentuated as the years went by, in Aberdeen by the time of the 1862 report of Watson's school the controversy was described as 'an occurrence almost forgotten'. One reason may be that the two Aberdeen school were not competing to attract support from the same sources, as both had their backers. Watson commented that 'As the Churches had entered warmly into the dispute, there was soon no want of funds, and in the year ending 1847 both schools were in a prosperous and satisfactory condition'.[35]

Juvenile School of Industry (1845)

Originally known as the Soup Kitchen School on account of its temporary location in the Kitchen premises in Loch Street, the Juvenile School aimed to extend the principle of prevention by casting the net wider to catch children aged six to nine, whereas the first school had mostly catered for boys between eight and fourteen. The experience of the first few years of the boys' school had shown that 'there is little hope of reclaiming many of them, if they have been previous convicted of crime, for long accustomed to habits of vagrancy'.[36]

Once again, well-established local procedures assisted Watson's venture. 'The decision to bring beggar children to the Kitchen', reported the *Aberdeen Journal* in May 1845, 'was taken by the Town Council in an effort to clear the streets of "youngling beggars of both sexes ... whose clamorous and pertinacious importunities for alms" were "subject of general complaint"'.[37] Authority for this was found by stretching the vagrancy clause of the 1829 Aberdeen Police Act,[38] which, as

Thomson later admitted to the 1852 Select Committee, he had 'not the slightest doubt ... was highly illegal, but at the same time it was highly expedient...'.[39] Instruction was given to the police to round up children found wandering, on the understanding that the Sheriff himself would take responsibility for the exercise. Thus, on 1 May 1845, seventy-five children found themselves at the Soup Kitchen, where they were washed and given breakfast. As happened on the first day of the original school in 1841, they were informed that they would not be forced to return the next day, but begging would no longer be tolerated. According to Thomson's account, all except four were there waiting next morning. Watson's proud claim was that 'in a few hours juvenile vagrancy was finally extinguished in Aberdeen, and has never raised its head again'.[40]

The Child's Asylum Committee (1846)

One lesson of the early months of the Juvenile School was to confirm the importance of dealing with a child when he took his first steps towards vagrancy or crime. A second was that some parents seemed to be deliberately sending their children out to beg in order to gain admission to the school. The establishment of the Child's Asylum Committee in December 1846 was intended to deal with both of these problems by scrutinising admissions to decide whether a child merited a place in one of the schools, whether it should be restored to its parents or whether it had a claim for parochial relief. An example of the way the committee operated can be seen in its December 1847 report. By October of that year it had dealt with thirty-four cases of petty crime and thirty-six of vagrancy. These were disposed of as follows: twenty-seven to the industrial schools, twenty-five delivered up to parents and six to the police for trial as criminal offenders, the remainder being admonished and dismissed.[41] Thus, the committee was not only a further refinement of the policy of prevention; it also demonstrated the closest co-operation so far between charity and authority. Watson is reported in the *Aberdeen Journal* as saying that the committee

> is composed of representatives from the Magistrates, Commissioners of Policy, House of Refuge, Schools of Industry, and Parochial Boards; so that it may be said to be representative of the whole of the public bodies of the town. Their influence is so unquestionable that nobody can find any fault with them.[42]

Above all, Watson's personal involvement at all levels ensured a consistency of approach. As the Free Church newspaper *The Witness* recognised in an article on industrial schools, 'It is no ordinary advantage to have the acting magistrate of the district at the head of such an undertaking'.[43]

The Industrial Schools Association (1851)

Further co-ordination was achieved when, in March 1851, the committees of management of the Boys' School and the Juvenile School were amalgamated to form the Industrial Schools Association of Aberdeen. The two girls' schools, whose existence was a result of religious disagreements, continued to be managed independently. By now, the managers of the Industrial Schools Association considered their schools to have passed the experimental stage and it is noticeable that in the early fifties these institutions began to be referred to as the 'Aberdeen system'. Around this time, too, influential accounts of the development of the schools were published by Watson in *The Juvenile Vagrant and the Industrial School* (1851) and Thomson in *Social Evils* (1852), the implication being that they felt able to speak with authority on the basis of ten years' experience. The feeling that the theory of industrial schools had now been vindicated is also reflected in the content of the annual reports. Thomson's remarks to the annual meeting of Sheriff Watson's Female School in 1855 summarise the stage that had been reached:

> in previous years the reports had to argue the propriety of carrying on these schools, and of the principles on which they were established; but these things were now so thoroughly recognized, that long reports and speeches were quite unnecessarily, and the schools might be left quietly and steadily to carry on the work undertaken by them.[44]

Principles of the 'Aberdeen system'

By the mid-1850s industrial schools on the Aberdeen model had been established in many other towns in Scotland and England, though the systematisation of a network of schools in one town and their integration with existing agencies were above all the distinguishing features of the Aberdeen system. This success gained the schools a national reputation, enhanced by Mary Carpenter's complimentary description of them in her influential book *Reformatory Schools* (1851), which devoted much space to 'Aberdeen, *where alone the system has been fairly tried…*'[45] In her account, Carpenter summarises the factors which contributed to its success:

> the sphere of operation was sufficiently limited to be subject to direct influence from the plan adopted; the individuals most active in carrying it out were influential, and secured the co-operation of members of the different branches of municipal legislation and of charitable institutions; while the evident utility of the plan called forth such willing pecuniary co-operation throughout the town, that the proceedings of the committee were not shackled by want of money.[46]

While rightly appreciating the importance of other local agencies' support to the success of the schools, Mary Carpenter does overestimate the amount of backing they received, as there is plenty of evidence that precarious finances made Watson's gradual approach all the more necessary. Looking back in 1872 on the origins of the schools in his *Chapters on Ragged and Industrial Schools,* he sums up the financial state of each school on its opening by saying that 'the first school began with a subscribed capital of £100, the second with about £20, and the two last entirely on credit'.[47] Tenure of premises was uncertain, and all the schools moved to different buildings at some stage. Public support fluctuated and Thomson singled out the end of 1843 as a crucial period for the Boys' School as public interest waned and admissions had to be temporarily suspended. It was only generous support from the Town Council and the trustees of a charitable trust set up by John Gordon of Murtle that enabled the school to continue. Watson spoke in December 1845 of the insecure position of the recently opened Soup Kitchen School,[48] and by 1847 it had carried on its work in four different premises in the space of two years.

If financial constraints dictated a step-by-step approach, the principles of the system were themselves formulated gradually in the light of experience. Initially, of course, Watson acted upon certain fundamental presuppositions, the first and most important of these being that 'every child has a right to food, clothing and education, either from its parents or the public'.[49] Certainly, efforts to provide these in Aberdeen did not commence with Sheriff Watson. In the 1830s the Rev. A.L. Gordon of Greyfriars Parish Church published an address on the need to educate the poor which led to a number of parochial schools being set up, and the one in Gordon's parish even included some industrial training, as a printer was employed to teach his trade to the pupils. Where Watson went beyond such efforts was in attempting to provide for a class which existing educational facilities could not reach: children whose parents did not want to educate them. The provision of meals as an enticement differentiated the industrial schools from all other schools in the city for, as Thomson put it, 'It is manifest mockery to offer a starving child training or instruction, without *first* providing him with food'.[50] Thus, 'the combination of food, teaching, and industrial training form together the distinctive peculiarity of these schools',[51] the cost of the food being partly offset by the proceeds of the children's industrial work, in order to impress upon them the necessity of earning their bread. The work was not just intended to occupy the pupils' time but was specifically geared to local trades that would enable the children to be readily absorbed into the labouring population when they left school. This was the scene in the Juvenile School in about 1850: 'Thirty boys seated on low stools are actively employed in knitting herring nets. Ten or a dozen small children are busy filling the netting needles, two or three are unwinding the twine...'.[52]

However, this training was not to take place in a setting which cut the children off from their homes. The promoters of industrial schools had witnessed the harmful effects of the hospital system on pauper children and maintained that 'Family ties are the foundation laid by the Creator himself for the good order of society; whatever tends to break them up ... must be evil'.[53] Related to this was the attempt to interest the parents in the work of the school, and soirees were held at which parents and friends were invited to tea. One such event, reported in the *Aberdeen Journal* for 25 August 1847, is described as 'another effective step in the right direction of social love'.

If the provision of meals and the maintenance of the home connection remained fundamental features of the Aberdeen schools, other aspects developed over time. For example, the very success of the schools in tackling juvenile vagrancy led to fluctuations in the type of children attending. Only seventeen were admitted to the schools by the Asylum Committee in 1851, compared to ninety-five in 1847.[54] As this class diminished, it became more difficult to fill the schools, and places were granted to children whose parents applied for their admission, being unable to feed them. Judging by figures quoted by Thomson, the majority of these were admitted. In 1850, for example, of 108 applicants, only 10 were refused admission and 2 were referred to the Poor Law authorities.[55] Care was taken, though, to ensure that no parent took advantage of the free education offered by the schools. In May 1849 the roll of the Juvenile School was reduced by seventeen, as a sub-committee appointed to look into the state of the parents discovered that 'from the resumption of work at some of the manufacturies, and the improvement in trade, several of the families were in better circumstances than when the children were admitted – they therefore recommended that their children should be dismissed.'[56]

Another relevant factor might be that at the date of the widening of the categories eligible for admission, Aberdeen was particularly well served with industrial school accommodation, having a boys' girls, two girls' schools and one mixed school, their combined capacity being in the region of 350 pupils.

A further way in which the schools evolved over the years was in their relationship with existing institutions. Initially other social service agencies had assisted the industrial schools, but as the schools expanded their operations they began to encroach upon areas formerly catered for by these agencies, in particular the House of Refuge and the Boys' and Girls' Hospitals. Moreover, the establishment of Parochial Boards after the 1845 Poor Law Act added a further dimension to the city's social services.

An example of this can be seen from the experience of the House of Refuge. Although the first industrial school was opened as an extension of the Refuge's provision for children, with boys who had no homes being lodged there, the Refuge managers discovered there were disadvantages from their point of view:

> While these schools are relieving this institution of the burden of most of these children who have a home to go to, they are annually drawing off, in a much greater proportion, the revenue which before was received from the public by the latter Institution (House of Refuge) alone.[57]

More serious still from the point of view of the Refuge was the fact that its very existence was being questioned in the light of the recent Poor Law Act. The two city parishes – St. Nicholas and Old Machar – opened their own poorhouses, thereby catering for many of those formerly housed in the Refuge. The new Poor Law arrangements impacted on the industrial schools, too, as the financing of relief by assessment and the systematisation of allowances drew attention to the fact that many children on the roll of the schools were entitled to parochial aid. Of sixty-three children on the roll of the Boys' School in April–May 1847, forty-six were chargeable to parishes. Reluctant to dismiss the children and hand them over to the care of the parochial boards which might not provide adequately for their education, the school decided to keep the children and make 'an earnest and urgent appeal ... to the parochial boards for a grant to the school, in consideration of the benefits therein derived by the children'.⁵⁸ The parochial board of St. Nicholas made a gesture in this direction in September 1847, giving a donation of £30 to the school on condition that it received all children with a claim on the parish,⁵⁹ and a similar arrangement was presumably made with Old Machar parish. By May 1849, the seventh annual report of the Boys' School stated that of ninety-six children attending the Boys' School, forty-seven were paupers, and the schools continued to press for more realistic grants from the boards.

After 1854, a further factor has to be taken into account in shaping the system: the effect of government legislation. In the early years of industrial schools in Aberdeen there was less enthusiasm for state intervention than in other cities. The 1845 report of the Boys' School sounded a note of confidence and independence:

> It has been frequently suggested that an application should be made to Government for a grant to the Schools. Your Committee have deemed this inexpedient. They consider that those who reap the advantage should pay the price; and the public have rendered such an application unnecessary, inasmuch as the funds in the hands of the Treasurer, at the close of the year, amounted to £124.⁶⁰

In the same year, the managers of the Soup Kitchen congratulated themselves that 'it is apparent to all that our streets are now well nigh cleared of [juvenile] applicants for casual charity'.⁶¹

A decade later, both the financial state of the schools and their success in suppressing vagrancy were far less convincing. The roll of the Juvenile School had been declining since 1851, and it was being maintained out of its reserve fund, while the Boys' School reported a decrease in subscriptions and a poor response to an appeal to the city churches.⁶² Attendance figures, too, were erratic. Alexander Thomson said in 1855 that 'the power of the law was required to counteract the evil dispositions of the parents who withdrew their children from the schools'.⁶³ Most serious of all was 'the startling and most painful fact, that in the last two years, not less than 18 children, who had been at one or other of the Industrial Schools, have been committed to prison...'⁶⁴ In a report on juvenile delinquency submitted to the Aberdeen Prisons Board in 1855, Alexander Thomson put forward a possible explanation:

> Our neglected population has outgrown the means of instruction and training provided for them. Since the last Industrial School was opened in 1847, there has probably been addition of 8000 to the population of Aberdeen ... but no additional provision of Industrial Schools has been made for them, though something has been done by opening ordinary schools in neglected localities. The Committee can only express their desire that there were more Industrial Schools.⁶⁵

The conclusion which seems to emerge is that although the industrial schools became consolidated into a system in the early 1850s, this system reached a stage beyond which it could not develop on its existing footing, and turned to government for assistance. Aberdeen, then, in common with Edinburgh and Glasgow, hoped the state would support existing local arrangements by providing further legal powers and funding. At the same time, the Industrial Schools Association was concerned that the schools would retain their original characteristics. In a letter to M.D. Hill, Thomson emphasised that in the proposed Act the schools should be given the full title of 'Juvenile Ragged Industrial Feeding School', thus giving 'the sanction of the legislature to the two leading principles on which they proceed, viz:- industrial training and feeding'.[66] Given this, it was Thomson's hope that 'It may reasonably be expected that the working out of the new law will necessitate the establishment of additional Industrial Feeding Schools in all our towns'.[67]

Notes

1 Population of Parliamentary Burgh of Aberdeen (Parishes of St. Nicholas and part of Old Machar), 1801–51:

   1801:   26,992
   1811:   34,640
   1821:   43,821
   1831:   56,681
   1841:   63,288
   1851:   71,973

   Source: *Census of Great Britain, 1851 Population Tables, Vol. II* (London, 1852), p. 66.
2 P. Seed, 'Types of Conceptualisation of Ascribed Client Need in Social Service Provision' (Aberdeen University, Ph.D thesis, 1976), p. 11.
3 A.A. McLaren, *Religion and Social Class: The Disruption Years in Aberdeen* (London and Boston, 1974), p. 7.
4 Ibid., p. 2.
5 W. Watson, *Pauperism, Vagrancy, Crime, and Industrial Education in Aberdeenshire, 1840–1875* (Edinburgh and London, 1877), p. 18.
6 Of the two Aberdeen parishes (the other being St. Nicholas), Old Machar tended to have less poverty, and enclosed the residences of the wealthy.
7 J. Lindsay, *The Scottish Poor Law: its Operation in the North-East from 1745 to 1845* (Ilfracombe, 1975), p. 54.
8 M. Angus, *Sheriff Watson of Aberdeen: the Story of his Life and his Work for the Young* (Aberdeen, 1913), p. 22.
9 Ibid., p. 21.
10 Ibid., p. 55.
11 Ibid., p. 21.
12 Ibid., p. 58.
13 Ibid., p. 59.
14 Rev. George Smeaton, *Memoir of Alexander Thomson of Banchory* (Edinburgh, 1869), p. 2.
15 *The Spectator,* 29 May 1869, p. 655.
16 Smeaton, op. cit., p. 2.
17 Ibid., p. 27.
18 Ibid., p. 31.
19 Ibid., p. 180.
20 Ibid., p. 367.

21 Ibid., p. 181.
22 Ibid., p. 23.
23 Angus, op. cit., p. 82.
24 William Watson, *Chapters on Ragged and Industrial Schools* (Edinburgh and London, 1872), p. 6.
25 *The History of the Workhouse or Poor's Hospital of Aberdeen* (Aberdeen, 1885), p. 3.
26 Jean Lindsay, *The Scottish Poor Law: Its Operation in the North-East from 1745 to 1845* (Ilfracombe, 1975), p. 107.
27 Report of the Committee appointed by the General Meeting of Subscribers to the proposed Establishment of a House of Refuge for the Destitute, and Asylum for Children [n.d.].
28 *The New Statistical Account of Scotland*, Vol. XII (Edinburgh and London, 1845), p. 82.
29 William Watson, *The Juvenile Vagrant and the Industrial School: or, 'Prevention better than Cure'* (Aberdeen, 1851), p. 9.
30 Alexander Thomson, *Social Evils: Their Causes and Their Cure* (London, 1852), p. 66.
31 William Watson, *Chapters*, p. 14.
32 Ibid., p. 14.
33 *Aberdeen Journal*, 30 December 1846.
34 *Aberdeen Herald*, 26 December 1846.
35 Watson, *Chapters*, p. 15.
36 Third Report of the Committee of Management of the Juvenile School of Industry, 1847–8, p. 10.
37 Lindsay, op. cit., p. 100.
38 Section 171 of the Police Act stated that a beggar apprehended by the police would be warned that if he was found begging again within forty-eight hours he would be liable for up to sixty days in Bridewell.
39 SC 1852, para. 3035.
40 Watson, *The Juvenile Vagrant*, p. 15.
41 *Aberdeen Journal*, 29 December 1847.
42 15 September 1847.
43 *The Witness*, 24 February 1847.
44 *Aberdeen Journal*, 21 March 1855.
45 Mary Carpenter, *Reformatory Schools* (London, 1851), p. 236.
46 Ibid., p. 225.
47 William Watson, *Chapters on Ragged and Industrial Schools* (Edinburgh and London, 1872), p. 15.
48 *Aberdeen Herald*, 13 December 1845.
49 *Aberdeen Banner*, 17 July 1846.
50 Alexander Thomson, *Social Evils* (London, 1852), p. 69.
51 Papers on the Aberdeen Industrial Feeding Schools in A. Thomson's papers, New College, Edinburgh.
52 William Watson, *Should I subscribe to the Industrial School? or Reasons for the Education of Pauper Children* (Aberdeen, 1850), p. 7.
53 Alexander Thomson, *Industrial Schools* (Aberdeen, 1847), p. 12.
54 Alexander Thomson, *Social Evils* (London, 1852), p. 117.
55 Ibid., p. 116.
56 Fourth Report of the Juvenile School of Industry, 1849, p. 7.
57 *Aberdeen Journal*, 25 August 1847.
58 Quotations and figures from *Aberdeen Journal*, 7 September 1847.
59 *Aberdeen Journal*, 28 April 1847.
60 *Aberdeen Herald*, 26 April 1845.
61 Ibid., 5 July 1845.
62 Seventh Report of the Aberdeen Industrial Schools Association, 1856–7.
63 *Aberdeen Journal*, 20 June 1855.

64 [Alexander Thomson], Report by Committee of Prisons' Board of the County of Aberdeen to the Board, on the Causes of the Remarkable Increase in Juvenile Delinquency in the County of Aberdeen (18 July 1855), p. 19.
65 Ibid.
66 Letter to M.D. Hill, Esq., on Juvenile Ragged Industrial Feeding Schools, p. 3.
67 Report by Committee of Prisons' Board, p. 19.

6 Ragged school rivalry

The Original versus the United Industrial School in Edinburgh, 1847–1854

The name of the Rev. Thomas Guthrie, D.D. will always be associated with the institution he founded in 1847, the Edinburgh Original Ragged School, which lived on as Dr. Guthrie's Boys' and Girls' Schools until as recently as 1985. Yet his key achievement was not so much to found a school or devise a new approach to the problem of juvenile vagrancy and crime; his role was, rather, one of publicising and persuading, initially through writing his famous *Plea for Ragged Schools* in 1847. More than any other figure, Guthrie spread the message of ragged schools throughout Scotland, the UK and beyond, and played a crucial part in the campaign for support from the state. His genius was perhaps best summed up in the tribute paid to him after his death by the Rev. William Robertson of New Greyfriars parish, who had set up his own ragged school in 1846, some months before Guthrie's:

> It matters little who it was that established the first Ragged School in Edinburgh or in Scotland. It is not the single school which Thomas Guthrie established ... which is his real monument, but the hundreds of Ragged Schools which the powerful pleading of his eloquent tongue and pen has planted in half the cities of the British empire.[1]

But Guthrie was not only a ragged school pioneer; he was also a leading figure in the recently formed Free Church, and his stance on religious instruction in the Edinburgh school quickly led to controversy. This chapter will examine (i) the significance of Guthrie's life and work; (ii) the relationship between his school and previous attempts to set up similar establishments in Edinburgh; (iii) the extent to which the subsequent development of the city's industrial schools was shaped by sectarian division.

'A really gude man': Rev. Dr. Thomas Guthrie (1803–1873)

A group of drinkers in an unlicensed public house in Victorian Edinburgh were discussing their opinions of the local clergy. 'I'll tell ye a gude man, a really gude man', said one. 'Tam Guthrie. He's different frae the ithers: he practises mair than he preaches.' The story is no doubt apocryphal, and Dr. Guthrie might not have entirely welcomed the endorsement as he was a firm believer that preaching and social action were inseparable. To a large extent, it was his success in the first area that explains his achievements in the second.

An examination of the earlier stages of Guthrie's career reveals why he was the perfect candidate to become what Samuel Smiles called 'the Apostle of Ragged Schools'.[2] The skills which he honed in the pulpit were seamlessly transferred to the platform of the public meeting and to the printed page. As *The Times* noted in September 1860,

> Dr. Guthrie is the greatest of our pulpit orators, and those who have never heard him will probably obtain a better idea of his wonderful eloquence from his work on Ragged Schools than from his published sermons … The writer is himself under the influence of a mastering passion, and he carries his readers along with him, by the help of a strong, clear style and a boundless store of illustrations…[3]

Unlike many preachers of his day, Thomas Guthrie was not 'a son of the manse'. He was born in Brechin, Angus, on 12 July 1803, the twelfth child of David Guthrie, a merchant 'engaged in many departments of business – a banker, grocer, seed-merchant, ship-owner'[4] who was also Provost or chief magistrate of the city. Thomas' early education was in a local school run by a humble weaver. 'There were some half-dozen of us who sat on stools', he recalled, 'conning our lessons to the click of his shuttle, while he sat weaving, gently reminding us from time to time of our tasks, by the use of a leather thong at the end of a long stick'.[5] As soon as the children could recognise letters and sound out words, they moved straight into reading the Book of Proverbs. Looking back on these days in his unfinished autobiography, Guthrie trenchantly remarked: 'What a contrast to the silly trash of modern schoolbooks for beginners, with such sentences as, "Tom has a dog"; "The Cat is good"; "The Cow has a calf"!'[6] Cynicism about new-fangled teaching methods, it seems, is nothing new in Scottish education.

Guthrie went on to receive more advanced schooling at the hands of university-trained teachers in other establishments in Brechin and it was there that signs of his combative spirit emerged. He gained a reputation as the best fighter among the boys, and would challenge opponents with one hand tied behind his back. It was not only his classmates that he was prepared to take on. Asked in class to read a passage aloud, his reply was 'Not ready, sir!', which would usually secure another half-hour's preparation time from the teacher. However, on this occasion,

> something had put him into a savage humour. So, without more ado, he discharged it on me, springing from his seat to haul me from mine, and say, with fury in his face, as he struck the table with clenched hand – I'll *make* you ready!" Well, no doubt … I should have bowed my head to the storm, whereby I would have come off little the worse. But my blood got up, and I refused to read one word. Blows had no more effect on me than on an iron pillar. My class-fellows stood trembling. The attention of the school was wholly turned on the struggle. Transported with rage at the prospect of being baffled by a

boy, he dropped the strap for a ruler, and beat me black and blue with it on the head. He might have broken my skull; he could not break my resolution, and at length gave it up ... Seeing me return next day with a brow and face all marred and swollen, he regretted, I believe his violence, and was very gracious. I had no choice but to return. My parents were wiser than my teacher, my mother telling me, when I said I would not return but tell my father how I had been used, 'You had better not; he will lick you next!' We were brought up hardier *louns* than the present generation, and did not get on any the worse in life for that.[7]

Whatever might be thought of the pedagogical methods employed, they evidently produced results, for Guthrie was able to enrol at Edinburgh University at what he later called the 'preposterously early age of twelve years'.[8] There he followed a wide-ranging course comprising, among other subjects, Latin, Greek, literature, moral philosophy, logic (which he considered at the age of thirteen to be 'a farrago of nonsense'[9]), mathematics and divinity. 'I was a mere boy, pushed on too fast at school, and sent to the University much too soon.'[10] Here, too, he got into scrapes, on one occasion gathering a crowd in the college yard as he challenged a fellow student to a fight for making a fool of his Brechin accent. On his own admission, 'beyond the departments of fun and fighting, I was no way distinguished at college'.[11] But there was no doubt that the country lad who had 'shot up into 6 feet 2½ inches without the shoes by the time he was seventeen years of age'[12] was well able to look after himself.

In his autobiography Guthrie does not say much about experiencing any strong sense of a call to be a preacher. While unquestioningly endorsing the religious attitudes of the day – believing, for example, that the strict observation of the Sabbath, which he concedes

could not be very agreeable to the volatile temperament of the young ... was the means of training them to those habits of patient endurance, obedience, and self-denial, to which, as much as to their good school education, Scotsmen owed their success when they went forth ... to push their fortunes in the world[13]

– he does not, as his sons point out in their memoir of their father's life, 'ever speak much of his own spiritual history'.[14] It was his parents' wish that he would become a minister and it was assumed that his father would use his influence to find a patron who would provide Thomas with a living.

As expected, the possibility of 'one of the largest charges and best livings in Scotland' was soon within his grasp. All he was required to do was to pay his respects to the leader of the Moderates, the anti-Evangelical party within the Established Church, or rather – as Guthrie saw it – 'sell my liberty to him, "my birthright for a mess of pottage"'.[15] Needless to say, he refused to do so and another candidate was appointed in his place.

While waiting for a suitable charge, Guthrie took himself off to Paris in 1826, ostensibly to pursue further study at the Sorbonne. This was the first time he had been outside Scotland, and he first spent some weeks in London, thereafter crossing the Channel and finding lodgings in the French capital in the Rue Cassette and later on Quai St. Michel. Notwithstanding his initial horror at the 'rampant' Popery and infidelity, Guthrie seems to have got on remarkably well in the country, making friends in his *pension*, learning the French language, attending classes at the Sorbonne, witnessing operations carried out by famous surgeons, viewing corpses in the Morgue and even visiting 'a celebrated gambling-house in the Palais Royal' where he reckoned that those who had 'staked and lost their all went to throw themselves into the Seine, and fill the tables of the Morgue'.[16]

He returned to Scotland in May the following year to find that, once again, siding with the Evangelical party in the Church cost him preferment, confirming his resolution to 'do my utmost to hurl [the Moderates] from power'.[17] He next spent two years working in a bank in Brechin managed by his elder brother, a period which he reckoned to be 'not the least valuable part of my training and education'.[18] At length he was inducted to the living of Arbirlot, near Arbroath, in 1830, a parish populated by farm workers and weavers. It was here that he refined his manner of delivery, avoiding 'dry disquisitions' and developing a style rich in anecdote and illustration. 'I resolved', he said, 'to spare no pains, nor toil, nor time in careful preparation, in making my descriptions graphic, my statements lucid, my appeals pathetic, in filling my discourses, in fact, with what would both *strike* and *stick*'.[19] Lord Cockburn (1779–1854), Solicitor-General for Scotland, considered that 'Guthrie is our greatest preacher, and though never courting vulgar popularity ... he is pre-eminently the orator of the poor'.[20]

Guthrie soon found himself drawn into the ecclesiastical controversies of the day, speaking at often rowdy public meetings. The burning issue was the abolition of patronage: its opponents believed that, instead of a wealthy patron choosing the minister of a parish church, the decision should be in the hands of the congregation. Many saw a parallel with what was happening politically: just as the 1832 Reform Bill started the process of transferring political influence from the few to the many, it was felt that the people should have a say in the appointment of their ministers.

It was only a matter of time before a man of Guthrie's talents was called away from a quiet country parish to a larger sphere of influence. He resisted all such requests until he was eventually persuaded to become assistant minister at Old Greyfriars Church in Edinburgh in 1837. Guthrie was now in closer proximity to many influential figures, such as Graham Speirs, Sheriff of Midlothian; Fox Maule, MP for Perthshire; and the Lord Advocate, Lord Murray, all of whom were later to support the ragged school movement. A key figure in securing Guthrie's move to Edinburgh was his 'most intimate friend', Alexander Murray Dunlop, later to be MP for Greenock and sponsor of the 1854 legislation for the support of Scottish industrial schools.

Moving from his rural idyll to the 'foul haunts of darkness, drunkenness and disease' in which so many of Edinburgh's citizens lived changed Guthrie's priorities. He could not but contrast the 'heartless, hopeless, miserable condition of the people – the debauched and drunken mothers, the sallow, yellow, emaciated children' with 'his happy country parish ... with health blowing in every breeze, and blooming in the rosy cheeks of infants laughing in their mothers' arms, and of boys and girls on their way to school'.[21]

In the same year that he moved to Edinburgh, the Old and New Greyfriars parishes decided to create a new parish and erect another church building with a schoolroom underneath the sanctuary. It was to this new charge, St. John's, that Guthrie was appointed minister on its opening in 1840. He immediately embarked upon visitation of the poor in their homes and a traditional parish school was opened in 1842. This was free to boys and girls living in the parish, while children from other parishes were charged 2d. per week 'exclusive of writing and arithmetic, and three pence per week including these Branches'.[22]

It was, however, some time before Guthrie could devote himself wholeheartedly to helping such children. Scotland was in a ferment over the patronage issue which culminated in the Disruption of the Church of the Scotland in 1843, when over one third of the ministers left to form the Free Church, losing their livelihoods, manses and churches in the process. Guthrie vacated the charge in which he had laboured for such a short time, to found Free St. John's with the seceding congregation. In support of the new denomination, he set himself the huge challenge of touring the length and breadth of the country, using all his skills of persuasion to raise money for the Manse Fund, an effort which produced the sum of £116,370 in less than a year.

Guthrie was therefore absent from Edinburgh during much of 1845–1846 but, on completion of this task, he turned his attention again to the provision of education for destitute children. Convinced 'that it was impossible to raise the lower classes in towns, unless through the means of the rising generation',[23] he proposed to open a school attached to his new church, but the opposition of some of his office-bearers put an end to the scheme and led him to attempt the foundation of a school on a wider basis by publishing his famous *Plea for Ragged Schools* in early 1847.

Edinburgh already had plenty of schools and endowed hospitals, but Guthrie argued in his *Plea* that these institutions were not reaching those who most needed help. The hospitals were, moreover, residential, whereas Guthrie believed that the proper place for a child to be brought up was in a family home. Yet, where poor children had been living at home and even attending a day school, the poverty of their parents often meant they were withdrawn and sent out to work or beg. Ordinary schools were irrelevant in such cases. 'What man of sense, – of common sense, – would mock with books a boy who is starving for bread?'[24] asked Guthrie. His answer was simple: 'since he cannot attend your school unless he starves, give him food; feed him, in order to educate him; ... by that powerful magnet to a hungry child, draw him to school.'[25] Food and education were to be supplemented by industrial work which would have 'the double advantage of lessening, by its profits, the expense of maintenance, and forming in the children habits of industry, which will fit them for an honest and useful life'.[26] In any case, the cost of providing the schools was far outweighed by the financial burden of the arrest, trial and imprisonment of young offenders, a point he drove home in one of the aphorisms which gave his speeches and writings such a powerful impact: 'it is better to pay for the education of the boy, than pay for the punishment of the man.'[27]

There was, of course, nothing particularly original in these suggestions. Guthrie readily acknowledged that the concept of the 'ragged school' had already been put into practice by Sheriff Watson in Aberdeen in 1841 and, as will be seen, there were a number of precedents in Edinburgh itself which, like those in Aberdeen, originated in conjunction with existing agencies. It is interesting to note that Sheriff Watson had visited Edinburgh in about 1845 in an attempt to stimulate the establishment of an industrial school there, but found that 'the City ... was unwilling to listen to any appeal for the really destitute to be cared for in so humble an institution as an industrial school...'[28]

It was Thomas Guthrie's great achievement to change this apathy into enthusiasm. By 1847 he has a considerable track record as a fund-raiser, as his experience with the Free Church Manse Fund had shown that his powerful eloquence could not only move hearts but also open wallets. Many years later, the philosopher Bertrand Russell would observe that 'What is distinctively human at the most fundamental level is the capacity to persuade and be persuaded'.[29] When Guthrie issued his *Plea* the time was right for his skills of persuasion to be brought to bear on a public ready to be won over.

Figure 6.1 Rev. Dr. Thomas Guthrie

Source: *Autobiography of Thomas Guthrie, D.D.: And Memoir by his Sons*, Rev. David K. Guthrie and Charles J. Guthrie, M.A., London, 1877

Ragged schools in Edinburgh: precedents and pioneers

Chapter Three, which dealt with developments in the twenty years following the Tron Riot in Edinburgh, showed how precedents for the reformatory treatment of convicted young offenders could be found within the penal system. Similarly, the ragged industrial schools should be seen in the context of earlier attempts to assist vulnerable children by the traditional agencies providing poor relief and education.

Long before the nineteenth century, Edinburgh had numerous endowed hospitals. In 1628, George Heriot, a goldsmith, had bequeathed his fortune for the purposes of providing free education for children of deceased or impoverished burgesses and freemen, and also for the children of ordinary poor citizens. His example was followed by other prominent local figures and in 1847, the year of Guthrie's *Plea*, the *Edinburgh Almanack* listed nine such endowments. Guthrie wrote that 'instead of the "Modern Athens", Edinburgh might be called – the City of Hospitals'.[30] His satirical comment was prompted by the fact that these institutions had by this time been diverted from the original intentions of the founders. The statute of Heriot's, for example, had stated that no children should be admitted 'if their parentis be weill and sufficientlie able to menteyne yame since the intentioun of the Founder is onlie to relieve the puire',[31] yet by the mid-nineteenth century the sons of well-off shopkeepers were being educated there in an ornate Gothic-style building.

Admittedly, the Heriot Foundation had made an attempt to cater for the poor and by 1847 had opened seven juvenile and three infant schools, catering for about 3,000 children. But these were not always situated in the poorest areas and they gave education to the families of decent labourers or tradesmen rather than to the 'perishing' classes most vulnerable to criminal involvement. Moreover, as a consequence of the Irish potato famine, the number of Irish-born inhabitants of Edinburgh more than doubled from 7,100 in 1841 to 15,317 ten years later. This led to overcrowding in the wynds of the Old Town and outbreaks of fever. Nine-tenths of the fever-stricken in 1847–1848 were Irish,[32] and the death of many parents combined to produce the further problem of destitute orphans.

In October 1845 the Governor of Calton Jail, Mr. John Smith, prepared a 'letter to the Governors of George Heriot's Hospital and circulated among the Ministers of Edinburgh' in which he drew attention to the fact that in the previous three years 740 children under the age of fourteen had been sent to prison in Edinburgh for crime, and proposed that existing agencies should provide a ragged school, 'as Heriot's old and invaluable bequest appears to comprehend the claims of these unfortunate outcasts...'[33] Whether or not the letter was acted on by the Governors in unknown, but Smith's initiative found a sympathetic response from at least one of the ministers, the Rev. William Robertson (1805–1882) of New Greyfriars Church, whose parish included the slums of the Grassmarket.

Robertson inherited a tradition of social concern from his predecessor, the Rev. John Julius Wood (1800–1877). The Session Minutes of New Greyfriars Church for 15 May 1842 record that 'owing to the ignorance of Sunday School children', Wood had obtained the permission of the Governors of Heriot's Hospital to use their schoolroom in Heriot's Bridge for one hour each weekday evening, the teacher to be appointed by the Session.[34] Wood joined the Free Church at the Disruption in 1843 but Robertson continued his concern for the poor, organising a house-to-house visitation which revealed the extent of destitution in the Grassmarket area, including the fact that 250 children were receiving no education whatever. A school was accordingly opened towards the end of 1846.

In what sense can this venture be described as a ragged or industrial school?[35] Schools run by parish churches were widespread in Scotland, but the fact that Robertson's provided meals differentiates it from an ordinary parish school. This practice, judging by the Kirk Session records, seems to have been adopted some time during 1847, changing the character of the school: those who had made a small contribution to their schooling left, and more non-payers filled the places. Although the other hallmark of a ragged industrial school – industrial training – seems to have been confined to sewing instruction for girls, the school appears to have successfully grafted the ragged school concept onto the parochial tradition.

At about the same time as Robertson, an attempt was made by one of the Police Court magistrates, Bailie James Mack, to open an industrial school under the terms of Section 69 of the Scottish Poor Law Amendment Act of 1845, which permitted parochial boards to make provision for the education of children receiving relief. Mack further hoped to provide for very poor children who were not eligible for relief, and delinquents convicted of small thefts, but it was considered more expedient to confine the planned school to strictly poor law cases in case the legality of the venture was challenged. Mack is quoted in the *Edinburgh Courant* of 21 February 1846 as stating that industrial training 'ought to be the grand object in view'. The Parochial Board approved the plan in principle but, owing to the difficulty in finding suitable premises, the school did not open until June 1847.

Hence, both Robertson's and Mack's schemes originated from within the circle of existing institutions and practices, one from the tradition of parish education provided by the church and the other from the poor relief authorities. What they were able to achieve was therefore limited: Robertson's was a parish school for the children of the New Greyfriars area, meaning there was a territorial restriction, while Mack's provided only for children eligible for poor relief, thereby excluding immigrants. Compared to these ventures, Guthrie's proposal extended the ragged school concept in two ways. Firstly, it was to be managed by a committee independent of ecclesiastical or poor law authorities, and was open to children from any part of the city. Secondly, where Robertson's school was funded mainly from church collections and Mack's from the poor rates, Guthrie planned to raise a public subscription.

Before examining Guthrie's institution in more detail, it is worth commenting on the confusion of nomenclature that arises in connection with these schools. The term 'ragged school' came from England, where it was applied to voluntary schools, often held in the evenings, which offered rudimentary schooling. Sheriff Watson preferred the term 'industrial school', which stressed the importance of training that would help the child become a productive member of society. Watson argued that 'The term Ragged … should be disjoined from the Industrial School, as being in no sense applicable; for although the children may have been ragged when they entered, the rags soon disappear...'³⁶ However, the designation was perpetuated by the title of Guthrie's *Plea*, although – in a final ironic twist – Guthrie states on the last page that he did not like the name and suggests 'Destitute schools' as a better title. After the legislation of 1854, the terminology became more consistent and the schools were officially known as industrial schools.

Guthrie's Original Ragged School

In her history of philanthropy in Victorian Scotland, Olive Checkland observes that 'religion was a source equally of stimulus and strife'.³⁷ Nothing demonstrates the truth of that statement more clearly than the subsequent development of ragged industrial schools in Edinburgh. Christian social concern led to the founding of the first school of this type in the city by Robertson but when Guthrie popularised the ragged school idea, his insistence that children should be taught 'the truths of the gospel, making the Holy Scriptures the groundwork of instruction'³⁸ was soon challenged by those who felt this policy was designed to exclude children from Roman Catholic backgrounds.

Initially, religion provided a 'stimulus' in the sense that Guthrie made an unashamed appeal to public benevolence. 'Our trust is in the almost omnipotent power of Christian kindness', he wrote, and his *Plea* quickly achieved its objective by appealing to the heart, using what the *Edinburgh Review* called 'pictures and passion' rather than facts and figures.³⁹ As Guthrie himself put it, the effect was like 'a spark among combustibles'.⁴⁰ Almost every newspaper published extracts and within a few weeks £700 had been raised. A public meeting was convened by the Lord Provost, Adam Black, in the Music Hall on 9 April 1847 at which a constitution was unanimously approved, and the ragged school began its work that summer in premises in Ramsay Lane near the entrance to Edinburgh Castle.

While Guthrie opened the hearts of the public with his prose, Alexander Maclagan (1811–1879) made an even more directly emotional appeal through his poetry. After reading the *Plea*, the Perthshire-born poet published a little volume in support of Guthrie's efforts, entitled *Ragged School Rhymes*. In the preface he maintains that 'The pieces ... were written to suit the Capacity of the Children of the Ragged Schools', but they are likely to have had far more impact on the consciences of the middle classes. One typical poem, *The Lost Found,* tells how 'A servant of the Lord' comes upon 'a little starving child' whose parents are dead. The last verse drives home the message:

> When o'er the face of nature sweeps
> The wintry winds so wild,
> When ye are warmly clad, O think
> Upon the Ragged Child!
> When tables groan, then think upon
> The heart that breaks for bread;
> And when the blazing fagots burn
> Think of the houseless head.⁴¹

But it was not only the general public who offered their support: Guthrie was proud to record that 'Foremost among the friends of the cause ... were the judges of the land',[42] including Sheriff Graham Speirs, Sheriff of Midlothian and the Lord Advocate, Lord Murray. The involvement of magistrates ensured that their discretionary powers could be used to send young offenders to the school rather than prison, some years before this was provided for by legislation. The credit for this arrangement was due to Sheriff Andrew Jameson, who was also chairman of the school's Acting Committee. In December 1848 he wrote: 'I have frequently taken it upon me to send very young offenders to the schools instead of the prison, having first made careful inquiry into the circumstances of each case...'[43] In March of that year, 78 of the 265 children on the roll of the ragged school had passed through the police court on one or more occasion. However, emphasis was placed on the fact that only children for whom there was no other provision would be admitted. In an interesting parallel to the present-day debate on immigration and the benefits system, the ragged school stipulated that only those who had been living in Edinburgh for at least a year could be admitted, so that Irish immigrants would not flock to the capital knowing that their children would be provided for by the school. Children with a claim on the poor law were likewise excluded. Much was made of these safeguards to ensure that donations were not abused, or that the school was not taken advantage of by parents who could afford to educate their children.

In addition to backing from the legal establishment, Guthrie had the encouragement of influential Free Church colleagues such as Thomas McCrie, R.S. Candlish and James Begg, all of them future Moderators of the General Assembly.[44] And it was here that, in the words of Guthrie's biographer, 'a difference of opinion arose, based on those sectarian cleavages which have been Scotland's curse for the last two hundred years'.[45] A mere five days after the school opened, a polite enquiry was made about the school's policy towards Roman Catholic children by 'a Protestant Dissenter' in the columns of *The Scotsman*, eventually drawing an unequivocal statement from John Cook on behalf of the Acting Committee, of which he was a member, that Catholic children could not be excused from religious instruction. In view of this, the Catholics of Edinburgh, under the direction of their bishop, Dr. Carruthers, proposed another school under a general committee comprising both Catholics and Protestants, in which pupils would receive separate religious education.

A further public meeting took place on 2 July, during which both sides of the argument were aired. In one of the principal speeches, Lord Murray said that

> I have no sympathy with the Roman Catholics in religious views ... but still I must acknowledge that they are a religious body; and why should they not have the same security against sectarian bias which is given to every sect of Protestants?[46]

But Murray's reasoning proved powerless in the face of Guthrie's impassioned oratory. If he saved a child, he would claim the right to bring it up in his faith. 'I shall bind the Bible to the Ragged Schools; ... and there I take my stand.'[47] Only five hands were raised against his motion, leaving those who objected no alternative but to leave and open their own school. This commenced its work on 30 November 1847 in South Grey's Close, High Street, with fifty children and was known as the United Industrial School, Guthrie's thereafter adopting the title of the Original Ragged School.

Original versus United

Though the Free Church newspaper, *The Witness*, denounced the United as 'the Roman Catholic Ragged School',[48] this was inaccurate. The principle on which it was based can be summed up as 'combined instruction in things secular, separate in things religious'. There were more Protestants than Catholics involved in setting it up; Guthrie himself was invited to be a Director though, not surprisingly, he declined.

Figure 6.2 The Edinburgh United Industrial School
Source: *Cassell's Old and New Edinburgh,* Volume 2, London, Paris and New York, N.D.

Over the entrance to the Original School on Castle Hill – still visible today – was a depiction of an open Bible with the words 'Search the Scriptures', an indication of the strongly Protestant form of religious instruction upon which Guthrie and his supporters insisted. Yet, while he would never countenance any compromise with 'Popery', Guthrie was anxious to ensure that the school was non-sectarian in the sense that it was not exclusively associated with his own denomination, the recently formed Free Church, and he was happy to work with supporters from the Established Church, Episcopalians and Dissenters. The United School's willingness to accommodate both Protestant and Catholic religious teaching was a rare example of toleration for its time, and to this day such arrangements are unusual in Scottish schools. A recent scholar who has written about the history of the United School, Peter Mackie, describes it as 'as a unique symbol, in the nation's capital, of inter-denominational education'.[49]

As religion was the only significant area of disagreement, in practical terms the two Edinburgh schools exhibited little difference. A typical day at the Original Ragged School lasted nearly twelve hours:

7.30 a.m.: washing and play
9.00 a.m.: breakfast
9.30 a.m.: school
12.30 p.m.: play
1 p.m.: industrial work
2.00 p.m.: dinner
2.30 p.m.: school
4.00 p.m.: play
4.30 p.m.: industrial work
6.30–7.00 p.m.: supper; change clothes; dismiss[50]

Both schools had a comparable admissions policy, giving preference to children convicted of vagrancy or petty theft. Of 292 children in the Original School in October 1850, 88 had been sent there for vagrancy or theft by the magistrates. At the United School, too, 'There is one class of claimants who are never, except in very peculiar circumstances, refused, those who are sent from the Police Office'.[51] In spite of its *raison d'etre* being to allow Catholic children to receive instruction in their own beliefs, the United followed the Original in refusing admission to children of recently arrived Irish immigrants who had been resident in the city for less than a year. The fact that both institutions received annual donations from the police funds (£100 in the case of the Original School and £50 for the United, which was half the size) suggests that the magistrates impartially approved of the work of both.

On the other hand, the United School claimed in its fourth Annual Report that it gave more prominence to industrial work, providing 'training in skilled labour', and statistics were quoted to suggest that children leaving the United School found it easier to get jobs: 56 per cent at the end of 1854, compared to only 18.5 per cent of those from the rival establishment.[52] The Original, by contrast, stressed in 1852 that as far as industrial training was concerned, the aim was simply to train the children to habits of industry, rather than to fit them for particular trades ... Fourteen years – the age when the children leave school – is early enough for a boy to begin to learn the particular trade by which he is to earn his livelihood.[53]

Thus children were employed in relatively unskilled activities such as assembling cardboard boxes used by shops and tailors or, in the case of girls, prepared for domestic service. Evidently there is more than an element of poetic licence in the *Ragged School Rhymes* which depict pupils preparing for roles as printer, sailor, blacksmith and builder:

> OH! I will be a builder –
> Hurrah for square and rule! –
> Oh! I will be a builder
> Of many a Ragged School.[54]

A further difference was that the Original School felt the need for legal powers to detain children – Guthrie told the annual meeting in January 1854 that it was not difficult to attract children to the school, but it was quite another matter to keep them there. During that year almost half the roll had been lost by desertion or removal by parents. For its part, the United School claimed that the disappearance of children in an irregular manner was 'an extremely rare event'[55] and consequently did not seek new powers of detention. The writer of a 'comparative view' of the two schools in 1855 suggested that because children were given superior industrial training leading to specific jobs, they were more settled in the United School and less likely to abscond. Another contributory factor might be that the Original School was more regimented than its smaller counterpart, in which it was consequently easier to establish an individual relationship with the pupils. For example, except in cases of extreme necessity, the United School did not provide clothes, so that there was a 'great variety of raggedness'; in the Original, meanwhile, children were provided with a uniform during school hours only, which gave them a 'clean but penal or pauper-like aspect' which *The Scotsman* thought 'cannot but be humiliation to any boy possessing even the germ of self-respect'.[56] The Committee of Management explained that

> their own rags will in the meantime be subjected to deodorizing by fumigation, and will be again put on before leaving the school at night. This precaution is necessary, both to prevent the school-clothing from being pawned or sold by the parents, and to preclude its being used as bedclothes...[57]

If this policy appears somewhat draconian, it is understandable in view of the fact that, during the first eight months of the school's existence, several children, the industrial teacher, the schoolmistress and the medical attendant all died from fever.

It should, however, be borne in mind that both schools had an interest in emphasising such differences of approach, as they were in competition with each other in pursuit of donations from the public. The Original School had the inestimable advantage of having as its figurehead the eloquent and popular Dr. Guthrie, who was backed by members of the Free Church and its newspaper, *The Witness*. But if the United School lacked a charismatic personality, it had the influential figure of Lord Murray and the support of *The Scotsman*. From the standpoint of the treatment of juvenile delinquency and vagrancy, one wonders whether the young offender would have discerned much difference in routine between the two schools. Ironically, the religious policy in Guthrie's school does not seem to have deterred applications from Irish Catholics: the third Annual Report of the Original School stated in 1850 that 'the great bulk of applications have, during the past year, been made, as in former years, by Irish beggars'.

The divergence of opinion over religious instruction in the ragged school was not fatal, since it resulted in two schools to deal with the juvenile problem instead of one. If the claim of Guthrie's sons in their biography of their father that 'In direct proportion as the various Ragged Schools filled, the portion of the jail appropriate to juvenile delinquents emptied'[58] sounds a little too good to be true, the surviving statistical evidence does suggest that the combined efforts of the schools had an impact on juvenile crime in the capital city. Figures for the city Bridewell between 1811 and 1840 demonstrate that juvenile and adult commitments rose and fell in a parallel way. From 1847 onwards, however, total commitments increased whereas juvenile commitments declined, suggesting that some additional factor was operating. There is evidence that a considerable number of children who appeared in court were sent directly to the schools. In December 1850, for example, 103 children in the Original School were classed as 'police subjects'.[59] Edinburgh police court returns for the period 1852–1868 reveal a consistent decrease in the number of children appearing before the court for trial between 1852 and 1861; thereafter the figures fluctuated, although always at a lower level than any year since 1856.[60]

By that stage, a national system to provide for destitute and delinquent children was developing. Having demonstrated what voluntary effort could achieve, Guthrie took on a new role, proving to be as passionate a campaigner for legislation and government aid as he had been for the original ragged school concept.

Notes

1. *Autobiography of Thomas Guthrie, D.D., and Memoir by his sons, Rev. David K. Guthrie and Charles J. Guthrie, M.A.* (London, 1877), p. 445.
2. Samuel Smiles, *Self-Help* (London, 1903), p. 366.
3. *Autobiography of Thomas Guthrie, D.D.*, p. 475.
4. Ibid., p. 15.
5. Ibid., p. 22.
6. Ibid., p. 23.
7. Ibid., p. 29.
8. Ibid., p. 210.
9. Ibid., p. 42.
10. Ibid., p. 41.

11 Ibid., p. 40.
12 Ibid., p. 38.
13 Ibid., p. 17.
14 Ibid., p. 219.
15 Ibid., p. 54.
16 Ibid., p. 79.
17 Ibid., p. 84.
18 Ibid., p. 86.
19 Ibid., p. 153.
20 Lord Cockburn, *Circuit Journeys* (Edinburgh, 1889), p. 187.
21 *Autobiography of Thomas Guthrie, D.D.*, p. 157.
22 Session Minutes, St. John's Church, Vol. I, 11 October 1842.
23 *Autobiography of Thomas Guthrie, D.D.*, p. 316.
24 Thomas Guthrie, *A Plea for Ragged Schools* (Ninth edition, Edinburgh, 1847), p. 17.
25 Ibid., p. 21.
26 Ibid., p. 21.
27 Ibid., p. 29.
28 William Watson, 'The Spread of the Aberdeen System in Scotland' (Manuscript in Aberdeen Public Library).
29 Quoted in Charles S. Mack, *Business Strategy for an Era of Political Change* (Westport, Connecticut, 2001), p. 158.
30 Thomas Guthrie, *A Plea for Ragged Schools*, p. 6.
31 Quoted in 'Report on the Condition of the Poorer Classes of Edinburgh and of their Dwellings, Neighbourhoods and Families' (Edinburgh, 1868), p. 65.
32 J.E. Handley, *The Irish in Modern Scotland* (Cork, 1947), p. 35.
33 SC 1852-3, p. 434.
34 Session Minutes, New Greyfriars Church, 15 May 1842.
35 The school is referred to in the Session Minutes as a 'ragged school'.
36 Letter of Sheriff Watson in 'Ragged Schools in Relation to the Government Grants for Education. The Authorized Report of the Conference held at Birmingham, January 23rd, 1861' (London and Birmingham, N.D.), p. 83.
37 Olive Checkland, *Philanthropy in Victorian Scotland* (Edinburgh, 1980), p. 256.
38 Report of a Discussion regarding Ragged Schools ... held in the Music Hall, Edinburgh, on Friday 2 July 1847 (Edinburgh, 1847), p. vi.
39 Quoted in *Journal of Henry Cockburn*, Vol. 2, 1831–54 (Edinburgh, 1874), p. 174.
40 *Edinburgh Evening Courant*, 10 April 1847.
41 Alexander Maclagan, *Ragged School Rhymes* (Edinburgh, 1851), p. 16.
42 *Edinburgh Evening Courant*, 10 April 1847.
43 Rev. Thomas Guthrie, *A Second Plea for Ragged Schools* (Edinburgh, 1849), p. 57.
44 In passing, it is interesting to note that one of the ministers who presided with Guthrie at the public meeting in April was Rev. William Innes, who had written an account of his conversations with the three youths executed at the time of the 1812 Tron Riot.
45 Oliphant Smeaton, *Thomas Guthrie* (Edinburgh and London, 1900), p. 81.
46 Report of a Discussion regarding Ragged Schools ... held in the Music Hall, Edinburgh, on Friday 2 July 1847 (Edinburgh, 1847), p. 16.
47 Ibid., p. 37.
48 *The Witness*, 3 July 1847.
49 Peter Mackie, 'Inter-denominational Education and the United Industrial School of Edinburgh, 1847–1900', *The Innes Review*, Vol. XLIII, No. 1, Spring 1992, pp. 3–17.
50 Timetable as outlined by Guthrie in evidence to the 1852-3 Select Committee.
51 Fifth Annual Report of the Committee of the United Industrial Schools of Edinburgh, 1853, p. 8.
52 'Public Education: the Original Ragged School and the United Ragged School of Edinburgh; being a comparative view of their recorded results' (Edinburgh, 1855), p. 10.

53 Fifth Annual Report of the Committee of the United Industrial Schools of Edinburgh, 1853, p. 16.
54 *Ragged School Rhymes*, p. 57.
55 'Public Education....', p. 11.
56 *The Scotsman*, 22 October 1865.
57 'Eight Months Experience of the Edinburgh Original Ragged or Industrial Schools, Castle Hill and Ramsay Lane; conducted on the principles advocated by the Rev. Thomas Guthrie. Reported by the Committee of Management' (Edinburgh, 1848), pp. 18–19.
58 *Autobiography of Thomas Guthrie, D.D*, p. 459.
59 Alexander Thomson, *Social Evils* (London, 1852), p. 134.
60 Reports and Returns, Edinburgh Police.

7 'A better model'

The influence of the Scottish approach in England

It is clear that, by the start of the 1850s, the initiatives taken by charitable individuals, magistrates and prison officials in response to local needs had produced a number of innovative methods of dealing with destitute and delinquent children in Scotland's three major cities. It is equally clear that those involved in this process had discovered that local efforts could only go so far in addressing the problems and that state intervention was desirable. This was secured by legislation in 1854 and thereafter developments were shaped less by local circumstances than by the national framework. Before examining this process in detail, it would be convenient at this point (i) to summarise the distinctive features of the pioneering institutions founded in Aberdeen, Edinburgh and Glasgow discussed in the preceding chapters; (ii) to evaluate their impact south of the border; and (iii) to examine the various factors which led to different approaches being taken in Scotland.

Distinctive features of the Scottish institutions

Scotland's main contribution was undoubtedly the development of day industrial feeding schools which aimed at preventing children becoming delinquents rather than reforming those who had already committed crimes. These institutions were first set up by Sheriff Watson in Aberdeen in 1841, and it was his success in persuading the police to round up all vagrant children in the city that enabled the schools to expand until by 1851 there were four, catering for around 300 children.

In October 1845 William Chambers, the publisher, visited the Aberdeen schools and published an influential account of them in his *Edinburgh Journal,* which, according to the fifth report of the Aberdeen Boys' School, was the means of extending the industrial school concept to Glasgow and Edinburgh. Other Scottish towns were quick to follow Aberdeen and in the majority of cases Watson was involved, either directly or indirectly, in the initial stages. Sheriff Hugh Barclay of Perth[1] wrote to him in September 1841 and a School of Industry was opened there in January 1843, although, in opposition to Watson's views, it had a dormitory where boys were lodged overnight instead of returning home. During a stay at Bridge-of-Allan, Watson published a letter in the local newspaper stating that he had seen more begging children there in a week than in the previous twelve months in Aberdeen, a remark which prompted the Sheriff-Substitute of Stirling to set up an industrial school in August 1849. The publication of Watson's correspondence with a Mr. Ingram of Stranraer had the same effect there, with a school being opened in 1850.[2]

The movement was given a still greater impulse by the Rev. Thomas Guthrie, whose powerful *Plea for Ragged Schools* raised sufficient money to open the Edinburgh Original Ragged School in 1847, followed shortly after by the United Industrial School which, unlike Guthrie's, allowed separate religious instruction for children from a Roman Catholic background.

In the space of a few years, then, day industrial schools had sprung up in most Scottish towns. It is important to recognise the distinctiveness of these schools. Crucially, they were non-residential: both Watson and Guthrie strongly believed that parents should never be entirely relieved of their responsibilities. Again, the Scottish industrial schools had little in common with English ragged schools, in spite of the fact that they were often referred to by the same name, though both Watson and Guthrie are on record as disliking this designation. Whereas English ragged schools provided rudimentary lessons in reading, writing and arithmetic in the evenings, Watson's system not only took charge of children for twelve hours a day, but provided industrial training and meals in addition to intellectual instruction. As Guthrie told the Royal Commissioners on Scottish schools,

> in regard to London, six-sevenths of the ragged schools are not feeding-schools at all; the children are taken in two or three hours in the evening, and the attendance is most irregular ... I venture to say, there is not such regular attendance anywhere as in our ragged schools, because the children know that they get no porridge unless they come there.[3]

Further, while children might attend a Scottish industrial school for up to five years, the object of the evening ragged schools was 'to pass them away as quickly as possible when fit for it'.[4] Hence, the possibilities of providing any kind of industrial training were very limited, in contrast to the Scottish schools where this was seen as a central concern. The English schools aimed to impart a basic Christian education to neglected children who 'from their poverty or ragged condition [were] prevented attending any other place of religious instruction',[5] but the Scottish schools were specifically intended to combat juvenile vagrancy and delinquency. It could be said that the impulses which motivated the reformatory movement in England gave rise to day industrial schools in Scotland. The difference was that the Scottish schools attempted to catch the delinquent at an earlier stage of his evolution – before he committed an offence, not afterwards. As one of the ministers connected with the Greenock school put it graphically, 'While other institutions reserve their efforts till the fire gets ahead and then ply their buckets to extinguish a towering conflagration, the Ragged Schools watch the latent combustion and extinguish the first spark that appears'.[6]

While the day industrial schools wished to reduce juvenile vagrancy, their rationale for doing so was the belief that 'to prevent juvenile delinquency, it was requisite also to prevent juvenile vagrancy',[7] this being seen as the first step on the road to crime. At the annual meetings of subscribers to the schools, there was almost always at least one speaker who gave an outline of the criminal's career such as the following:

> In most cases, from the criminality of their parents, but in some, from their extreme poverty, these children do not receive from them the first elements of education; poorly clothed and poorly fed, they are rarely placed at school, and many, perhaps, are never led to a place of worship; ... They commence by idling about the streets when they ought to be at home or at school; they soon learn to beg to supply their pressing want, and from this the transition is easy to the commission of petty thefts for the same purpose; and so, from step to step, till the little boy or girl ... soon becomes a frequent inmate of our prison cells.[8]

By this reasoning, then, prevention was better than cure, and the industrial schools served the function of 'diminishing the stream of crime, by cutting off one of its larger tributaries'.[9]

The prominence given to the idea of prevention has to some extent overshadowed other, equally significant, developments in the treatment of juvenile crime in Scotland in the same period. The fact that Scotland also pioneered reformatory institutions has tended to be overlooked and in the 1840s Scotland appears to have been at least as advanced as England in this respect. An 'Abstract of Returns of the Names of Charitable Institutions for affording temporary Refuge to young Offenders when discharged from Prison in England', to be found in the Parliamentary Papers for 1849, lists a number of prisons which sent released juveniles to places such as the Refuge for the Destitute in London; however, only two of the institutions mentioned were specifically for juveniles: the Philanthropic Society's school and the Asylum for Juvenile Offenders at Stretton-on-Dunsmore, Warwickshire. Yet Scotland was also pioneering similar institutions at the time. The Dean Bank Institution for the Reformation of Female Delinquents opened in Edinburgh in 1832 and Glasgow's House of Refuge for juvenile male offenders, which dates from 1838, became the largest reformatory school in Britain and the only one to have a special Act of Parliament to regulate its operation. The size of this institution, and the influence it exerted in England, demonstrates the fact that in the early 1840s Scotland was providing for the reformation of actual, as well as for the prevention of potential, juvenile offenders. Indeed, it is noticeable that, while day industrial schools were to be Scotland's main contribution to the treatment of juvenile delinquency, each major city had set up, or had attempted to set up, a reformatory institution in the 1830s – prior, that is, to the advent of industrial schools.

One must beware, however, of attempting to define schools rigidly as either 'industrial' or 'reformatory' at this stage, for this is to impose on the 1840s the terminology of the post-1854 period. The distinction was not yet clear-cut; the ideology of a dual system of industrial schools for preventing delinquency and reformatory schools for treating it had not yet developed. In Scottish institutions there was generally less rigid categorisation of inmates; both convicted and destitute children were to be found in the same school, in contrast to the trend of opinion in the English reformatory movement. Sheriff Watson said that there was no need to deal with convicted children separately from those who were only destitute, for in reality they belonged to the same class, whereas (for example) Captain W.J. Williams, Inspector of Prisons for the Home District, believed that 'combining penal and pauper schools would be fatal to the effect of both'.[10] While in England reformatory institutions were strictly for juveniles released from prison, in Glasgow destitute boys could apply for admission to the House of Refuge without having been in prison, and the Girls' House, opened in 1840, had separate wings for girls convicted of crime and for those 'who, from extreme destitution, might be in danger of going astray'.[11]

Perhaps the most significant difference between Scottish and English practice in the 1840s was that in England magistrates lacked the power to commit children to reformatory institutions whereas in Scotland there are many instances of magistrates sending children to industrial schools instead of prison, prior to the legislation of 1854. In Aberdeen, petty offenders were frequently handed over by the police to the Child's Asylum Committee, a body composed of representatives of the magistrates, police commissioners, poor law authorities and industrial schools, whose function was to decide whether such cases should be sent to the schools. Similar examples of magistrates using their discretion were examined earlier in relation to Glasgow and Edinburgh, and the reasons for this will be considered later in this chapter.

The wider influence of the 'Scotch system'

As the Scottish industrial schools were in operation for a number of years before anything similar was set up in England, the most prominent figures in the reformatory movement there showed a good deal of interest in the experiments being carried out north of the border, and looked to the Scottish schools as models. Mary Carpenter remarked that 'In some of the large towns of Scotland, the experiment [of industrial schools] has been tried ... and its success removes from us all excuse for not making similar efforts'.[12] No less a figure than Charles Dickens, in a lengthy article published in *Household Words* in 1851, extolled the achievements of the Aberdeen schools: 'Aberdeen has done an act of real charity and good sense here, blessed itself and blessed these poor vagrants.'[13]

In addition, evidence presented by representatives of the Aberdeen and Edinburgh schools and the Glasgow Houses of Refuge before the Select Committee of 1852–3 made a vital contribution to the committee's resolution that 'the Ragged Schools existing in England and Scotland, ... especially the ragged industrial feeding schools, at present supported by voluntary subscriptions or, as in Glasgow, by local rates, have produced beneficial effects...'[14] William Locke, Honorary Secretary of the London Ragged School Union, told the 1852 sitting of the Select Committee that there were schools run according to what he called 'the Scotch system' in Manchester, Liverpool, York and Westminster.[15] In many of these instances, Sheriff Watson's advice had been sought. In July 1846, for example, he received a letter from the committee of the proposed ragged school in Manchester which had not yet decided whether to operate as an evening school or as an industrial feeding school. On Watson's advice, they opted for the latter. The following year, he received a similar request from the Rev. Mr. Yorke, Rector of St. Philip's, Birmingham, stating that the committee there had decided 'to profit by the example set by Scotland'.[16] At least fifteen English towns followed the Scottish lead in this respect.[17]

If Watson's experiments provided the pattern, Guthrie's speeches supplied the passion. One adulatory writer singled out his 1855 address on ragged schools at the Exeter Hall in London as the 'high water-mark' of his oratory, making him 'a familiar name all over Europe'.[18] Guthrie, in fact, became so prominent a national figure that Lord Shaftesbury, who had been President of the Ragged School Union since its formation in 1844, was 'depressed' by a report in *The Times* which implied that Guthrie was the originator of these schools. According to his biographer, Shaftesbury

> claimed that Guthrie had only been occupied with his own school in Edinburgh. He [Shaftesbury] would have thought that Ragged Schools were a speciality with him and lamented the denial of his achievement because it crippled his influence and dried up public liberality towards him.[19]

If the story related in the *Memoir* of Guthrie written by his sons is to be believed, his influence even spread as far as Barbados. A merchant who had visited Scotland was shipwrecked on one of the West Indian islands and lost all his belongings. The only thing that survived was a copy of *A Plea for Ragged Schools* which was washed ashore. As his name and address was written on it, this was returned to him and proved to be 'the cause of a Ragged School movement in that far-off isle of the sea'.[20]

The achievement of the Scottish industrial schools up to 1854 was summarised by Alfred Hill, a barrister, in a paper read to the National Reformatory Union in 1856:

> While, therefore, I fully admit the urgent necessity of Reformatory Schools for the reclamation of young criminals, I think that the experience of Scotland justifies me in hoping that the general establishment of Industrial Schools would greatly diminish the number of the class requiring such treatment. In Scotland, Industrial Schools were established earlier and have been carried to a greater extent than elsewhere, and with more tangible results.[21]

Significantly, in 1857 Hill was himself one of the framers of the bill which extended to England the provision of the Scottish Industrial Schools Act of 1854.

The influence of the Scottish schools continued to be felt in the 1860s, and they were often praised by the government inspector, Rev. Sydney Turner. In his 1862 report, for instance, he wrote that

> We cannot have a better model for our English Industrial Schools than those of Scotland, and especially those in Aberdeen whose success laid the foundation of the system which the Industrial Schools' Acts recognise.[22]

The Glasgow House of Refuge exerted a similar influence on the development of reformatories. In 1839 an article in *The Spectator* claimed that the Refuge was 'the only instance ... in the country' of an institution run on such principles and expressed the hope that it would 'before long meet with general imitation'.[23] This soon occurred at Liverpool, where the chief magistrate, Mr. Edward Rushton, said that the institution for juvenile offenders in the city was based on the Glasgow model,[24] while the Chaplain of Preston County House of Correction said that he had

> little doubt, from the result of experiments tried in Glasgow and elsewhere, that a well-organised house of refuge for the reception of young and destitute criminals on their discharge from prison, even if supported by the county funds, would tend upon the whole to diminish the county expenditure.[25]

Hence, by 1866, the *North British Daily Mail* was able to claim that the Refuge had been 'the fruitful parent and model of many similar attempts all over the kingdom'.[26]

The Scottish context

Why, then, did Scotland and England take different approaches to the juvenile problem? One clue can be found in an observation by J.D. Mackie in *A History of Scotland*. Reviewing the nineteenth century, he comments that 'The wind of progress which blew over the British Isles was the same on both sides of the Border, yet it did not blow upon identical countries; enough of the old Scotland remained to modify its operation...'[27]

Many of the differences of emphasis in the handling of social problems in England and Scotland can be accounted for in terms of the legacy of the 'old Scotland', particularly the country's unique legal and ecclesiastical system. Article XIX of the 1707 Treaty of Union stipulated that

> The Court of Session or Colledge of Justice, do after the Union and notwithstanding thereof, remain in all time coming within Scotland as it is now constituted by the Laws of that Kingdom, and with the same Authority and Priviledges as before the Union...[28]

In the same vein, the 'Act for securing the Protestant religion and Presbyterian Church government' outlined the constitution of the Church of Scotland and enacted that it should 'remain and continue unalterable'.[29] Legal practice obviously determined the way in which criminal offenders were sentenced while, in contrast to England, the Scottish Church had for centuries been in control of the administration of poor relief and the provision of education. These factors combined to produce a significantly different background against which developments in the treatment of neglected and delinquent children in Scotland were set.

Law

Nineteenth-century lawyers were well aware of the differences between English and Scottish law, and were fond of comparing and contrasting the two. James Paterson, of the Middle Temple, prefaced his *Compendium of English and Scotch Law* (Edinburgh, 1860) by saying that

> England and Scotland have long been running the race of civilization under similar circumstances. But it is well know that their laws are nearly as distinct as if each was a foreign country to the other. Though it may be true in a general sense that the result is now much the same in both countries as regards the main elements of rational liberty, yet the details of the respective processes by which this result is attained often differ widely.[30]

Here Paterson makes a distinction between legal principle and legal procedure which provides a convenient basis for a comparison of the status of juvenile offenders before the law in England and Scotland.

Under Scots law, as in England, there was no defined age of responsibility. David Hume states that children over the age of seven were liable to punishment as criminals, and that 'in fixing the measure of punishment to be inflicted on a pupil, the Court are not, and cannot be confined to dispense it, according to years and days'.[31] Sir Archibald Alison in his *Principles of the Criminal Law of Scotland* cites a case of youthful burglars being sentenced to death but notes that 'of all such cases of extreme youth it may be observed, that though the law is rightly allowed to take its course in pronouncing sentence, yet the royal clemency generally interposes to commute it to transportation'.[32]

While this legal principle was common to both countries, legal proceedings were significantly different. As Chapter One demonstrated, in England it was the responsibility of the wronged party to prosecute the culprit and the first significant legislation to allow for young offenders to be dealt with by a lower court was the 'Act for the more speedy Trial and Punishment of Juvenile Offenders' of 1847. By contrast, in Scotland 'The system proceeds upon the principle that it is the duty of the State to detect crime, apprehend offenders, and punish them, and that independently of the interest of a private party'.[33] Prosecution was in the hands of the Lord-Advocate, the Advocates-Depute and their local representatives, the procurators-fiscal. Again, summary jurisdiction had been widely used in Scotland since 1828, when Sir William Rae's 'Act to facilitate criminal Trials in Scotland'[34] had authorised a summary form of proceeding in the case of minor offences tried before a sheriff, who was empowered to impose a sentence of sixty days' imprisonment or a fine of £10. Under the terms of various local police acts, children could also be detained in police cells for up to three days.

Recent research by David G. Barrie and Susan Broomhall into the workings of Scottish police courts has revealed that 'by the end of the nineteenth century, they dealt with approximately 85 per cent of all crimes and nearly all offences and contraventions prosecuted in Scotland's largest towns and cities'.[35] Even in 1847 Lord Justice Clerk John Hope was able to tell the Select Committee that 'juvenile Offenders [in Scotland] are all tried in the first instance summarily, either in a Police Court or before the Sheriff, without Juries...'[36] Lord Cockburn, former Solicitor General, added that 'Our Scotch Magistrates possess and constantly exercise a Power of summary Convictions ... and the Jurisdiction is so useful that we can scarcely comprehend a System where it does not exist'.[37] Such evidence contributed to the 1847 Select Committee's recommendation that similar powers should be extended to English magistrates sitting in Petty Sessions.

Thus, the existence of public prosecution and the availability to the magistrates of summary powers combined to make the Scottish way of dealing with young offenders significantly different from the English.

Moreover, this system allowed magistrates a considerable amount of discretion – something which could have both negative and positive effects. One drawback was pointed out by the Inspector of Scottish Prisons, Frederic Hill, who wrote in his autobiography that:

> The difference which existed in the treatment of prisoners in various parts of the country was almost equivalent to a variety of laws respecting the same offence; so that a man was frequently punished, not according to the magnitude of his crime, but according to the latitude and longitude of the place where his crime was committed.[38]

Even within the same locality, the discretionary powers allowed to police courts meant that similar crimes could be punished in very different ways, depending on who was on the bench. An 1848 report on juvenile delinquency by the Aberdeenshire prison board cites the case of a prostitute who was convicted in the Police Court in July 1844 for breaking windows. She was sentenced to thirty days' detention and was warned by the magistrate that she would receive a more severe punishment if she repeated the offence. In October she was convicted of the same offence by another magistrate; this time she received a punishment of ten days in prison or a five-shilling fine.[39]

On the other hand, the advantages of the discretion allowed to magistrates become apparent when it is borne in mind that in many cases they were the very people who were active in promoting new approaches to the treatment of young offenders. Those who set up the ragged schools were often the same individuals before whom ragged children appeared in court. Earlier chapters have shown how men like William Watson, James Mack and Andrew Jameson used the discretionary powers available to them under law to send children to industrial schools. On occasion they were even prepared to go beyond the law, as Alexander Thomson of Banchory admitted. When magistrates ordered that all children found begging in Aberdeen should be taken to one of the industrial schools, he had not the slightest doubt that the proceeding was highly illegal, but at the same time it was highly expedient, and it has done a great deal of good; but several of the magistrates of the town gave their consent and concurrence, and, in fact, were managers of the school.[40]

It has been noted that one of the differences between England and Scotland was that a 'reformatory movement' developed in England to campaign for a change in the law, whereas in Scotland initiative tended to be directed towards localised solutions to the problem. The legal factors discussed above provide one explanation for this: English magistrates had to wait for a change in the letter of the law in order to do what the spirit of Scottish law already allowed.

Poor relief

If the law of Scotland worked to the advantage of magistrates and reformers dealing with young offenders, the reverse was true when it came to the Scottish system of poor relief. The early development of industrial schools in Scotland can to a considerable extent be viewed as a response to the shortcomings of the poor law, and the field of operation of these schools was defined in relation to the availability and extent of poor relief.

Looking back over the progress of the poor laws during the previous 200 years, Rev. Robert Burns of Paisley wrote in 1819 that 'In Scotland, there has always been an union of voluntary benevolence with compulsory enactment; In England, the system as exhibited in practice, has been, and is compulsory, in the most rigid sense of the term'.[41]

Historically, relief in England had been financed by assessing the inhabitants of the parish and administered by overseers appointed by the magistrates, whereas in Scotland poor relief was the responsibility of the landowners (heritors) and Kirk Session in the country parishes, and the magistrates, or a committee of managers appointed by them, in the burghs. An Act of 1579 permitted assessments but this provision was rarely resorted to, and poor relief was mostly paid for out of voluntary church collections. Furthermore, the Scottish system was essentially one of outdoor relief. Although Edinburgh had its Charity Workhouse, Glasgow and Paisley their Town's Hospitals, and some towns had poorhouses, the institutionalisation of paupers was not a feature of the Scottish poor law. In England, on the other hand, after the passage of the Poor Law Amendment Act in 1834 there were 587 poorhouses by 1839.

In view of the dependence on voluntary contributions, it is not surprising that far less was spent on poor relief north of the border. In 1835–1837, for example, the average per head of population was 1s. 3 ¾ d. in Scotland, compared to 6s. 10 ¼ d. in England – not because there were fewer paupers in Scotland but because the allowances were inadequate and many of those who were destitute were not legally entitled to relief.[42]

In short, the Scottish system of poor relief was no longer of relevance to the new industrial society of the nineteenth century. Distress in the Highlands and Ireland led to the migration of starving people in search of food and work, especially to Glasgow. Yet, as these immigrants had no settlement in the south of Scotland, they were not entitled to parish relief. Workers were at the mercy of forces over which they had no control, but there was no provision for the able-bodied who were thrown out of work during the frequent periods of economic recession. Paisley, for example – a town in which virtually the whole of the working population was dependent on the shawl-manufacturing industry – suffered repeated outbreaks of commercial distress in 1840–1843, yet the unemployed were not eligible for parochial relief. In June 1842 there were only about 700 paupers on the roll, with the result that it was necessary to have recourse to outside help, and a relief fund was set up.

Captain Miller, Superintendent of Glasgow police, remarked that many thefts were committed by people in distress rather than by hardened criminals. Very often, he said,

> the property stolen was of very trifling value, consisting of articles of provision, weights from shop counters, and liquor measures from public houses: in other instances the articles consisted of bed clothes taken from lodging houses where the parties had resided, and which had been put by them in pledge, with the intention, it is believed, in many cases, of redeeming and restoring them, after the pressure of the necessity which had prompted the commission of the offence had ceased.[43]

In the same way, throughout his prison reports Frederic Hill argues that, as the poor law failed to relieve the poor, they were forced to turn to crime, and he extolled the superiority of the English system: 'How far the workhouse in England must remove the formidable difficulty experienced by many liberated prisoners in Scotland, in affording asylum till such persons can get work, it is needless to dilate on.'[44]

There were various attempts to tackle the shortcomings of the poor laws in the 1820s and 1830s, the most notable being the experiment conducted by the Rev. Dr. Thomas Chalmers (1780–1847) in his Glasgow parish of St. John's between 1819 and 1823. He had divided his large and densely populated parish into more manageable areas, each under the charge of an elder of the congregation, to organise the distribution of poor relief from what he called the 'four fountains of benevolence': self-help, the help of relatives, the help of neighbours and, if all else failed, the help of the rich. However, critics of Chalmers considered that such an attempt to encourage independence among the poor by restoring the friendly spirit of the country community was not suited to an age when economic cycles rather than moral failings accounted for poverty:

> Chalmers wished to revert to what he regarded as the older social system of Scotland, but it did not occur to him that the new industrialism and the economics on which it was based – and which he himself accepted – made this an anachronism.[45]

Private charities similarly attempted to counteract the inefficiency of the poor law. During the cholera epidemic of 1832, a House of Refuge for the Destitute was set up in Edinburgh to relieve vagrants who were not entitled to parochial relief. Glasgow, too, had a Night Asylum, opened by public subscription in May 1838. The destitute gravitated towards such institutions from all parts of the country. In the night refuge of the Edinburgh institution, for example, of 4,334 persons given shelter from 10 July to 30 September 1840, 2,502 came from outside the locality.[46]

Such ventures, however, were only palliatives, and the failure of attempts to revive or supplement the old system of relief gave rise to a growing advocacy in Scotland of the principles of the 1834 English Poor Law Amendment Act, with its centralised administration, indoor relief and finance by assessment. The chief proponent of this approach was Dr. W.P. Alison, Professor of Medicine at Edinburgh University, who, in an influential pamphlet, argued that the destitution prevalent in Scottish cities was proof of the failure of the voluntary system, and wrote that

> it seems to me, that the administration of the poor Laws in England is so greatly more favourable to the comforts of the poor, and to the health and happiness of all classes of the community, that I can hardly doubt of the disposition of many persons in Scotland to wish them to be placed on a similar footing here…[47]

The Disruption of the Church of Scotland in 1843 lent additional weight to such arguments. When one-third of the ministers left to form the Free Church, the burden of financing parish relief from depleted collections became even greater for the Established congregations. Finally, a wave of economic distress hastened the appointment of a Commission of Inquiry in June 1843 and its findings formed the basis of the Poor Law Act which followed. Although the right to relief was still not extended to the able-bodied in times of distress, in many respects Scottish law was brought into line with that of England: the Church was relieved of the responsibility of poor relief; a central Board of Supervision was established, with parochial boards at the local level, under an inspector of the poor; parishes were permitted to unite for the purposes of forming workhouses; assessments gradually replaced voluntary contributions. By 1856 Sir George Nicholls, a former poor law commissioner, could conclude his *History of the Scotch Poor Law* by saying that

> The divergence which took place between the theory of the Poor Laws in England and in Scotland, as well as in their practical application, appears now therefore to have been in a great degree corrected, and the systems of relief in the two countries are again approximated although still far from being identical.[48]

Children under the Scottish Poor Law

While the institutionalisation of children in workhouses was favoured in Victorian England, Scotland had a long tradition of 'boarding out' pauper children. Glasgow, for example, had its Town's Hospital, opened in 1733, but by 1830 one of the regulations stated that

> The Hospital is no longer a receptacle for the maintenance and education of the young. It has been judged much more conducive to their present health and future prosperity, that they should be boarded at a cheap rate with decent families in the country.[49]

The practice continued after the 1845 Act. A case of neglect, arising from the negligence of the assistant inspector of St. Cuthbert's parish, Edinburgh, led the Board of Supervision to investigate the question of boarding out, yet, on the whole, they considered its advantages to outweigh its drawbacks because 'The instincts of domestic attachment are developed ... and the children ... acquire the habits of thought and action of those with whom they associate and cease to be a separate class'.[50] Results for Glasgow in 1860 appear to corroborate this: of 397 children who had been boarded out, 362 were reported to be 'of good character' and thirteen 'of bad character'; five had been convicted of crime, six were in the poorhouse and eleven had died.[51]

Nevertheless, the social upheavals of the 1830s and 1840s had given rise to a class of children for which the poor law did not cater. Moreover, children were particularly vulnerable to the shortcomings of the poor relief system. The Governor of Glasgow Bridewell, William Brebner, drew attention to the fact that the lack of relief for the unemployed affected not only adults but also children:

> the poor law in Scotland affords no relief to those who are able to work, even though they are quite unable to obtain work; and the consequence is, that many persons, and even children of 12 or 14 years of age, are almost driven into crime when trade is bad...[52]

One of the most serious results of this was pointed out by Frederic Hill, who noted that

> Owing in part to the want in Scotland of any means short of an application to the highest court of law to compel parishes to take charge of destitute children, many such are sent to the prisons with their parents.[53]

At Greenock, for example, Hill discovered that a whole family, including three children, had recently been in prison; the parents and elder son as offenders, and an eight-year-old boy and a baby because there was no other place for them.[54]

Consequently, we find contemporaries viewing the Scottish poor law as one of the causes not only of crime in general, but of juvenile crime in particular. At a meeting in Dundee in 1846 for the purpose of setting up an industrial school, it was stated that

The mischiefs and miseries of juvenile delinquency ... are, as a general rule, more painful in Scotland than in England. The great cause of this is the want of a poor-law. There is no resource but mendicancy for the widow left with a family, and denied all relief, or allowed at best a pittance which mocks her necessities.[55]

Once again, private charities were attempting to alleviate the problem. A substantial proportion of the inmates of the Edinburgh House of Refuge and the Glasgow Night Asylum were children, and Edinburgh had so many orphan hospitals and schools endowed for the education of the poor that Guthrie said that the capital might be called 'the City of Hospitals'.[56] Such agencies, however, did not reach the very lowest class – the starving children whose presence on the streets of the cities could no longer be ignored. In 1849 Guthrie estimated that there were nearly 2,000 such children in Edinburgh, while in Aberdeen the city police reported 280 in their area in 1840.

The revised poor law brought little improvement in this respect. The result of a test case in 1849 made it clear that 'children living with parents who are not proper objects of relief, have no claim to be supported independent of them'.[57] William Lindsay, an unemployed cotton-spinner, had applied to the inspectors of the poor in the Gorbals parish of Glasgow for relief for his four children on the grounds that he had found it impossible to obtain work, and was consequently unable to support them. The Court of Session pronounced in favour of the parochial board, arguing that although Lindsay was eligible for occasional relief or charitable assistance, the wording of his petition, which demanded aid as a right, could not be upheld.[58]

The inadequacies of poor law provision for destitute children thus provided a powerful negative impulse for the establishment of industrial schools and other child-care establishments. The extent to which the Scottish institutions supplemented the deficiencies of the poor law was often remarked upon by observers who were familiar with the poor relief systems of both Scotland and England. Thomas Tancred, in a description of the Glasgow House of Refuge, says that the number of vagrant children on the streets of the city showed the need for such institutions, 'Particularly in Scotland, where the want of an uniform and efficient system for the relief of destitution leaves so many helpless beings no other alternative but crime or starvation'.[59]

Frederic Hill's view of the industrial schools was that they fulfilled a function in Scotland which was not necessary in England: he praised the Scottish industrial schools but added that 'in England, where there is a comprehensive poor-law, providing ... for destitution and want of every kind, ... I look upon such establishments as unnecessary, and likely to produce more harm than good'.[60]

Previous chapters have shown that, even though the shortcomings of the poor law were a factor in giving rise to industrial schools, it remains true to say that the schools were very much in the Scottish poor law tradition. For example, the reluctance to keep industrial school children overnight in dormitories coheres with the Scottish tradition of non-institutionalisation of children. Similarly, the idea of boarding out poor law children in ordinary working-class homes, which was thought to provide a family attachment for children who had been deprived of parental care, was carried over into the ideology of the Aberdeen system. It should also be remembered that both Watson and Guthrie had had experience of residential provision for poor children in the form of the Orphan Hospitals at Aberdeen and Edinburgh and their conviction that such institutions were harmful helps to explain their insistence that children should not be lodged in industrial schools. In *The Orphan Country*, Lynn Abrams has demonstrated how the same preference for boarding out rather than residential care was a characteristic of Scottish methods of caring for children from broken homes: 'between 1845 and 1914 up to 90 per cent of Scottish children dependent on poor relief were boarded out and there was little change in the inter-war period.'[61]

If industrial schools filled a gap in the poor relief system, they could become to some extent an agency of it, and work in co-operation with it. The practice established in England by the 1834 Poor Law Amendment Act was to educate children in union schools attached to workhouses. The corresponding Act for Scotland in 1844 did not contain an equivalent provision, but section LXIX enacted that 'it shall be lawful for the parochial board to make provision for the education of poor children who are themselves or whose parents are objects of parochial relief'. This clause could be interpreted as applying to industrial schools, and we have seen how Bailie Mack planned such a school in Edinburgh, financed entirely from the revenue of the poor law assessment.

There are numerous other examples of co-operation between schools and parochial boards. In Glasgow, the industrial school was a joint venture between voluntary support and the poor law authorities, though in its early stages it was only the City Parochial Board (the largest one) which gave the plan wholehearted support. In Perth, boys were sent to the School of Industry and paid for by the parochial boards; in 1855, twenty-one out of the school's fifty-two pupils were supported in this way.[62] At Pollokshaws, near Glasgow, an arrangement was made for children under the care of the parochial board to be lodged and educated at the industrial school which had been opened there in 1856, the board having given £100 for the erection of a dormitory, and paying eight shillings per month for each child.[63] In 1872 there were 493 children boarded out by the City Parish of Glasgow, some of them at industrial schools.[64] Thus, the traditional method of boarding out worked in harmony with the industrial schools; in a sense, the children were 'boarded out' at the schools. Sydney Turner could therefore hold up this practice as another Scottish example worthy of imitation: in his 1875 report he expressed the hope that 'the liability of parishes to aid in the support of children chargeable to them to a reasonable amount may be extended to England'.[65] By 1877 he summed up the differences between Scottish and English industrial schools by remarking that

> In estimating the relative results of the English and Scottish schools, it must be remembered that in Scotland the certified industrial school takes the place in a large number of cases of the pauper or union school, and that a considerable

proportion of the children sent to these school are sent 'as without proper guardianship'.[66]

Schools and poor law boards did not always work in harmony, however. As will be seen in Chapter Eight, when legislation governing industrial schools was passed in 1854, some schools found themselves in conflict with certain boards which were not willing to contribute to the upkeep of pauper children in industrial schools, preferring to provide for them more cheaply themselves.

Education

At first sight the state of education in mid-nineteenth century Scotland appears little different from that of England. In 1833, 9 per cent of the population of England and Wales was at school, whereas the corresponding figure for Scotland in 1834 was 9.6 per cent – hardly evidence of a significantly better educated populace. However, as with so many aspects of Scottish history in this period, a different tradition lies behind the apparent similarities.

The key distinction was that in England educational reformers sought to establish the principle of universal education, while in Scotland they sought to revive it. The Scottish appreciation of the benefits of education dates back to the Reformation, when John Knox's *First Book of Discipline* (1560), which outlined the organisation and practice of the reformed Church of Scotland, envisaged a system of national education based on the parish unit and controlled by the Church. While this ambitious scheme was never fully put into practice, the principles on which it was based gained acceptance in the succeeding centuries. James Scotland states that it was not the custom to have special schools for poor children: provision was made for them in parish schools, and in many towns it was stipulated that one of the teacher's duties was to instruct poor children free.[67]

The principle of universal schooling, then, was established in Scotland centuries before England, and this legacy was of considerable importance in the nineteenth century. The demand for the education of the poor in England was largely a result of the industrial revolution, with fears of unrest, Luddism, revolution, vagrancy and crime all contributing to the educational movement. These dangers were no less real in Scotland, but the difference was that national education had already been attempted there for other reasons. Whereas the education that arose in nineteenth-century England was designed to keep the poor in their place and to preserve the naturalness of the class structure ('provision should be made for instructing the labouring classes in these circumstances which have the greatest influence over their condition'[68]), in Scotland education had traditionally enabled those of humble origins to rise in the social scale. One historian writes that in the Scottish parochial school, pupils 'of all degrees of society sat at the same benches side by side'.[69] The poor but scholarly 'lad o' pairts' is a familiar figure in the annals of Scotland – men like Robert Burns, Thomas Carlyle and J.M. Barrie began their education in this way.

Moreover, it was widely believed that education had had beneficial and visible social effects in Scotland, and English writers held up the northern kingdom as an example in this respect. 'The quiet and peaceable habits of the Scottish peasant, [writes Rev. T. R. Malthus], compared with the turbulent disposition of the ignorant Irishman, ought not to be without effect upon ever impartial reasoner.'[70] Scottish writers, for their part, were most willing to perpetuate this reputation. Even as late as 1816 James Cleland, in his *Annals of Glasgow*, quotes some rather dubious statistics showing Scotland in a highly favourable light compared to England and Ireland with regard to the proportion of commitments for trial to the population of each district, and considers this to 'exhibit the effect of education on the moral conduct of the lower classes...'.[71] Samuel Whitbread, Whig MP for Bedford, was even more dogmatic in Parliament in 1807:

> Search the Newgate calendar. The great majority of those executed in London every year were Irish; the next in order were English, and the last Scots. This was in exact proportion with their respective systems of education among the lower orders.[72]

The problem with this attractive notion of the superiority of Scottish education was that it had not kept pace with social change. In 1780, when the population of Scotland had been about one million, there were 907 parish schools; by 1831 the population was 2.4 million but the number of parish schools had only increased to 1,005.[73] The greatest need was where the population had grown fastest – in the cities. The Church had not been inactive: some congregations opened sessional schools, so-called because the Kirk Session ran them and appointed the master. By the 1860s Glasgow had forty such schools. But the main initiative had passed into private hands; in the early 1830s there were about three times as many private schools as parish schools. Many were 'adventure' schools which could be set up by anybody, irrespective of qualifications, and were not supervised in any way. In 1857 there were about 1,500 of these, a third in the Glasgow area,[74] fulfilling the Rev. George Lewis's 1834 prophecy that Scotland was becoming 'a half-educated nation, both in the quantity and quality of her educational institutions...' He posed the question, 'are we satisfying ourselves with the past fame of Scotland as an educated nation, unconscious of the change in the numbers and character of her population, and the fixed condition of her educational institutions?'[75] Lewis saw the solution in terms of a revival of the parochial system under Church control, as Chalmers had argued in connection with poor relief. 'Had the parish churches of Glasgow multiplied with the population, the schools would have multiplied also.'[76]

Lewis' vision may have seemed plausible in 1834, but nine years later the Disruption made it hopelessly impracticable. The established church lost the majority of its Evangelical ministers and the men of spiritual energy and vitality were mostly to be found in the new denomination – including industrial school pioneers such as Watson, Thomson, Guthrie, Murray Dunlop and Sheriff Andrew Jameson. As one American observer wrote, the Free Church 'seems to me all in one great revival ... I should like to spend three months in the Free Church, to try and find out the secret of their ardour'.[77]

The Disruption had an immediate and profound effect on education in Scotland. As teachers in parish schools who left the established church were dismissed from their posts, the Free Church quickly opened new schools as well as building its own churches.[78] Thus, in less than a decade, as a parliamentary return of 1851 demonstrates, Scottish education was being conducted by a wide variety of agencies (see Table 7.1).[79]

Such diversity produced obvious anomalies which had to be addressed. The established church still possessed 'school endowments enormously out of proportion to the number of the population adhering to her, and at least two-thirds of what she says she hath ought to be taken away from her'[80] – a situation which gave rise to a call for a 'comprehensive and unsectarian System of Education'. The 1861 Parochial and Burgh Schoolmasters' Act was one stage in this process. Teachers were no longer obliged to subscribe to the Confession of Faith, and were no longer to be under the jurisdiction of the local presbytery. The process culminated in the 1872 Education Act, which went further than its English counterpart, transferring education to the control of the Scottish Education Department, which was responsible for the distribution of grants and for inspection, while at the local level school boards with the power to levy rates took over existing schools.

All this forms the background to the development of ragged industrial schools and, as was the case with the poor relief system, these schools incorporated numerous aspects of existing educational practice. The industrial schools should be understood as one method employed in extending to the 'dangerous' classes the long-established Scottish custom of making education available to all. As *The Witness*, the Free Church newspaper, commented, reviewing Guthrie's *Plea*,

> there are two classes of uneducated poor in Edinburgh, - the *hundreds* of that lowest class of all, on which Mr. Guthrie proposes to operate, and the *thousands* of that low class which comes in direct contact with it, though yet separate and apart, on which Dr. Chalmers and his coadjutors have been operating for years.[81]

Scottish educational tradition also helps to explain some of the differences between the types of teaching given in Scottish and English ragged industrial schools. In English reformatory, industrial and ragged schools intellectual instruction was

Table 7.1 Agencies providing education in Scotland, 1851

Number of Schools	Counties	Burghs
Established Church of Scotland	1765	270
Free Church	601	167
United Presbyterian	21	33
Roman Catholic	9	29
Non-denominational	1274	657

usually restricted to a minimum – 'Our object is to teach them that which will be of use to them in after life, and no more'[82] – whereas Scottish industrial school children received teaching which was 'just the same as they would get in nineteen-twentieths of the ordinary schools in Scotland'.[83] In Aberdeen industrial schools children were held to have a right to education, whether or not their parents paid for it. Watson believed that even children from the very lowest class had within them 'the elements of greatness'. 'Few things', he wrote, 'have afforded me greater satisfaction than to see young men educated at an industrial school showing the superiority of this teaching by taking rank before the youth of a higher grade who had been worse educated'.[84] Guthrie was thrilled to meet a former ragged school pupil who graduated from Edinburgh University.

Sometimes Sydney Turner criticises the methods by which results were achieved. In his first report, for example, he describes the master at Dumfries ragged school as 'efficient, though I think too fond of learned books and difficult subjects of instruction, Latin roots, prefixes & c. Such lessons and questions seemed hardly appropriate in a school for ragged children of so young an age.'[85] Such criticisms nevertheless serve to illustrate how the traditions of Scottish teaching were carried on into the industrial schools. One could hardly expect otherwise, considering that most of the teachers recruited to ragged industrial schools had previously taught in parish, sessional or other schools connected with the churches, and many of them could say with William Cairnduff, Headmaster of Edinburgh's United Industrial School, that 'the system of education pursued is precisely similar to that in which I formerly conducted a parish school'.[86]

Similarly, the theory that education would help prevent crime was not the preserve of industrial schools. The arguments put forward in favour of industrial schools were often applied to education in general; Lewis, for example, warns that 'if the nation will not pay for the schoolmaster, to prevent crime, it must pay tenfold for the repression of social disorder, and for coercing an unhappy, dissolute, and reckless population'.[87] David Stow (1793–1864), a Glasgow merchant, was shocked by conditions he observed in the city and the question perpetually recurred with growing urgency: 'Can nothing be done to stem this deepening torrent of degradation and vice?'[88] His answer was infant schools and a system of teacher training, enterprises which his biographer sees as being part of a network of crime prevention. He asks: 'Why not carry the blessings of such a system of training as that instituted by Mr. Stow, abroad through all those uncultivated districts out of which reformatories are drawing their inmates? Prevention is better than cure...'.[89]

There are, therefore, many connections between industrial schools and the wider Scottish educational background. These schools were based on two traditional principles: the value of a literate working class, and the effect of education in preventing crime. The establishment opened in 1820 in St. John's Parish, Glasgow, by Dr Chalmers illustrates how the traditional parish school was the forerunner of the ragged industrial school. His social work was based on the belief that the Church should take a personal interest in the poor, taking education and worship to them, rather than simply setting up schools and churches in the hope that the poor would attend. His school was no different from the traditional parish school, providing the same educational curriculum; but, by taking education to those who really needed it, it anticipated the rationale of Watson and Guthrie's industrial schools – in the latter case only the method, the provision of food as an incentive, differed. Similarly, in the 1840s the Rev. William Robertson's ragged school in Edinburgh was an extension of his congregation's sessional school, and Guthrie's school had a precedent in the parish school of St. John's.

Thus, as was the case with Scottish legal procedure and poor relief, an examination of the tradition of parochial education sheds light on many of the distinctive features of the Scottish approach to the treatment of destitute and delinquent children in the mid-nineteenth century. The point was well summarised by Rev. Dr. Macduff (1818–1895), minister of Sandyford Parish, Glasgow, who highlighted the continuity between ragged schools and educational values dating back as far as the Reformation. Having heard Guthrie give an address on Scottish education at a conference in Geneva, he wrote: 'Many thanks... for your Geneva speech; it stirred a chord in many hearts. I wish that old John Calvin had heard it. Ragged schools would have had a chapter in the "Institutes"!'[90]

Notes

1 Sheriff Hugh Barclay (1799–1884), author of *Juvenile Delinquency, Its Causes and Cure* (Edinburgh, 1848).
2 Information taken from manuscripts of Sheriff Watson in Aberdeen Public Library, Local Collection.
3 First Report by Her Majesty's Commissioners appointed to inquire into the Schools in Scotland. PP 1865, XVII (3483), p. 246.
4 Evidence of William Locke, Honorary Secretary of the Ragged School Union, Report from the Select Committee on the Education of Destitute Children, PP 1861, VII (460), p. 5.
5 See Geoffrey B.A.M. Finlayson, *The Seventh Earl of Shaftesbury, 1801–85* (London, 1981), p. 251 ff.
6 *Greenock Advertiser*, 17 June 1851.
7 Quotation from the Aberdeen Child's Asylum Committee, 1850, in Mary Carpenter, *Reformatory Schools*, p. 233.
8 Aberdeenshire Prison Board Report on Juvenile Delinquency, quoted in Alexander Thomson, *Industrial Schools; their Origin, Rise and Progress, in Aberdeen* (Aberdeen, 1847), p. 38.
9 Ibid., p. 36.
10 SC 1852, para. 189.
11 The Glasgow Girls' Reformatory, or Juvenile Department of the Females' House of Refuge. From 1840 to 1860 ([Glasgow], 1860), p. 3.
12 SC 1852-3, p. iv.
13 Charles Dickens, 'Lambs to be Fed', in *Household Words*, 30 August 1851, p. 548.
14 SC 1852, paras. 3307–3311.
15 William Watson, 'English and Irish Industrial Schools' (Manuscript in Aberdeen Public Library).
16 E.A.G. Clark, 'The Superiority of the "Scotch System": Scottish Ragged Schools and their Influence', *Scottish Educational Studies*, IX (1977), pp. 29–39.
17 Ibid., p. 35. 'Newcastle, York, Hull, Manchester, Stockport, Liverpool, Chester, Bradford, Bolton, Birmingham, Ipswich, Westminster, Southampton, and possibly Sunderland and North Shields.'

18 Oliphant Smeaton, *Thomas Guthrie* (Edinburgh and London, 1900), p. 88.
19 Finlayson, op. cit., p. 420.
20 *Autobiography of Thomas Guthrie, D.D., and Memoir by his sons, Rev. David K. Guthrie and Charles J. Guthrie, M.A.* (London, 1877), p. 488.
21 Carpenter, *Reformatory Schools*, p. 37.
22 Fifth Report, RIS, PP 1862, XXVI (3034), p. 22.
23 Quoted in the *Glasgow Herald*, 25 November 1839.
24 Ibid.
25 Eighth Report of the Inspector of Prisons of Great Britain, IV Scotland, Northumberland, and Durham, 1841, p. 67.
26 *North British Daily Mail*, 22 February 1866.
27 J.D. Mackie, *A History of Scotland* (Harmondsworth, 1964), p. 330.
28 *The Acts of the Parliaments of Scotland* (1824), Vol. XI, p. 411.
29 Ibid., p. 403.
30 Op. cit., p. vii.
31 David Hume, *Commentaries on the Law of Scotland Respecting Crimes* (Edinburgh, 1819), Vol. I, p. 35. For a detailed discussion of legal opinions on age, maturity and capacity in Scots law, see David G. Barrie and Susan Broomhall, *Police Courts in Nineteenth-century Scotland* (Farnham, 2014), Vol. 2, pp. 81–87.
32 Op. cit., p. 664.
33 William Forsyth, 'Criminal Procedure in Scotland and England' in *Essays Critical and Narrative* (London, 1874), p. 28.
34 9 Geo. IV. Cap. xxix.
35 Barrie and Broomhall, op. cit., Vol. I, p. 1.
36 SC 1847, Appendix, p. 66.
37 Ibid., Appendix p. 94.
38 Frederic Hill, *An Autobiography of Fifty Years in Times of Reform* (London, 1894), p. 129.
39 Aberdeenshire Reports on Juvenile Delinquency, 1848, p. 10.
40 SC 1852, para. 3035.
41 Rev. Robert Burns, *Historical Dissertations on the Law and Practice of Great Britain, and particularly of Scotland, with Regard to the Poor* (Glasgow, 1819), p. 69.
42 'Poor Laws and Pauperism', in *Poverty in the Victorian Age: Debates on the Issues from 19th Century Critical Journals*, Vol IV: Scottish Poor Laws, 1815–70 (Farnborough, 1974), p. 387.
43 Ibid., p. 400.
44 Tenth Report of the Inspector of Prisons of Great Britain, IV Scotland, Northumberland, and Durham, 1845, p. ix.
45 Andrew L. Drummond and James Bulloch, *The Scottish Church 1688–1843* (Edinburgh, 1973), p. 172.
46 'Poor Laws and Pauperism', p. 393.
47 W.P. Alison, *Observations on the Management of the Poor in Scotland, and Its effects on the Health of the Great Towns* (Edinburgh, 1840), p. 31.
48 Sir George Nicholls, *A History of the Scotch Poor Law* (London, 1856), p. 280.
49 *Regulations for the Town's Hospital of Glasgow: With an Introduction, containing a view of the History of the Hospital, and the Management of the Poor* (Glasgow, 1830), p. x.
50 *Edinburgh Evening Courant*, 28 December 1852.
51 *Reports on the Boarding-Out of Orphans & Deserted Children and Insane belonging to the City Parish, Glasgow* (Glasgow, 1872), p. 5.
52 Seventh Report of the Inspector of Prisons of Great Britain, IV Scotland, Northumberland, and Durham. p. 67.
53 Ibid., p. 14.
54 Ibid.
55 *Edinburgh Evening Courant*, 21 September 1846.
56 Rev. Thomas Guthrie, *A Plea for Ragged Schools* (Ninth ed., Edinburgh, 1847), p. 6.
57 A. Murray Dunlop, *The Law of Scotland regarding the Poor* (Edinburgh and London,

1854), p. 29.
58 Full details of the case are in the collection of documents entitled 'Glasgow Poor Law Cases, 1848–9', Mitchell Library, Glasgow.
59 *Journal of the Statistical Society of London,* VI (1853), p. 253. Thomas Tancred was a member of the Children's Employment Commission which investigated the condition of children who were not under the protection of the Factory Act.
60 Eleventh Report, Inspector of Prisons Scotland, PP 1846, XX (740), p. 483.
61 Lynn Abrams, *The Orphan Country* (Edinburgh, 1998), p. 39.
62 Alfred Hill, *Train up a Child…*, p. 15.
63 First Annual Report of the Pollokshaws Industrial School, 1857, p. 8.
64 *Reports on the Boarding-Out of Orphans & Deserted Children and Insane belonging to the City Parish, Glasgow* (Glasgow, 1872), p.6.
65 Eighteenth Report RIS, PP 1875, XXXVI (1311), p. 50.
66 Twentieth Report RIS, PP 1877, XLII (c.1796), p. 9.
67 James Scotland, *The History of Scottish Education* (2 Volumes, London, 1969), Vol. I, p. 90.
68 *The Quarterly Journal of Education* I (1831), p. 217.
69 S.J. Curtis, *History of Education in Great Britain* (London, 1948), p. 513.
70 Rev. T.R. Malthus, *An Essay on the Principle of Population* (Seventh ed., London, 1872), p. 439.
71 James Cleland, *Annals of Glasgow* (2 Volumes, Glasgow, 1816), Vol. II, p. 423.
72 *Cobbett's Parliamentary Debates* IX (London, 1807), column 550.
73 Alexander Wilson, *The Chartist Movement in Scotland* (Manchester, 1970), pp. 9–10.
74 Scotland, op. cit., p. 263.
75 Rev. George Lewis, *Scotland a half-Educated Nation, both in the Quantity and Quality of her Educational Institutions* (Glasgow, 1834), p. 5.
76 Ibid., p. 42.
77 Dr. J.W. Alexander of New York, quoted in Iain H. Murray, 'Thomas Chalmers and the Revival of the Church', *Banner of Truth Magazine,* No. 198, March 1980, p. 3.
78 While this inevitably led to duplication in some areas, in others the Free Church school provided a good alternative to an inefficient parish one, and the rivalry often had a beneficial effect in raising standards. (See Scotland, op. cit., p. 252.).
79 *The Scotsman,* 4 November 1854.
80 Ibid.
81 *The Witness,* 20 February 1847.
82 Captain Donatus O'Brien, in evidence to SC 1852-3, para. 846.
83 Rev. Thomas Guthrie, ibid., para 384.
84 Quoted in Philip Seed, 'Types of Conceptualisation of Ascribed Client Need in Social Service Provision' (Aberdeen University Ph.D thesis, 1976), p. 56.
85 Second Report, RIS, PP 1859, Sess. 2, XIII, Pt. 2 (2537), p. 63.
86 First Annual Report, 1848, p. 16.
87 Lewis, op. cit., p. 44.
88 Rev. William Fraser, *Memoir of the Life of David Stow* (London, 1868), p. 19.
89 Ibid., p. 318.
90 *Autobiography of Thomas Guthrie, D.D.*, p. 487.

8 The emergence of a national system (i)

Reformatory and industrial schools legislation, 1854–1872

The history of the development of the various institutions for destitute and delinquent children in nineteenth-century Scotland is a tale of two halves. 1854 can be regarded as the turning point. Until then, a variety of local efforts contributed to the form the national provision would take; once legislation had been passed, however, individual institutions had to come into line in order to qualify for certification and grants. Before 1854, local provision moulded the national system; after 1854, the national system moulded local provision.

In retrospect, it is easy to discern an inevitability about this process. Even at the time, the inbuilt momentum towards the integration of voluntary agencies with statutory provision was recognised. In 1867 *The Scotsman* commented:

> It is obvious that no number of small circles will ever fill a large one; they may overlap each other, but they must always leave many intermediate spaces untouched. So no number of charities for specific purposes, no amount of individual effort, will ever overtake the needs of a large city.[1]

In a similar vein, Dr. George Bell, an Edinburgh physician with an interest in social reform, observed that 'If John Pounds alone saved ragged children by the dozen, surely society can save them by the thousand. If the active mercy of an obscure cobbler did so much, what may the mercy of a nation not effect?'[2] Remarks such as these anticipate the belief that state intervention could achieve more than charitable efforts.

UK-wide statutory provision quickly followed the recommendations of the 1852–3 Select Committee which itself had been appointed 'largely as a result of the spirited effort of Dr. Guthrie in this direction'.[3] The 1854 Youthful Offenders Act [17 & 18 Vict., c. 86] – sometimes referred to as Palmerston's Act, as it was passed when Lord Palmerston (1784–1865) was Home Secretary – applied to both England and Scotland and provided for the detention of convicted juveniles in reformatory schools after they had served at least fourteen days in prison. But there was also a separate Act passed the same year [17 & 18 Vict., c. 74] which applied to Scotland only, known as Dunlop's Act after its author, Alexander Murray Dunlop (1798–1870), Liberal MP for Greenock between 1852 and 1868, legal adviser to the Free Church of Scotland and 'intimate friend' of Guthrie. The Scottish Act met the demands of Guthrie and others by giving magistrates the power to send a vagrant child to a certified industrial school, the expenses to be charged to the parent or the parish. Most of its provisions were extended to England by the Industrial Schools Act of 1857 [20 & 21 Vict., c. 48] but, because industrial schools had been pioneered in Scotland, there remained a higher number of these north of the border until the late 1860s. It was only after further legislation in 1866, which permitted certain children charged with criminal offences to be sent to industrial schools, that these schools became widespread in England. Nevertheless, even in 1874 industrial schools were still more extensively used in Scotland than in England, in proportion to the size of the countries: more than one-third of children annually sent to industrial schools were committed in Scotland.

Figure 8.1 Alexander Murray Dunlop

Source: *Disruption Worthies: A Memorial of 1843* by Rev. J.A. Wylie, Edinburgh, 1881

By this stage, however, the Scottish schools had lost their distinctive features and certified industrial schools were run on similar lines on both sides of the border. Although Dunlop's Act applied to Scotland alone, it still had the effect of bringing the Scottish schools into greater contact with English approaches, particularly through the inspections carried out by Rev. Sydney Turner (1814–1879), who was appointed in 1857.[4] Although Turner warmly commended the Scottish schools, he considered that destitute and criminal children should be kept apart and preferred residential schools to day schools. It is noticeable, therefore, that within a few years these features began to die out in Scottish schools, and there evolved, as in England, two different types of school: reformatory for the convicted, industrial for the destitute. This chapter will trace the ways in which legislation and Home Office influence brought about this evolution.

Effects of the 1854 legislation

As Chapters Four, Five and Six demonstrated, by 1854 each of the main cities in Scotland had developed its own responses to the problem of juvenile delinquency in accordance with local needs; there was no 'reformatory movement' as in England. The Scottish schools were far from indifferent to the possibilities of legislation, but they looked to the state to assist existing schools rather than to help set them up. The viewpoint of the Scottish schools was well summarised by the Duke of Argyll, speaking at the annual meeting of the Edinburgh Original Ragged School in 1857:

> if it had been [Dunlop's] duty to go to Parliament to devise schools for educating the vagrant and criminal children, he would have been utterly unable to get any law on the subject passed ... But Mr. Dunlop was able to go to the House of Commons and say, 'You have nothing to do with founding schools; they are founded for you, and all that I ask is, that when children have been found in a vagrant condition, and likely to perpetrate crime, it shall be in the power of the magistrate, instead of sending them, as formerly, to prison, to send them to these schools'.[5]

The most significant alteration desired in Scotland was legal authority to ensure that pupils continued to attend the schools. Even when local police acts allowed sympathetic magistrates to send children to an industrial school, as in Aberdeen or Edinburgh, the schools did not have any legal powers to detain them for the length of time needed to make a genuine difference. Even the provision of meals proved insufficient to guarantee attendance. Consequently, when Dunlop sponsored a Bill in Parliament in May 1854 it aimed to 'give power to magistrates where delinquents were brought before them, to send them to school instead of to gaol ... and to charge the expenditure on county and parochial boards'.[6] There was clearly no intention to make any distinction between children who had already transgressed the law and those who were in danger of falling into crime. The full title of the original bill makes this plain: 'A Bill to render Reformatory and Industrial Schools in Scotland more available for the Benefit of juvenile Delinquents and vagrant Children.' A child under sixteen charged with an offence could, under the terms of the proposed Act, be sent to 'any Reformatory School, Industrial School, or other similar Institution', while vagrant children having no home, proper guardianship or 'lawful or visible Means of Subsistence' were to be dealt with in exactly the same manner.

A number of fundamental changes were made to the bill before it became law, however. The maximum age to which its provisions were to apply was altered to twelve, then to fourteen, and finally to fifteen. More importantly, the bill was amended to allow parochial boards the power to act as security for a child; a boy or girl entitled to poor relief could thus be withdrawn from the industrial school and boarded out by the parochial board or taken to an institution of its own. Dunlop later stated that he had only agreed to the inclusion of this clause very reluctantly, as he had 'had considerable difficulty in carrying the measure at all'.[7]

The difficulty he was referring to was the vigorous opposition of Roman Catholic MPs. In view of the dispute in Edinburgh over the religious education of Catholic children in the Original Ragged School, they objected to the first clause of the bill which allowed a sheriff or magistrate to send a vagrant child to an industrial school unless security was found for his good behaviour. Frederick Lucas (1812–1855), the Catholic journalist and MP for Meath, thought

> that a case of greater oppression could not be conceived than that a magistrate should be empowered by Act of Parliament to send a [Catholic] child to Dr. Guthrie's proselytising school, where it should be kept till the age of fifteen under the penalty of whipping and imprisonment.[8]

Dunlop was consequently forced to safeguard parents' rights and religious beliefs by adding the proviso that the magistrate should first inquire whether 'the Parents, Guardians, or other persons interested in such young Persons shall appear and find security for his or her good Behaviour'. In deciding which school to send a child to, the magistrate was to have 'due Regard to the religious Belief of such Child, or to any wish expressed by the Parents, Guardians, or other Relative as to the particular Institution to which such Child shall be committed or removed'.

These alterations prevented the Act from operating in the way originally envisaged and the vast majority of industrial school pupils remained voluntary cases. At the time of Sydney Turner's first Report in 1857–1858, only 7 out of 106 pupils at the Greenock Ragged School were under detention, 6 out of 230 at Kilmarnock, and 1 out of 34 at the Boys' School of Industry at Perth. As Turner commented of these and the other Scottish schools, the clause permitting the parochial boards to withdraw such children had 'almost neutralized the direct operation of the Statute…'.[9] Some boards had their inspectors of the poor stand security for children, and looked after them in their own schools, a procedure which was cheaper for the boards than contributing to an industrial school. Up to July 1856, thirty-four children had been committed to the Aberdeen schools under the Act. Of these, three had been withdrawn by parents and the rest remained; however, 'A much larger number seem to have been brought before the magistrates, but have not been sent to the school owing to security having been found for them, generally by the poor inspectors of the parishes...'.[10]

The controversy came to a head in Edinburgh in November 1855 over the case of a girl called Susan Guy. The parochial board of St. Cuthberts, to which she was chargeable, offered to stand security for her good behaviour, the parents having refused, but the magistrate persisted in committing her to the Original Ragged School. An action was accordingly raised by the board against the Superintendent of Police. The board urged that, instead of bringing such vagrant children to the police court, they should be handed over to the poor law authorities which would send them to their own schools. The magistrates had sent thirty or forty children to the industrial schools, which cost the board nearly ten pounds a week.[11] For their part, the police magistrates argued that for the board to stand as security for children was against the spirit of the Act, and was merely a means of saving expense. The Lord Justice General, the Rt. Hon. Duncan McNeill, however, decided in favour of the parochial board, as it was judged that 'Decidedly the parish is interested in keeping the child at home. The parish may, therefore, give the caution required by the Act'[12] – a pronouncement which led to the release not only of Susan Guy, but of forty-seven other children sentenced under the Act. By January 1857 there were only four or five children in the Original Ragged School sentenced by magistrates.[13] At the same time, some boards worked in harmony with the schools. In Glasgow, the City board had worked with the school since its establishment: Turner remarked in 1860 that Glasgow was the only city in which the Act had been fully adopted, and at the time of his visit that year as many as 72 out of 118 boys and 46 out of 98 girls were under sentence.

There were good reasons for the boards to co-operate with the schools, as the latter to some extent filled gaps in the poor relief system. During the 1860s and 1870s the boards, possibly because the increased availability of government grants relieved them of the burden of supporting the upkeep of many of the children in the schools, came to accept the value of industrial schools, and Turner's later reports frequently comment on the fact that in Scotland parochial boards contributed to the upkeep of children in the industrial schools and recommend the adoption of a similar practice in England.

Initially, Dunlop's Act came up against opposition from within the industrial school system as well as from some of the parochial boards. Some schools felt that the corollary of accepting warrant children would be a decline in subscriptions for the support of voluntary pupils, leading in turn to a greater reliance on children sent under magistrate's warrant, for whom government grants were received. A disillusioned Sheriff Watson wrote in 1872:

> Nearly all the industrial schools in Scotland are now certified, and while the number of voluntary inmates yearly diminishes, the number of warrant children yearly increases, and there is every appearance that all of them will soon become schools in name, and shelters, homes, or hospitals, in reality.[14]

This is in fact what happened, particularly after 1866, although the beginning of the process can be traced back to Dunlop's Act.

A further consequence of the acceptance of committed children in industrial schools was that it forced a reconsideration of the question of dormitory accommodation. A distinctive part of the ideology of Watson's and Guthrie's schools had been the fact that children were allowed home in the evenings. Initially, there was some doubt as to whether schools were obliged to become residential in order to qualify for a certificate under Dunlop's Act. The confusion arose over the interpretation of the phrase in the Act which said that children could be committed to an industrial school 'to be detained therein'. The Lord Advocate, Lord Moncrieff, hesitated over certifying schools, because he believed 'that, in most if not all, of these institutions in Scotland there is no adequate accommodation for lodging the pupils; and on the other hand, attendance as mere day scholars would not carry out the objects of the Act'.[15]

In practice, the provision of dormitory accommodation was an inevitable result of the acceptance of children sent by magistrates. When a school had only two or three such cases, they might be boarded out with suitable families, as was the Scottish custom with poor law children. As the number of committed cases increased, however, it was more convenient and cheaper for schools to accommodate them on their premises. The directors of the United Industrial School, for example, decided in December 1859 that 'licensed as the institution was under Mr. Dunlop's Act, it was essential that sleeping places should be provided for the children sent to the institution under that Statute'.[16]

Where managers of schools did not approve of these tendencies it would theoretically have been possible for the schools to continue on their original basis, without applying for certification under the Acts, which were only permissive legislation. In practice, the schools considered government finance and legal backing so imperative to their continued existence that most, with the exception of Sheriff Watson's Female School in Aberdeen, were prepared to accept the side-effects of the Acts which they did not particularly welcome.

We have seen how the mixing of destitute and convicted children was a characteristic of all the Scottish pioneering institutions in the 1840s. Hence, with the passing of legislation in 1854 some schools received certification under both Palmerston's (reformatory schools) and Dunlop's (industrial schools) Acts. At the time of Turner's first Report there were four such institutions: Greenock, Paisley, Stranraer and Inverness. Turner did not, however, approve of this arrangement, and was critical of the schools in which 'convicted children are mixed with paupers and day-school scholars, a practice which I cannot think defensible or safe'.[17] Dunlop's original Bill was not intended to preclude the mixing of different types of children in the one school, but in June 1856 an 'Act to make further Provision for rendering Reformatory and Industrial Schools in Scotland more available for the Benefit of Vagrant Children' [19 & 20 Vict. c.28] was passed which stipulated that no more schools were to be certified under both Acts.

The clause thus created a distinction between reformatory and industrial schools in Scotland which had two important consequences. First, the practice of treating different classes of children in the same school died out, and paupers, delinquents and destitute children were dealt with separately. The Govan Parochial School in Glasgow, for example, was part of the parish poorhouse and was certified under Dunlop's Act, but planned to give up the certificate when the last four children detained under the Act were released. The Greenock Poorhouse, which had been certified as a reformatory under Palmerston's Act, gave up its certificate in 1860, the directors having resolved not to continue mixing convicted, pauper and vagrant children, and the institution returned to its original purpose as a poorhouse.[18] In the same year, the Stranraer Industrial School, on Turner's advice, was moved out of the poorhouse premises and thereafter received children only under Dunlop's Act, while the Inverness Ragged School transferred to a new building and admitted only those sent under Palmerston's Act, becoming known as Inverness Reformatory.[19]

The second consequence of the amending Act was to necessitate the provision of reformatory schools in the strict sense of institutions certified under Palmerston's Youthful Offenders Act. Previously children convicted of delinquency were often sent to industrial schools; now they were required to be sent to reformatory institutions. But, as the industrial schools had formerly fulfilled this function in much of Scotland, there was a lack of suitable reformatories in many cities. Edinburgh and Aberdeen, for instance, had pioneered industrial schools and had emphasised the prevention of delinquency rather than the reformation of the delinquent; it had therefore not been considered necessary to provide separate reformatories. On 17 September 1856 *The Scotsman* pointed out that

> It is quite clear that while so few certified Reformatory Schools are in existence, the reformatory system cannot have a chance of being fairly carried out in Scotland; and in this matter we are very far behind our neighbours in the south.[20]

Accordingly, steps were taken to provide reformatories in both cities; the Oldmill reformatory in Aberdeen, accommodating fifty boys, was opened in March 1857, followed two years later by the Wellington Farm School in Edinburgh.

Thus, a pattern of having separate institutions in each city, one under Dunlop's and one under Palmerston's Act, was becoming established. Glasgow was the only Scottish city which already had both a reformatory and an industrial school, prefiguring the arrangements which were to become general in Scottish and English cities.

The new emphasis on reformatories in Scotland was a result of greater contact with English approaches, through government inspection and grants. Similarly, the introduction of certified industrial schools into England was a result of Scottish experience. In 1857 most of the provisions of Dunlop's Act were extended to England, and the debt to the Scottish schools was specifically acknowledged in the Commons by Sir John Pakington (1799–1893), Conservative Member for Droitwich and one of the MPs prominent in the Reformatory and Refuge Union:

In this matter [he said] they were only copying the example set by their enlightened neighbours in Scotland ... They ... led the way in the establishment of reformatories for the guilty; and again, by the adoption of the Act of the honourable member for Greenock (Mr. Dunlop), they had been pioneers to us in reclaiming the neglected and intermediate class in whose behalf this bill had been introduced.[21]

As in Scotland, the Act took some time to have any significant effect. The evening ragged schools which were widespread in English cities were unsuitable for transformation into certified industrial schools. Moreover, under the English Act only children convicted of vagrancy could be detained in industrial schools. The ragged schools affiliated to the Reformatory and Refuge Union objected to the stigma of a magistrate's committal. Thus by 1861 Mr. A.O. Charles, Secretary of the Union, stated that there were only 420 children in certified industrial schools in England, and of these a mere twenty were under magistrate's warrant. Turner frequently remarked how it would be desirable if England were to follow Scotland's lead in the use of industrial schools. 'It is impossible to visit [the Scottish schools]', he wrote in his 1860 report, 'without regretting that the Industrial Schools Act ... is not more generally adopted and acted on in England'.[22] 'To complete the reformatory system', he added, 'we need a large extension of these cheaper and more directly preventive schools...'.[23]

By 1857, then, increased contact between Scottish and English approaches had been brought about. While reformatory schools outnumbered industrial schools in England, and industrial schools outnumbered reformatory schools in Scotland, there was nevertheless legislation providing for both types of school in each country, and the foundation was laid for the dual system of schools which developed in the 1860s. However, to view Dunlop's Act as confirming in law a system which had been worked out empirically at a local level – 'a distillation of the experience of the early Scottish schools'[24] – would only be partially correct. While the Act fulfilled some of the Scottish aspirations, such as the necessity for legal powers of detention and the provision of financial support by the state, the practical effect of the measure was to alter some of the fundamental features of the Scottish system and, through the separation of delinquent and destitute children and the change from day to residential schools, make possible the future standardisation of procedure in England and Scotland alike. In short, Dunlop's Act, while resulting from Scottish initiatives, did not consolidate the Scottish schools into a distinct system but began the process of amalgamating approaches north and south of the border.

Standardisation of procedure in England and Scotland

Developments in the 1860s confirmed the trends initiated by the 1854 Acts. Home Office policy was to eliminate voluntary cases from industrial schools by giving grants for the support of committed cases only. As a result, the number of voluntary pupils declined, a process which was carried a stage further by the 1861 Industrial Schools Consolidating and Amending Act (Scotland) [24 & 25 Vict., c.

132] which allowed children under twelve convicted of a criminal offence to be sent to an industrial school. In 1866 the law was made the same for both England and Scotland, after which parallel systems of industrial and reformatory schools operated on both sides of the border. The stages of the completion of this process must now be examined.

(i) The withdrawal of government grants

Under the Minute of the Committee of Council on Education of 2 June 1856, grants were given to 'schools wherein Children of the Criminal and Abandoned Classes may be reformed by Industrial Training'. Such schools qualified for the payment of half the rent of their premises; a third of annual costs of tools and materials for industrial work; grants towards books and equipment; and supplementation of teachers' salaries. In addition, a capitation grant of fifty shillings per annum was given for every child who was fed as well as taught at the school. This support was in accordance with the recommendation of the 1852–3 Select Committee that such schools 'should not be excluded from the aid of the National Grant, under the distribution of the Committee of Council for Education...'.[25]

However, on 31 December the following year the minute was abruptly superseded by one with far less generous terms. Grants were now to be limited to certified schools, and the allowance of half the rent was payable only for the part of the building in which industrial training was given. The terms relating to teachers' salaries, books and materials were unaltered, but the fifty-shilling capitation grant was reduced to five shillings for voluntary scholars and increased to £5 a head for each child committed by the magistrate.[26]

The withdrawal of this support was the most controversial aspect of the relationship between the government and the industrial schools in the period between 1857 and 1861. The issue of restricting grants to certified cases became a focal point for the discussion of questions which had already been raised by the operation of Dunlop's Act: the suitability of voluntary scholars in certified schools and the role of charitable support vis-a-vis government supervision and finance.

The reduction of grants for non-warrant children was designed to further the policy of withdrawing such children from industrial schools altogether. The objective of the Committee of Council was 'to encourage the transformation of those Ragged Schools which are organised as asylums or refuges into certified Industrial Schools'.[27] Agreeing with this, *The Scotsman* argued that the class which did not qualify for reformatory schools or for poor law schools could be left to private benevolence, for 'the encouragement of Ragged Schools by government aid encouraged the pauperization of the masses'.[28] It was feared that some parents who could afford to pay for their child's education were using the ragged schools as a means of obtaining free schooling.

The new policy was received by a storm of protest from the schools, and it is hardly surprising that much of the organised opposition came from Scotland, for the system of mixing voluntary and warrant cases, and the ideology of prevention rather than cure, were the distinctive characteristics of the Scottish schools, and both were under threat. Guthrie and others attempted to reverse the Committee of Council's decision. Deputations were sent to the Committee in every year between 1857 and 1860, but were told that

> the parliamentary grant is made for *educational purposes*; that Ragged and Industrial Schools are not to be viewed as purely *educational* institutions, but as means of repressing crime and vagrancy; and, therefore, that no aid can be granted to them beyond what they are entitled to under the existing Minutes.[29]

Guthrie campaigned on the basis that ragged and industrial schools should be entitled to the same support as other educational institutions. A conference held in January 1861 in Birmingham to discuss the matter concluded that 'the Government grant does not reach the neglected and morally destitute'; since 'the Ragged Schools which provide for them cannot permanently stand by voluntary aid alone … it is the duty of the State to give liberal financial aid to such schools…'[30] Grants were given to upper-class schools, denominational schools and universities, but the ragged schools received a pittance, claimed Guthrie. 'We ought to have been first, and we have been put last.'[31]

Moreover, the withdrawal of the grants left the schools doubly worse off, for their increasing dependence on government aid led subscribers to think that their contributions were no longer required. Even the Aberdeen schools were unsuccessful in their attempt to persuade churches to take collections on their behalf. In January 1861 it was stated that the withdrawal of capitation grants would reduce the amount received by the Aberdeen schools from government sources to £8 instead of £320 as before.[32] In the same way, the reports of the United Industrial School in Edinburgh in this period are full of urgent pleas for funds. Not only were the operations of some schools circumscribed by the removal of grants for unconvicted children; the very principles on which they were based – prevention rather than cure – were undermined. Just as it had been argued that it would be better for the government to pay for children to go to an industrial school, rather than to wait until they were convicted and pay for their maintenance in prison, so it was now argued that it would be better for the government to give an allowance to voluntary pupils in industrial schools rather than to wait until they were committed and then pay for them at the higher rate. As Mr. Charles Ferguson, headmaster and superintendent of the United School, told the 1865 Commission on Scottish Schools,

> … if Government would give a certain sum for what we now call voluntary children – those that are not convicted – we would be able to take more into the school; and consequently the very same class that in a year or two afterwards, if they were not admitted on the charity, would likely be sent to us under warrant at 4s. 6d. a week.[33]

The grants policy appeared to be geared towards the English idea of reforming offenders rather than the Scottish idea of preventing children becoming offenders in the first place. Guthrie ridiculed the government for giving more money to reformatory than to industrial schools:

> think of the Government refusing money to save a man's leg, but giving him money instead to buy a wooden leg when the limb is cut off ... They give much more to those who cry out for reformatories than to those who demand prevention.[34]

Attempts made by Sir John Pakington and the Edinburgh MP Adam Black to bring the question up in Parliament made little headway, but hopes were raised when Sir Stafford Northcote, MP for Stamford, secured the appointment, at the request of the Birmingham Conference, of a Select Committee 'to inquire how the Education of Destitute and Neglected Children may be most efficiently and economically assisted by any Public Funds'. Its recommendations, however, simply ratified the procedure already being followed. The argument of representatives of Scottish schools – that the schools would be prepared to accept grants on the same basis as other schools, that is, for educational purposes only – was rejected by the Committee on the grounds that

> Aid to Ragged Schools and other Institutions where children are fed, or fed and lodged is really aid in relief of the poor rate, and this is true even when the aid is given as salary to a master for such a payment sets at liberty an equal sum to be employed in feeding and lodging.[35]

The object was to ensure that children were dealt with in the appropriate schools: those convicted of crime should be sent to reformatories, vagrant children should be sent under warrant to certified industrial schools and paupers should be dealt with by the parochial boards. 'No child', said the Committee, 'should be encouraged to go to a Ragged School, for whose education provision can be made elsewhere'.[36]

However, these proposals were again based on English rather than Scottish experience. In Scotland there were no other schools suitable for the children who voluntarily attended the industrial schools. The line followed by the Select Committee was applicable only to England, with its Union schools and poor relief for able-bodied persons and their families, and the proposals of the Committee reveal its misunderstanding of the function of industrial schools in Scotland, particularly of their relationship with the poor relief system. Outdoor relief for able-bodied paupers made destitute through unemployment was the exception rather than the rule in Scotland, where such parents were more likely to send their children to an industrial feeding school.

It is not surprising, then, that the debate over grants to ragged schools at the Birmingham conference made many English delegates more aware of the difference between the English and Scottish schools. In the words of Robert Hanbury, MP for Middlesex,

The Scotch institutions are those mainly known by the name of Feeding and Industrial ragged schools, while our schools for the most part in England, and entirely in the metropolis, are not Industrial Schools, and not Feeding Schools, but purely and simply educational. Therefore I foresee great difficulties in our unanimously agreeing upon the measure of aid to be granted...[37]

Nevertheless, the grants were not restored in either country. When the Revised Code was introduced in 1862 ragged schools could apply for grants, but, as Mary Carpenter argued, the regulations were framed for a higher class of school; 'payment by results' was inapplicable to ragged schools, in which the results aimed at were not 'purely intellectual'; moreover, schools had to have certificated teachers before they could receive support, whereas it was the teacher's 'moral influence' which was of paramount importance for a ragged industrial school.[38]

The question of government aid for voluntary scholars in certified industrial schools continued to be raised in the 1860s, but without the same force. There was a softening of official attitudes: when representatives of schools gave evidence to the Royal Commission on Scottish schools in 1867–1868, the Commission recommended that 'some small assistance might be granted towards meeting the cost occasioned by the voluntary inmates at such Institutions, and by the children attending them for instruction and receiving food as day-scholars'.[39] But by this stage the number of voluntary cases had diminished still further, and indignation at the withdrawal of government support for them had subsided correspondingly. The greater the number of warrant children in the schools, the greater was the amount of government grant received for their upkeep, which helped to offset the lack of allowances for day scholars. Captain Dempster, the Secretary and Treasurer of the Edinburgh Original Ragged School, complained that grants were not given for all children attending the school, but nevertheless conceded that the present sum of four shillings and sixpence a head paid for warrant cases was 'a very good allowance'.[40]

The fact, then, that demand for the restoration of grants for unconvicted children in industrial schools died down may be attributed to the greater reliance of the schools on committed cases, and for an explanation of this we must examine the legislative changes of the 1860s which further widened the class of juveniles which could be sentenced to detention in an industrial school.

(ii) Consolidating legislation, 1861 and 1866

In 1861 the English and Scottish Industrial Schools Acts were consolidated and simplified, and the types of children who could be sentenced to such schools were both defined more precisely and extended to include criminal offenders as well as vagrants. Experience of the English Industrial Schools Act of 1857 had shown that few magistrates were prepared to commit children under so vague a charge as 'vagrancy'. In 1861, therefore, the offences were clearly defined (as they had been in the Scottish Act of 1854) as begging, wandering without visible means of subsistence and keeping the company of reputed thieves. Furthermore, any child under twelve charged with an offence could now be sentenced to an industrial school, such children being thereby kept out of prisons. The schools could also admit children under the age of fourteen whose parents could not control them.

Three months later, Dunlop and David Mure, MP for Bute, introduced a bill to extend these provisions to Scotland. As had happened in 1854, the bill was amended in committee to safeguard the position of the parochial boards, and a clause was added to the effect that a child chargeable to a board was to be sent to a school run by that board, if one existed. In July the bill came in for heavy criticism from the *North British Daily Mail*, on the grounds that it 'interferes with the principles of constitutional liberty':

> Here is a bill which, upon *mere appearances*, proposes to deprive a subject of his freedom ... If a child is 'apparently' under 14 – if he is found 'placing himself in any street' so as to excite, in the imagination of a policeman or 'any person', the notion that he is under 14, and has an intention of asking or receiving a copper – he may at once be captured and conveyed to a cell, to be dealt with as a Magistrate may direct.[41]

Once the bill had become law, there were reports of cases which seemed to confirm these fears. In November, for example, it was reported that 'in Greenock so many children are being sent summarily to the Ragged School that there is a danger that zeal may outstrip the discretion of the magistrates'.[42] It was alleged that a girl called Ann Mary Small was at the door of a shop being asked to run a message in return for a biscuit when she was spotted by a ragged-school teacher who conveyed her to the magistrate, by whom she was sent two hours later, without her parents being informed, to the industrial school for a period of five years. While not every case was as extreme as this one, the Act clearly increased the number of juveniles sentenced to the schools, as can be seen from figures in Turner's annual reports (see Table 8.1).

In 1866 the Acts relating to reformatory schools in England and Scotland were consolidated into the one statute, the Reformatory Schools Act [29 & 30 Vict., c. 117], Scotland ceasing to have separate legislation. The same was done for the industrial schools by 29 & 30 Vict., c. 118, which made some minor amendments, permitting them to allow children out on licence and making provision for contributions from county and burgh rates, on the same basis as reformatories. Thus, as

Table 8.1 Children sentenced to Scottish industrial schools, 1862–1867

| | Number of children sentenced to Scottish Industrial Schools: | | |
	Boys	Girls	Total
1862	82	49	131
1863	162	76	238
1866	592	359	851
1867	717	397	1114

Turner said, 'the law was made uniform for both Scotch and English schools',[43] marking the end of a phase in the history of the Scottish institutions.

The vexed question of religious instruction was largely settled at this time by a clause which stipulated that a minister of the child's persuasion was allowed to visit the school during the period set aside for religious instruction. Peter Mackie states that this provision appears to have been influenced by the United School which had been founded on the basis of 'combined instructions in things secular, separate in things religious'. He also notes that this arrangement did not turn out to be a model for other similar schools because the availability of state funding now enabled Roman Catholics to set up their own reformatory and industrial schools on a denominational basis, leaving the United School 'as a unique symbol, in the nation's capital, of inter-denominational education'.[44]

Conclusion

The consequence of the legislation of the 1860s was to blur the distinction between reformatory and industrial schools. Through the admission of young offenders to the latter class of institution, convicted and destitute children were again mixed, as they had been in the Scottish industrial schools of the pre-1854 period. By 1870, Sydney Turner could look back over the development of the system, and say that

> The position of certified industrial schools … completely changed, and though still called by the name of schools they are in fact but reformatories of a milder sort, and so institutions of a corrective and not a merely educational character.[45]

The statistical information contained in Turner's reports reveals how in other respects Scottish and English schools developed in similar ways in the 1860s. Certified industrial schools were of two types, states the 1868–1869 report: in one, day scholars attend in addition to warrant cases; in the other, all the children are lodged and boarded under magistrate's order. 'The Scotch Schools', continues Turner, 'were generally of the former description, but are now mostly of the latter'.[46]

Moreover, industrial schools expanded in the same way in both countries. Once industrial schools began to take convicted offenders, the number sentenced to reformatories tended to stabilise. As the table on page 126 demonstrates, the number of children in reformatories in England and Scotland declined in the early 1870s, and remained fairly level for the rest of the decade. Between 1864 and 1874 the number of offenders in reformatories increased slightly, but there was a dramatic increase in the number of children in industrial schools in the same period.

Certified reformatory and industrial schools were regulated by the same Acts in England and Scotland from 1866 onwards, and with the exception of various issues arising from the Scottish poor law, the schools were conducted on similar lines in both countries. Between 1854 and 1861, legislation and government grants moulded the various schools into a dual system of preventive and reformatory institutions, to which potential and actual offenders could be committed by magistrates. As Mary Carpenter put it in an address 'on the Consolidation of the Reformatory and Industrial Schools Acts' at the Social Science Congress held in Sheffield in 1865, 'There has been no contradiction in the different amendments; all have tended only to develop more perfectly the original intention, and little has been added which was not foreshadowed in the first act'.[47] The Education Acts of 1870 (England) and 1872 (Scotland) mark the natural conclusion to this process since by providing education for all they put an end to the presence of voluntary pupils in certified industrial schools, a class which had been steadily diminishing since 1854. Yet, as Chapter Ten will demonstrate, even in the era of universal schooling, the type of school pioneered by Watson and Guthrie still had a role to play.

Appendix

Table 8.2 Number of juveniles detained in reformatory and industrial schools from 31 December 1859 to 31 December 1874

	England		Scotland	
	Reformatory	Industrial	Reformatory	Industrial
1859	2570	–	696	–
1860	3035	–	768	–
1861	3488	592	890	486
1862	3570	531	966	423
1863	3671	805	1025	654
1864	3681	957	1089	822
1865	3820	1172	1121	912
1866	4140	1518	1205	1089
1867	4585	2525	1303	1493
1868	5805	3574	1354	2189
1869	5100	4564	1376	2831
1870	5314	5345	1359	3420
1871	5265	6148	1347	3776
1872	5356	7120	1325	3785
1873	5513	8060	1269	3780
1874	5536	8530	1256	3743

Note: Totals include juveniles in schools under magistrates' orders, those released on licence and those who had absconded.
Source: Reports of the Inspector of Reformatory and Industrial Schools

Notes

1 Quoted in a pamphlet entitled *How to Relieve the Poor of Edinburgh without increasing pauperism* (Edinburgh, 1867), p. 6.

2   George Bell, M.D., *Blackfriars' Wynd Analyzed* (Edinburgh, 1850), p. 27.
3   Oliphant Smeaton, *Thomas Guthrie* (Famous Scots Series, Edinburgh and London, 1900), p. 86.
4   Turner was one of those of whom it has been said that 'for the most part [the members of the Victorian Inspectorate] did not interest themselves in certain things because they were servants of the State; rather, they were servants of the State because they were interested in these things, because they had formed opinions which an official position allowed them to translate into action' (W. L. Burn, *The Age of Equipoise,* London, 1964, p. 223).
5   Quoted in *Autobiography of Thomas Guthrie, D.D. and Memoir by his Sons* (London, 1877), p. 472.
6   *Hansard's Parliamentary Debates,* Third Series, CXXXIII (London, 1854), col. 588.
7   *Edinburgh Evening Courant,* 27 November 1860.
8   *Hansard's Parliamentary Debates,* Third Series, CXXXV (London, 1855), col. 434. Catholic hostility to the Bill is understandable as so many of the children eligible for industrial schools were Irish immigrants.
9   First Report, Reformatory and Industrial Schools, PP 1857-8, XXIX (2426), p. 17.
10 Alfred Hill, *Train up a Child in the Way he should Go: A Paper on the Industrial Schools of Scotland, and the Working of Dunlop's Act* (London and Bristol, N.D.), p. 17.
11 *Edinburgh Evening Courant,* 8 December 1855.
12 Ibid., 20 December 1855.
13 Ibid., 15 January 1857.
14 William Watson, *Chapters on Ragged and Industrial Schools* (Edinburgh and London, 1872), p. 22.
15 *Edinburgh Evening Courant,* 16 December 1856.
16 *The Scotsman,* 26 December 1859.
17 First Report, RIS, PP1857-8, XXIX (2426), p. 17.
18 Third Report, RIS, PP 1860, XXXV (2688), p. 7.
19 By 1866 the only schools which mixed voluntary and certified pupils were those in smaller towns where the number of young offenders would not justify the maintenance of separate industrial and reformatory schools, such as Stirling, Dumfries and Greenock.
20 *The Scotsman,* 178 September 1856.
21 *Edinburgh Evening Courant,* 7 March 1857.
22 Third Report, RIS, PP 1860, XXXV (2688), p. 19.
23 Ibid., p. 20. Although based on Dunlop's Act, the English equivalent was not as wide-ranging: it applied to 'any child who may be found begging or committing an act of vagrancy', whereas Dunlop's Act could be enforced in the case of a child 'found begging, or not having any home or settled place of abode, or proper guardianship, and having no lawful or visible means of subsistence, … found wandering, though not charged with any actual offence'. It was consequently a recommendation of the 1861 Education Commission that Dunlop's Act be extended to England in all its aspects. (Report of the Commissioners appointed to inquire into the State of Popular Education in England, PP 1861, XXI Pt. 1 (2794), p. 400 and p. 550.)
24 E.A.G. Clark, 'The Superiority of the 'Scotch System': Scottish Ragged Schools and their influence', *Scottish Educational Studies,* IX (1977), pp. 29–39.
25 SC 1852-3, p. iv.
26 'Minute of the Lords of the Committee of Privy Council on Education', 31 December 1857, PP 1857-8, XLVI (2315).
27 *The Scotsman,* 4 August 1858.
28 *The Scotsman,* 6 July 1861.
29 'Ragged Schools in relation to the Government Grants for Education. The Authorized Report of the Conference held at Birmingham, January 23rd. 1861' (London and Birmingham, N.D.), p. viii.
30 *The Spectator,* 26 January 1861.

31 First Report by Her Majesty's Commissioners appointed to inquire into the Schools in Scotland, PP 1865, XVII (3483), p. 246.
32 *Aberdeen Herald*, 12 January 1861.
33 Third Report by Her Majesty's Commissioners appointed to inquire into the Schools in Scotland, PP 1867-8, XXXIX (4011), p. xlviii.
34 *The Scotsman*, 26 January 1861.
35 Report from the Select Committee on the Education of Destitute Children, PP 1861, VII (460), p. iii.
36 Ibid.
37 'Ragged Schools in relation to the Government Grants for Education. The Authorized Report of the Conference held at Birmingham, January 23rd. 1861' (London and Birmingham, N.D.), p. 53.
38 *Transactions of the National Association for the Promotion of Social Science, 1864* (London, 1865), pp. 441–442.
39 Third Report by Her Majesty's Commissioners appointed to inquire into the Schools in Scotland, PP 1867-8, XXXIX (4011), p. xxv.
40 Ibid., p. xliv.
41 *North British Daily Mail*, 10 July 1861.
42 Ibid., 15 November 1861.
43 Tenth Report RIS, PP 1867, XXVI (2889), p. 19.
44 Peter Mackie, 'Inter-denominational Education and the United Industrial School of Edinburgh, 1847–1900', *The Innes Review*, Vol. XLIII, No. 1, Spring 1992, pp. 3–17.
45 Thirteenth Report RIS, PP 1870, XXVI (c.170), p. 16.
46 Twelfth Report RIS, PP 1868-9 XXX (4183), p. 18.
47 *Transactions of the National Association for the Promotion of Social Science, Sheffield Meeting, 1865* (London, 1866), p. 217.

9 The emergence of a national system (ii)

The effects of legislation on individual schools

In *Caring for Children in Trouble*, Julius Carlebach outlined how the 1854–1866 legislation altered the character of reformatory institutions all over the country. As schools now had the power to detain inmates, they no longer needed to hold out incentives to entice children to remain; discipline became more severe and, since low running costs were considered evidence of good management, profits from industrial work came to be valued more than its efficacy in moral training. Some institutions admitted too many children in order to qualify for more government money, which was given on a per capita basis.[1]

This chapter revisits the pioneering Scottish institutions discussed earlier – principally the Aberdeen and Edinburgh industrial schools and the Glasgow House of Refuge – with the aim of assessing the extent to which each of these changed significantly in the period between 1854 and 1866, when locally devised systems were required to adapt to a national framework governed by legislation, certification and inspection.

Aberdeen Industrial Schools

The Juvenile School was the first to take advantage of Dunlop's Act in Aberdeen, and noted its impact with approval within a few months of being certified in June 1855. In the first year thirty-one children were sent to the school under warrant, and the legislation also had beneficial side-effects on the voluntary cases. The 1859–1860 report states that desertions had declined as a result of the act: not one had been recorded during the previous year, the reason probably being that although the school did not have legal control over voluntary pupils, the children knew that if they stopped attending of their own accord, they were likely to be taken up by the police under the Act and committed to the school.

At the same time, the Act also led to changes in some of the original practices. In common with every other industrial school, those in Aberdeen found that a decrease in voluntary contributions and the acceptance of government aid were two sides of the same coin. School reports had been complaining for a number of years that since the system had become established and had lost its novelty, donations had been declining,[2] but the process was accelerated by the introduction of state aid. The 1854–1855 report which announced that the Committee of Council had authorised a grant also noted that public support had decreased and that the school was being maintained out of its reserve funds. As the grants amounted to no more than £40 12s. 6d. in 1857–1858, the school would have found itself in a worse position than before, had it not been for a donation of £500 from Dr. William Henderson of Caskieben (1792–1877), a distinguished local medical practitioner, and the support of the Free Church. Even worse, the grants were themselves diminished in 1858. One expedient adopted in the light of this was the foundation of an association to organise the collection of annual subscriptions from the County of Aberdeenshire, expanding the basis of support beyond the bounds of the city.

Meanwhile, the girls' schools had continued to subsist entirely on voluntary support, and making ends meet was no easier for them than for the other schools. In February 1861, for example, Sheriff Watson's school reported that its appeal to the churches had been disappointing and that it was £100 in debt. Watson nevertheless affirmed that 'the school had never asked [for] any grants from Government and he believed never would'.[3] In 1872 he was still holding up the school as an example of the continued viability of the original, voluntary management:

> In the boys' and girls' certified industrial school in Aberdeen there are 206 boys and 55 girls under warrant, and only 62 boys and 9 girls free; and the Government grant on account of the former must exceed the whole cost of the school, while the uncertified girls' schools are maintained solely by local subscription as efficiently as the other, and at considerably less expense.[4]

But by 1870 the other girls' school, the Female School of Industry, found reliance on charity anachronistic in an age of state support; it was certified in December, thus marking a further absorption of the original, local system into the national one.

Financial considerations had the additional effect of altering the type of industrial training given to the children in the schools which had a mixture of government voluntary cases. As Watson explained in an unpublished manuscript,

> When the schools were supported entirely by voluntary subscription and when the children could leave when they liked it appeared to me that unskilled labour requiring little supervision was the most suitable and teasing hair and oakum, net making and wood chopping were the chief occupations. But when the Industrial Schools Act came into operation, and under it children could be retained in School for several years it seemed right that they should be employed in some kind of skilled labour, by means of which they might, if so inclined, obtain a living when they went out.[5]

The prisons inspector Frederic Hill sheds some more light on this in his autobiography, where he explains that

> As many of the boys would become farm-labourers, it was considered well to give them some knowledge of rocks and soils; they were, therefore, encouraged

to bring to school specimens of every kind of rock or earth they could find, till ... a very practical, though small, geological collection was formed.[6]

The idea may well have come from Alexander Thomson himself, as the study of geology was one of his many hobbies.

It was nevertheless some time before the expanded industrial training got under way, and Sydney Turner's reports contain frequent references to the inadequacy of the arrangements. Even as late as 1867 he complained that 'The industrial training of the boys is still very imperfect, little being done beyond a little tailoring and picking horsehair'.[7] But by 1870 the Industrial Schools Association's report stated that industrial profits amounted to over £241, explaining that occupations such as teasing hair had been given up and replaced by tailoring and knitting, which were more profitable.

The acceptance of warrant cases at the schools again raised the question of residential accommodation. In a draft report to the Aberdeenshire Prison Board to be found among Thomson's papers written about 1861, he refers to 'long and very anxious discussions as to whether or not it was desirable to *lodge* the children in connection with the schools, and only a small majority decided in the negative'.[8] Although Thomson and Watson consistently opposed these moves, by the late 1850s the Juvenile School had a dormitory for its committed cases. Annual balance sheets reveal that a considerable sum was spent on the boarding of children: £219 in 1857 and £251 in 1858. While these figures include the expenses of both those kept in dormitories and those boarded out with labourers' families, it is clear that the principle of children returning to their own homes at night was no longer strictly adhered to.

Watson never deviated from his belief that home connections must be retained at all costs, maintaining to the end of his life a belief that 'parent and child should never be separated except in extreme cases'.[9] This is the most likely explanation of the fact that the Boys' School which he founded in 1841 was not certified until 1860–1861, in spite of the fact that the Boys' and the Juvenile Schools had been under the same management for a decade. Nevertheless, as happened in the rest of Scotland, an increasingly large proportion of the roll of both schools was made up of children committed by magistrates, with a corresponding decline in voluntary cases. For example, of 258 children in the Juvenile School in 1863, 48 were sent under the terms of the Industrial School legislation; by 1868 the figure was 201 out of 206, and by 1872 281 out of 310.[10]

The Oldmill and Mount Street Reformatory Schools, Aberdeen

Efforts to tackle juvenile delinquency in Aberdeen had been directed at its prevention through the eradication of vagrancy, rather than at the reformation of offenders who had been convicted. But Dunlop's Industrial Schools Act could not work to its maximum effect unless a reformatory institution was also available for the disposal of offenders who did not come under its terms. It was a measure of the success of the industrial schools in preventing juvenile crime in Aberdeen that a reformatory was not opened in the town until 1857, simply because there was little need for one. Yet the provision of such a school was considered increasingly desirable from about 1855 onwards, not only because of the effects of legislation, but also because there was an increase in the number of older juvenile delinquents. Criminal commitments between the ages of twelve and sixteen had dropped from 136 in 1848 to 90 in 1851, but thereafter increased annually, reaching 151 in 1855. The implication that the industrial schools alone were not preventing vagrants under the age of twelve progressing to delinquency was underlined by Alexander Thomson's concern that eighteen children who had been in the schools were sent to prison in 1853–1855. His recommendation was to set up more industrial schools, but as this coincided with growing interest in a reformatory, it was the latter type of institution which emerged as a solution to the problem.

Although it was opened in the period when the Industrial and Reformatory School Acts were beginning to exert more influence than local considerations, the Aberdeen institution owes its origin to the parent institution, the House of Refuge, to no less a degree than the first industrial school in 1841. The plan was prompted by the fact that the industrial schools and the new poor law had made the existence of the Refuge an anachronism in its existing form. The original intention of Dr. Watt's donation in 1836 had been to provide for destitute children, and in 1839 he gave a further gift of land worth £3,000 situated at Oldmill, three miles outside the city, for the same purpose. According to a later account, the Refuge had insufficient resources at the time to build a school there, so it encouraged other efforts to deal with children in the town, particularly the industrial schools. But by 1854 the situation of the Refuge was very different: other agencies now provided for the hungry, and the directors felt able to devote their resources to 'a higher object than mere alimentary relief, namely, the moral and religious instruction, and industrial training, of the inmates'.[11]

A large and extensive operation was envisaged, giving education and preparation for employment to many different groups, from vagrant children to alcoholics and released prisoners. However, when a Committee of Directors was appointed in September to draw up more precise plans, they proposed a less ambitious scheme for juveniles alone, which is best interpreted as an extension of the industrial school system. For example, whereas the industrial schools received children up to the age of fourteen, Oldmill would admit those up to sixteen. The institution, the directors hastened to add, 'should not be considered as in any way superseding the Industrial Schools in town, but as auxiliary to them'.[12] Children who, on their release from the industrial school, were in danger of falling back into their old ways could be admitted to Oldmill until, 'by the confirmation of good habits, the acquisition of some industrial pursuit and the ability to earn a livelihood, they were fit to be sent out into society'.[13]

These objectives are so similar to the original ones of the industrial schools that one suspects doubts were growing about the success of the existing facilities. It is clear, therefore, that the proposed use of the lands at Oldmill was determined by the need to supplement the efforts of the Refuge and the industrial schools.

When the institution opened in March 1857 it appears to have fulfilled a need: originally designed to accommodate fifty pupils, pressure on applications meant that it soon required to be extended. By 1862 it could hold 120, but the result of such rapid expansion was a debt of £1,800 by 1860 and £3,500 by 1862. The extension of the premises meant that cases from surrounding towns like Stonehaven, Peterhead and Fraserburgh could be accommodated, the institution thus serving as a reformatory for the North-East of Scotland. It is likely that contributions were received from these areas which helped to offset the upkeep of their cases.

Financial considerations, too, influenced the type of industrial work undertaken at Oldmill. The 1865 Report states that younger boys were employed in printing, carpentry and web-weaving which was carried on under contract for a city manufacturer. By far the most important – and profitable – activity was agriculture: of £479 raised by industrial work in 1862, £382 came from the proceedings of the market garden and farm, which in 1865 was extended from fifty-three to seventy-five acres. The directors considered that 'the success of the Institution is referable, in a large measure, to the healthy active outdoor employment which the farm has afforded for the boys',[14] an additional advantage being that the experience gained at the school enabled boys to find jobs on local farms when they were released.

The open situation of the school presented a temptation to boys who wished to abscond, and Sydney Turner, in his account of his first visit in 1858, attributed the number of desertions to lax management, although this is played down in the School's annual reports. But by 1860, he was able to report great improvement in the premises, teaching and discipline,[15] and it would appear that giving boys responsibility helped to maintain order: oversight of dormitories and even industrial departments, the serving of meals and the transportation of farm produce to Aberdeen were entrusted to senior boys. Even so, the 1860 annual report was perhaps stretching credulity by claiming that 'The Oldmill walls are the walls of Love'.

When a number of desertions occurred in 1862, it was the governor rather than the boys who came in for criticism, and the episode provides an interesting illustration of the extent of Home Office intervention in the running of reformatory schools. Turner recommended that Mr. Aiken, the governor, should resign. The directors were prepared to give him another chance, but Turner insisted on his dismissal, making it very clear that 'the Directors were not at liberty to consult their own feelings, as they might do in the case of a private charity'.[16]

This apart, the 1866 report was able to look back on ten years of successful work, pointing to the fact that the number of adults who had started their criminal careers under the age of ten had diminished. Although the building debt had not been cleared, the institution was self-supporting in other respects, while the policy of trust and responsibility was vindicated by the 1866 Reformatory School Act which extended the principle by allowing boys out on licence after eighteen months under detention. The success of the school may be partly accounted for by the fact that it was not a pioneering institution in the sense that the industrial school had been in 1841, and could consequently draw on the experience of working with delinquent children which had been gained over the years.

Logically, the next stage in the extension of the Aberdeen industrial and reformatory system was to open an equivalent reformatory for girls. In a lecture delivered to the Social Science Association which met in Aberdeen in 1863, Sheriff Watson argued that, while the industrial schools were adequate for younger girls, something more was required for the older age group. After analysing the criminal statistics for 1850–1860, he concluded that

> The increase of females of all ages and of those under the ages of 18, 19 and 20 is greater than that of males while of those of the age of 17 and under there have been fewer girls than boys. The reason is, that the number of girls attending the Industrial Schools is greater than of boys but there is no reformatory for Girls (there is one now) and when girls fall into crime after having left school they are sent to prison while Boys are sent to Oldmill Reformatory.[17]

As it was, girls under the age of sixteen were sent to Glasgow or Edinburgh from Aberdeen.

Once again, the girls' reformatory originated in connection with an already established institution. A Mr. William Harvey of Beadliston, Dyce, near Aberdeen, had left a legacy for the reformation of females in a penitentiary. As with Watt's lands at Oldmill, the Trustees of Harvey's mortification were not in a position to found an institution, and instead gave support to the Spital penitentiary, a home for prostitutes opened by public subscription in 1841. In June 1859, however, they acquired premises in Mount Street, Aberdeen, in which they opened a reformatory for fallen women. Evidently, little came of the attempt, as in March 1862 the home was closed, a new board of directors appointed and the premises reopened as Mount Street Reformatory School for Girls. While the management of the matron, Miss Meldrum, is praised by Turner in his reports, the institution never really played an important role in the treatment of juvenile delinquency in Aberdeen. Turner wished to see its 'capabilities for usefulness more fully developed'[18] but, although it could accommodate fifty to sixty girls, it never seems to have held its full complement and was closed in 1901, having no more than twelve inmates at the time.

By 1866 Aberdeen had completed its network of institutions for the treatment of juvenile delinquents. The Industrial Schools Association ran a school for girls and boys that was certified under Dunlop's Act, while, under Palmerston's Act, there was a reformatory for boys at Oldmill and for girls at Mount Street. A final streamlining of the system arrived with the 1885 Aberdeen Reformatory and Industrial Schools Act [48 & 49 Vict., c. 172], which united all the schools under one managing body. Each of these, directly or indirectly, could trace its origin to the House of Refuge, which had itself been child-oriented as a result of the wishes of its benefactor. The relationships between the institutions can be shown in the form of a diagram (see Figure 9.1).

The industrial school experiment in Aberdeen was the genesis of an approach to juvenile delinquency which spread nationwide and formed the basis of the legislation of 1854, which in turn modified the original plan to a considerable

The emergence of a national system (ii) 135

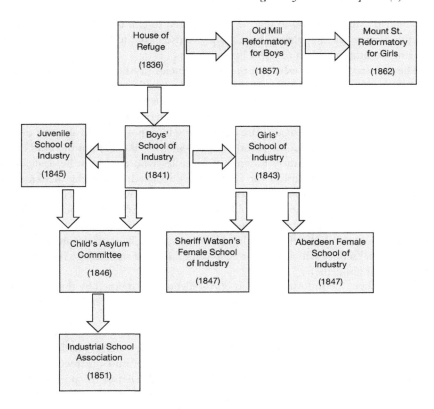

Figure 9.1 Connections between institutions in Aberdeen

extent. Watson, as we have seen, maintained that the original day system, without residential accommodation, was the best method. It is questionable, however, whether this would have worked as well in the 1860s as in the 1840s, when the balance between the schools and related institutions had altered, and when the state was the main source of income, rather than voluntary contributions. Moreover, when Watson looked back on the early days of the schools he sometimes tended to minimise the problems which had been experienced. In his thesis on social service provision in Aberdeen, Philip Seed quotes him as saying that

> In 1841 he established schools of industry ... that system had worked until the Industrial Schools Act came into operation. Then it was said we must take the children by night as well as by day, although it was proved that the parents had been greatly improved by the influence of their children who had been taught in Sheriff Watson's industrial school ... He had had no difficulty in getting children to his first school without any power at all but that which he chose to exercise.'[19]

The Sheriff omits to mention that he had required to enlist the help of the police and the magistrates in applying the vagrancy clause of the local police act in order to bring destitute children to the schools.

The industrial schools were not the only agencies in Aberdeen to change their form as the years progressed. In the 1840s the House of Refuge shaped the industrial school which was its subsidiary. During the 1850s the reverse was true, and the expansion of the industrial schools led to the contraction of the child-care aspects of the Refuge, which was in any case diminishing in importance on account of the existence of poorhouses. Consequently, in the 1860s the Refuge put the bulk of its resources into the reformatory training of juveniles who could not be dealt with in industrial schools, provision for adults being reduced to a night shelter. It is fitting, therefore, that in 1867 the Skene Square buildings which housed the House of Refuge and Boys' School were sold to the Industrial Schools Association and a shelter for the homeless was opened on a small scale in other premises in Upperkirkgate, the original boys' school thus ceasing to have a separate existence. The industrial school which had started as a subsidiary of the Refuge had by 1867 superseded it altogether.

Initially, then, the industrial schools of Aberdeen were defined by their relationship with other institutions for the relief of social problems. After 1854, legislation became the main factor in shaping the Aberdeen system, which gradually conformed to the emerging national pattern of certified reformatory and industrial schools. The loss of the distinctive local characteristics of the Aberdeen schools was only one aspect of a general trend in social policy in mid-nineteenth century Scotland, which was to provide for the education and relief of the poor by agencies which had a centralised rather than a localised direction.

Edinburgh Original and United Industrial Schools

While Dr. Guthrie campaigned as energetically for legislation and grants as he had for the original ragged school concept, the institution he founded was altered by the Acts as much as any other. But it was the rival United Industrial School which showed the greatest awareness of the erosion of its principles and fought to retain them in the face of changing circumstances.

Although both schools were certified during 1855, it was some years before this had any noticeable effect. The reason lay in the intervention of the parochial boards which meant that very few children were sent to either school under the terms of the Act. While Edinburgh was not the only place where this occurred, the effect was more apparent as the city board had an industrial school of its own, situated in part of the city workhouse, which was certified in April 1856. Presumably this was the school opened by Bailie Mack in 1847.[20] Given that children sent there by magistrates were treated as other poor law cases and boarded out, it is not surprising the board preferred children to attend its own school rather than contributing to their upkeep in one of the others.

As a result, progressively fewer children were sent to the Original and United Schools under the terms of Dunlop's Act. In 1856 forty children were committed to the United; in 1857, nineteen and in 1859, just two. Similarly, at the 1857 annual meeting of the Original School, Guthrie stated that only four or five children were under warrant, compared to thirty-nine the previous year. The directors highlighted the absurdity of the new system: a child was committed to the school under the Act; security was found for his good behaviour and he was released; his education and upbringing continued to be neglected and he was brought back to the school for admission as a voluntary case, the result being 'to deprive the directors of their legal claim under the Act against the parents of the Parochial Board, for the expenses incurred in their behalf'.[21] So, while the magistrates had attempted to enforce the Act, their efforts were – in the opinion of the schools – nullified by the hostility of the poor law authorities.

Because so few children were in the schools under the Act, the question of residential accommodation, which had been a cause of controversy in Aberdeen, had not yet become a serious issue in Edinburgh. In any case, the managers of the Original School were able to avoid any problems arising from mixing convicted and voluntary cases, or residential and day ones, by opening a market-garden extension at Marionville which acted as what Sydney Turner called 'a country colony'. Boys sent there were selected from those in the city centre Ramsay Lane premises, but by the early 1860s it was increasingly used as an annexe for the board and training of boys sentenced under the Act. In the same way, the United School recognised that, although 'it was not deemed consistent with the leading principles of the institution absolutely to sever the children from any vestige of a home that may remain to them', there were nevertheless 'many exceptional cases in which a child, if received at all, must have an entire home on the premises'.[22] Recognising also that sleeping places were essential for children sent under the statute, a dormitory for six boys and six girls was opened in December 1859.

Both schools benefited from the grants made available after 1856 and suffered correspondingly when these were withdrawn. The land at Marionville, for example, had been bought at a cost of £2,000 on the expectation of government finance. Guthrie led a deputation to the minister responsible, Adderley, to press for restoration of the grants, but without success. Moreover, as at Aberdeen, private donations had diminished as government aid became available. The Original School was the more fortunate of the two, for, while its grant had been cut from £847 in 1859 to £225 in 1860, it had been able – thanks to having the famous Dr. Guthrie as a figurehead – to raise £2,165 by a special subscription which warded off disaster for a time.

With grants being restricted to cases sent under Dunlop's Act, sheer necessity was an obvious reason for the schools to take in more of these cases. Simultaneously, changes in legislation were tending in the same direction, making it easier for children to be committed to the schools. The table in the Appendix to this chapter shows that from 1864 onwards almost two-thirds of the pupils in the United Industrial School were detained under the Industrial Schools Act. Successive annual reports show that the amount of money received from the state increased year after year from £195 17 shillings and fivepence in 1861 to £1,072 7 shillings and eightpence in 1864. This increased financial aid resulted in expansion of the premises: in 1864 two large dormitories and four new workshops were added to cope with the larger number of pupils, allowing the traditional emphasis on industrial training to be maintained. In 1865 it was claimed that the school kept a register of applications from employers and could find posts for four times as many children as they could supply.

Although this expansion was possible because of government aid, the school expressed concern at the side-effects of increased reliance on state finance. The falling-off in subscriptions meant that fewer and fewer voluntary cases were admitted, the result being that the preventive principles of the school were undermined, the institution taking on the function of a reformatory.

The problem came to a head in 1865, when the managers of the United School were faced with a decision which forced them to consider the school's identity. In July of that year an outbreak of typhoid fever drove home the fact that the premises in South Gray's Close were insanitary and that the children required far more outdoor exercise. This created 'a crisis in our history': should the school move to more healthy surroundings, which would mean that it was further away from the vicinity of the homes of the day scholars, in effect restricting admissions to certified cases? The Committee of Management argued that this would not mean that the children for whom the school was designed were being excluded, and their conclusion is significant as it marks an acceptance of the role of certified schools:

> The children are of the same class now as formerly, only a larger part now enter through one door of the school instead of entering it through another. And it was only what was to be expected if those withdrawn from the one category of entrants have gone to swell the other.[23]

In the event, a compromise was reached whereby voluntary scholars were enabled to continue; some children were boarded out until an extension containing an adequate dormitory could be built, while the slum clearance of the Edinburgh Improvement Commission made the neighbourhood of the school more spacious and healthy, so that by 1871 the government inspector could praise the school for its modernised accommodation.

The Original Ragged School similarly developed into a certified residential school, although the process took longer: it was not until the late 1860s that the number of pupils under the Industrial Schools Acts reached a level comparable with the United School. A likely explanation is that Guthrie was still able to arouse popular support for the school, and numerous avenues were explored to increase the amount of revenue from this source. In January 1863, for example, an attempt to encourage the working classes to support the school was made when a meeting for domestic servants was arranged and addressed by Guthrie. The outcome was the formation of 'The Edinburgh Servants Auxiliary Association in aid of the Original Ragged Industrial School'.[24] This, however, added little to the total income, and during the period 1863–1865 the school relied heavily on legacies. The credit balance in 1864, said the Earl of Dalhousie, arose more 'from the munificence of the dead than from the generosity of the living'.[25] Again, the school maintained its distinctive religious policy which, as was pointed out at the 1864 annual meeting, acted as an obstacle to the reception of children under the Act, the reason presumably being that the parents could object to the strongly Protestant and Biblical religious instruction. There are in fact some indications that the school became more rather than less rigid in its religious policy during the 1860s. At the 1864 meeting, the Rev. Dr. Alexander Duff (1806–1873), famous as a missionary to India, and Moderator of the General Assembly of the Free Church for that year, widened the gap between the two Edinburgh schools by insisting that the Original School was entitled to proselytise – something which Guthrie had always taken great pains to repudiate. 'If the Word of God took its effect on the heart and conscience of a child', said Duff, 'and the child became converted to God, it could not but become a Protestant...'.[26]

In addition to financial constraints and religious exclusiveness, problems relating to premises and management hindered a smooth transition from charity school to certified industrial school. The majority of children sent under the Act were detained at the Marionville branch outside the city, which frequently came in for criticism in the inspector's reports. In 1866, for example, disorderly behaviour and frequent desertions led to the dismissal of the master and it took his successor some time to restore discipline. It seems that the branch institution never operated satisfactorily and it was closed sometime after 1870. This step raised the problem of accommodation for convicted cases. The inspector's reports often point out that 'the premises are better adapted for their original purpose of a day school than for a school of detention'.[27] It was only in the second half of the 1870s that the school adopted many of the features of certified schools such as the United. In 1874 it was decided to separate the boys and girls and in 1875 girls were removed to premises in Leith Road, the house in which they had been lodged previously being used to accommodate boys who had formerly been boarded out through lack of space, thus carrying the institutionalised nature of the school a stage further until, by the end of the 1870s, the effect of the provision of elementary education by the School Boards had virtually eliminated the presence of day scholars at the Original as at other, industrial schools.

Reformatory institutions in Edinburgh

As in Aberdeen, the legislation of 1854–1861, by defining more precisely the classes of children who could and could not be admitted to the schools, created a need for a reformatory certified under the Youthful Offenders Act, transformed existing reformatories and refuges into certified institutions and stimulated the provision of further reformatory facilities.

(i) The Dean Bank Institution

Since its opening in 1832, the Dean Bank Institution for the Reformation of Female Juvenile Delinquents had been run as a modest home for about twenty girls, supported by charitable donations and the proceeds of laundry work and managed with a heavily religious emphasis, its aim being stated as 'nothing less than the salvation of some'. There was little change in the home during its first twenty years of existence – so much so that reports were not issued annually until 1856, and even then they recorded little worthy of comment on the grounds that 'the very nature of these institutions precludes the existence of incidents of a new and varied character'.[28] At about this time the Dean Bank premises, which consisted of a narrow two-storey house, were found inadequate and cramped, but as the original aim was 'to give the house the character, as much as possible, of a well-regulated, industrious, and religious family of the working-classes'[29] it was decided to open a second home rather than to move to a larger building, in order to preserve the all-important domestic atmosphere. As the 1859 report put it,

> as much juvenile crime is due to a lack of family life the committee have preferred two small houses to one large one ... where limited numbers might enable the matron to feel as a mother among those committed to her care.[30]

Another similar house was thus opened at Boroughmuirhead, and it was this institution which became certified as a reformatory, while the original one did not.

The existence of two comparable institutions, one a charity and the other receiving government grants and committed cases, enables the difference made by certification to be assessed. The reception of girls under the Reformatory Schools Act was not altogether an innovation for the two homes, as there already existed an arrangement with the Police Commissioners whereby suitable cases could be sent to Dean Bank directly from the Police Court. It seems that the management committee was not over-enthusiastic about this practice, but since they received an annual grant from police funds, they felt obliged to take in girls recommended by the magistrates. As the 1857 report suggests, these girls were regarded as a disruptive element, and as they were not under any legal restraint escapes were frequent. This also appears to have been an issue for the Boroughmuirhead branch after it was certified in 1858, as in his first few annual reports Sydney Turner continually draws attention to the efforts being made to prevent absconding. Things had begun to improve by the time of his 1861 report, in which he comments that 'admissions are now more carefully restricted, and the profligate and vicious girl, as far as possible excluded'.[31] While this remark might sound as if the home was now keeping out those who needed it most, Turner probably meant that reformatories should concentrate on those who were comparatively inexperienced in crime and who showed the greatest promise of reformation.

But a further problem now confronted Boroughmuirhead. The building in which its operations took place passed to new owners who did not wish to continue letting it out to the school. In May 1860 an appeal for funds was opened, by means of which £1,000 was raised, including a donation of £150 from the County Prison Board. A three-storey villa situated in three-quarters of an acre of land with a boundary wall was secured, the school assuming the name of the Dalry Reformatory. Although records are very incomplete, by February 1861 it seems that both houses were full up, and Dean Bank in particular was in urgent need of extension. At this point the question of amalgamating the two houses – recommended by Turner – was raised. Having observed the development of Boroughmuirhead and Dalry, the ladies in charge of Dean Bank were opposed to mixing voluntary cases with committed ones and, after considerable disagreement, the two houses were carried on under entirely separate management.

Now that the two houses were run on separate lines, their future pattern of development was more or less inevitable. The voluntary cases were phased out of Dalry as it expanded: eleven out of thirty-seven girls in 1863 were voluntary, five out of sixty-five in 1874. Meanwhile, Dean Bank continued as a refuge for destitute girls, who were usually recommended for admission by a city missionary who met them in the course of visitation of the homes of the poor. Those who had been guilty of minor crimes were not excluded, but girls were not received under warrant. Unlike other similar schools, Dean Bank managed to preserve its voluntary character right up to the turn of the twentieth century by virtue of its small scale. With the advent of a certified girls' reformatory for police cases, Dean Bank ceased to be of as much use to the police magistrates, with the result that in 1865 the annual police grant was diminished by £25, leaving the home £60 in debt. Nevertheless, its distinctive features were maintained and, unlike other schools, girls did not leave until a situation as a domestic servant had been found for them. As the 1868–1869 report pointed out, this was usually the weak link in the reformatory chain; when children were dismissed they often had no home or job to go to, and ended up in prison again.

The history of the Dean Bank and Dalry institutions thus provides another perspective on the effects of reformatory legislation. In most schools the pattern was for committed cases to increase at the expense of voluntary cases; this is what happened at Boroughmuirhead, and it was only by electing to rely entirely on charitable contributions that Dean Bank maintained its original domestic character and aims. Complete independence from government was rare in reformatories in the 1860s and it is largely because the proceeds of laundry work were sufficient to finance its limited operations that Dean Bank could survive on this basis. Like other schools, the history of Edinburgh's two girls' reformatories confirms that it was not possible to operate a charitably supported refuge and a government supported and certified reformatory under the one roof.

(ii) The Wellington Farm Reformatory School

At the time of the sittings of the 1852–3 Select Committee, Edinburgh had no school or refuge for the reception of boys convicted two or three times. It may be inferred that the ragged schools had made a sufficiently large impact on the extent of juvenile delinquency that there did not appear to be an urgent need for such an institution. Further, the fact that the ragged schools took in children who had been convicted of petty thefts must have contributed to the diminution of the number of young criminals. However, Guthrie told the Committee that he 'would rather those children should be in another school' and, like many others, recommended a dual system: ragged industrial schools for prevention, reformatory schools for cure.[32] Once the girls' institution at Dalry was certified as a reformatory, the lack of an equivalent institution for boys was all the more anomalous. Once again, the pattern was similar to Aberdeen, except that in the northern city the reformatory for boys preceded the one for girls.

The case for the establishment of such an institution was further strengthened by the amending Act of 1856, which, by enacting that schools could not be simultaneously certified as both industrial and reformatory schools, left Scotland with a shortage of schools of the latter class. Shortly after, *The Scotsman* drew attention to the need for a school of this kind in Edinburgh and a certain Bailie Thomas Russell aroused sufficient interest in the subject for a public meeting to be held in the Council Chambers in December 1858.[33] Even though the school – like Glasgow's House of Refuge twenty years earlier and Edinburgh's ragged schools ten years previously – originated from a public meeting called by benevolent men for the purpose of raising subscriptions, the situation with regard to the establishment of such schools was very different in 1858 than in 1847 or 1838. The fundamental difference between the Glasgow House of Refuge and what was to be known as the Wellington Farm School was, as Russell pointed out in a letter to *The Scotsman*, that the latter was not a pioneering venture. It did not, therefore, require justification of the principle of reformatory treatment. By March 1859 the acting committee appointed at the first meeting had drawn up a constitution for the school. It was to be run by 'the Edinburgh Association for the Reformation of Juvenile Male Offenders', the object being

> to promote the reformation of boys convicted of crime by training them to habits of industry in out-door and other employment, imparting to them an education of a plain and useful character, and endeavouring to bring them under the influence of religious principles.[34]

The school would receive boys sent by the magistrates and sheriffs, not just of the city of Edinburgh, but of the Counties of Midlothian and Peebles. At this time many reformatory and industrial schools all over Britain were placing greater emphasis on the value of outdoor work, and the Wellington Farm School is one instance of this trend. Thus the first annual report of the Wellington Farm School stated that 'the Directors consider that hard labour in the open air is one of the most essential parts of the reformatory discipline'.[35] Judging from Sydney Turner's description of the farm as being in an exposed situation, with soil 'requiring long and laborious cultivation to bring it into anything of a profitable state', it certainly offered plenty of scope for such training.[36]

The development of the school, which was certified in December 1859 and received forty-one pupils in its first year, can be seen in terms of a progression towards the aim of self-sufficiency. The school opened with a financial deficit of over £500 which made it necessary to keep down costs as much as possible, so that a good deal of use was made of the boys' labour. Hence, more time was spent working than in other schools: there were two to three hours of schooling per day and six or seven hours of work. As the directors quickly discovered, helping the school's finances and training the boys for independent living could be achieved by the same means. By 1860 the boys were employed in assisting the bricklayers and carpenters who were building an extended school room and dormitory and, as the 1861 Report points out, this work appeared to have given the boys an interest in the school so that attempted escapes were rare.

By the second year of operation, the directors felt sufficiently confident to take the idea of self-sufficiency a stage further, and decided not to ask the public for annual subscriptions, relying instead on the proceeds of industrial work and striving harder than most schools to recover parental contributions for the upkeep of boys under the terms of the Reformatory Schools Act. By 1866 the school had gone beyond supplying its own needs: as Mr. Craster, the Superintendent, said, 'Their goods were bought by merchants in all parts of the country, from Inverness to Berwick-on-Tweed'.[37]

The school used its financial independence to train the boys to self-reliance. In 1864–1865 an extension was planned in the form of a few cottages on the outskirts of the farm, to accommodate some of the staff and thirty or forty of the best-behaved boys, giving them a measure of freedom to prepare them for their release.[38] It is interesting to note that this practice, like the whole idea of a farm school, was adapted from Redhill, Surrey, which itself was modelled on Mettray in France. Unsurprisingly, Turner was full of praise for the school, as he himself had been in charge of Redhill from its inception until his appointment as inspector. In his comments on Wellington Farm in his 1867–1868 report, he writes that 'the school stands quite among the first of our reformatories…'.[39] He attributes its success to the policy of giving boys responsibility: there were few desertions, although they were allowed out of the school on errands such as transporting farm produce to town and were hired out to neighbouring farmers at certain times of the year, while older boys superintended the shoemaking and carpentry departments and one acted as cook.[40] It was largely to the efforts of Craster that credit was due for building up this trustworthy relationship. It was only in 1872 and 1873 that Turner suggests that the spirit of understanding had broken down, perhaps as a result of the school acquiring a further 150 acres and admitting a larger number of boys. Perhaps significantly, numbers dropped again the following year.

The Glasgow House of Refuge

Of all the Scottish institutions, the Glasgow House of Refuge was the one most profoundly affected by national legislation. As was shown in Chapter Four, Glasgow differed from Edinburgh and Aberdeen in that its most significant contribution to the treatment of juvenile delinquency was the formation of a large-scale reformatory establishment, rather than the provision of day industrial schools. Thanks to the passage of the city's local Juvenile Delinquency Act as early as 1841, the Refuge in effect had access to the kind of legislative and financial backing for which most other institutions had to wait until 1854. These local arrangements still remained in force after the arrival of national legislation until, eventually, the growing importance of industrial schools made the local Act obsolete and necessitated an overhaul of the city's facilities for dealing with convicted and potential delinquents. In the process, the House of Refuge, once held up as a model worthy of imitation throughout the United Kingdom, lost sight of its original purpose and suffered a dramatic and ignominious decline until it finally closed in 1887.

The Boys' and Girls' Houses of Refuge were certified under the Youthful Offenders Act on 15 November 1854 and the Boys' House was thereafter referred to as 'the Glasgow Reformatory Institution' as well as by the original designation. Magistrates now had the power to commit children directly to the institution, and the government provided a per capita grant, leading the number of inmates to increase considerably. By June 1855 nearly 100 offenders, mostly boys, had been committed to the Refuge under the terms of the Act,[41] and by the end of the year there were almost twice as many inmates than two years previously (286 compared to 155). In addition, commitments under the local Act continued: of 267 boys discharged between November 1854 and December 1858, 82 had been sent under the national Act and 194 under the local Act.[42]

To cope with the larger numbers, additions to the Duke Street premises were planned and by 1856 an extension containing a dining hall, a chapel and 'two tiers of well-ventilated dormitories' with accommodation for 150 boys had been added. The amenities were further increased by the addition of swimming baths and a new workshop with a steam engine. The total cost of the extensions amounted to £5,000 and the Refuge was now able to hold 400 boys.[43]

By enabling the premises to be expanded, the 1854 Act also facilitated a more ambitious system of training. The policy in this sphere was largely coloured by the views of the governor, Rev. A.K. McCallum (1816–1893). Whereas the first governor, William Gilchrist, had come from a prison background, having been Bridewell chaplain before his appointment in 1841, McCallum's idea was to build up the Refuge as a complete and comprehensive method of dealing with the delinquent. The Refuge, stated the 1858 report, should be 'a world on a small scale', aiming 'at bringing about, as far as practicable, what ought to be [the young offender's] condition in the world as a productive member of society'.[44] It was, he said, vitally important 'to train the boys as much as possible to the usual trades carried on in society – in short, to make the house a little world of its own'.[45] In 1855 the trades of blacksmith and cooper were added to the existing ones of tailoring, shoemaking, weaving, wood-splitting and carpentry, to be followed shortly afterwards by the introduction of bookbinding and printing. Subsequent annual reports bear the words 'Printed at the Reformatory Institution' on their front covers. In the tailoring department, uniforms were made for the police and Caledonian Railway[46] and it was boasted that 'we supply an outfit from a working man up to a city magistrate'.[47] Sydney Turner saw it as 'one advantage of a large institution that a great amount of work of various descriptions is furnished by the requirements of the establishment itself'.[48] The blacksmith's department, for example, produced farm implements for use at Riddrie and made most of the iron bedsteads for the dormitories. The importance of industrial work may be judged from the fact that over half the officers employed were involved in these departments.[49]

Industrial training accounted for half of a boy's day; the other half was spent in education, and in this direction too, the 1854 Act gave a stimulus to the efforts of the Refuge. The 1857 report to subscribers enumerated the advantages of certification: financial support towards the payment of teachers; grants towards books and materials; and the favourable influence of inspection. Sydney Turner refers in his 1860 report to some English reformatories like Redhill which had high educational standards and concludes that 'The Glasgow Reformatory ... is considerably superior to them all in its educational arrangements...'.[50] He attributes this superiority to the 'feeling and habits of Scotland', which placed education 'upon a different footing there'.[51] The emphasis was predominantly moral and religious: boys learnt a verse of the Bible by heart every day and a 'register of character' was kept. Marks were given for obedience, truthfulness and industry which determined a boy's privileges and could shorten the length of his stay in the institution. Teachers were encouraged to 'Pray, labour, look for conversions' and the boys were reminded that the rules of the house were 'designed to make you happy. They aim at your welfare for both worlds'.[52]

If the Youthful Offenders Act enabled the Refuge to expand its premises, industrial facilities and educational arrangements, it also had various negative effects. Whereas the 1841 local Act had contained a clause which left it to the discretion of magistrates to decide whether or not a child was sent to prison prior to voluntarily entering the Refuge, the 1854 stipulated a preliminary period of imprisonment and magistrates could now commit child offenders to the Refuge. The voluntary element was therefore not preserved in the way the managers hoped, and after the Act had been in operation for only a year their impression was that 'its compulsory aspect in the estimation of the young, produces on their minds, on admission, an unfavourable feeling against the House',[53] resulting in a number of attempted escapes.

The voluntary element was similarly an integral part of the system pursued in the Girls' House. A report issued in June 1850 discusses how compulsory detention had been tried at one stage but abandoned: 'When it became necessary to enforce residence, the whole house was roused and excited, and common cause was made with the refractory inmate, whose confinement served to remind the others of their own.'[54]

By contrast, when residence was voluntary it was claimed that the superintendents were regarded not as keepers, but as friends. Related to this was the method of treatment, based on reward rather than punishment. Girls who showed signs of improvement were promoted to the 'merit' ward where they received lessons 'no less entertaining than instructive' and were allowed 'an occasional walk into the country' and to wear 'frocks and bonnets for the Sabbath'.[55] Thus, the whole system of the institution depended on voluntary admission and the provision of incentives, and changes were inevitable after 1854; an 1860 report again mentions restlessness among the girls as a side-effect of compulsory detention. Certification created a dilemma for the school and the managers saw only too clearly the dangers which lay ahead – not just for the Girls' Refuge but for all such institutions: 'Perfect security no doubt is attainable by bolts and bars, and the other expedients of a prison, but the House would then ... become the very place to which it is designed to be a contrast.'⁵⁶

The change in the method of admission had other unexpected repercussions for the Boys' House. We have seen how the magistrates' increased powers led to a larger number of inmates. By 1858 the Refuge was overcrowded and the combined roll of the two Houses was about 600. The pressure on space was to some extent responsible for the opening of Roman Catholic reformatories in the city, the outcome of a dispute similar to that which had occurred in the Edinburgh Ragged School. Following a parliamentary debate on Scottish reformatories in 1856, a controversy arose in the Glasgow press in which the Catholics accused the Refuge of proselytising. Then, in 1858, a Catholic priest's request to visit Bernard Mooney, an inmate of the House, was rejected on the grounds that the religious training of the House was conducted on 'truly Catholic principles' based solely on the Bible, with no sectarian catechism. As children in the Refuge were destitute of education because of the neglect of parents and churches alike, the Commissioners had endeavoured to take the place of both, and therefore considered themselves responsible for the children's upbringing. To refute the charge of sectarianism, the directors pointed out that McCallum was a Baptist and the children attended services at St. Thomas's Methodist Chapel, 'being the nearest and most convenient church'.⁵⁷

Turner's opinion was solicited and he endorsed the Commissioners' stance. He recommended that 'sick Catholic boys or girls should be removed to the public Infirmary',⁵⁸ and added that if the Catholics were dissatisfied they should exert themselves to set up a Reformatory of their own. The Roman Catholic authorities took up the challenge and in June 1856 the Catholic Reformatory for Girls at Dalbeth was certified for thirty girls, in a former convent in idyllic surroundings near 'the banks of the little burn that flows peacefully towards the Clyde'.⁵⁹ In August of the following year a Catholic Reformatory for Boys was certified at West Thorn Mill, Parkhead, holding 100 boys and supervised by the Rev. A. Robertson with the assistance of five Benedictine brothers.

Although these institutions eased the pressure on the Houses of Refuge, the Boys' House remained the largest in the United Kingdom. Moreover, it was deliberate policy to keep inmates for a long period to break permanently their connection with their former way of life – a very different approach from that of Sheriff Watson and Dr. Guthrie, who consistently stressed the value of family links. The *North British Daily Mail* commented that 'Mr. McCallum considers that short courses of the reformatory school will prove almost as futile as short imprisonments, and that children should be kept in the institution till they attain majority'.⁶⁰

The larger number of inmates and the increased length of time for which they were detained lay behind the problems experienced by the institution in the 1860s. By 1861 the Refuge was apparently only outwardly efficient, its training having degenerated into a mechanical routine. In that year an assistant master complained to the inspector about the discipline of the school. Inferior officers, it appears, were able to punish boys indiscriminately, giving rise to resentment and attempted escapes. The Home Office made a careful enquiry and it is instructive to note Turner's diagnosis of the problem:

This gradual change from influence to discipline is the chief disease of all large institutions; and reformatories, depending for success so largely on the spirit that animates them, and being liable to suffer so much when they grow too large for individual oversight, or pass from a superintendence of personal interest to one of professional routine, it is essentially for the public interest that they should be confined within moderate limits of numbers.[61]

Although these weaknesses had been pinpointed, misgivings as to the methods and discipline of the institution continued. When the British Association met in Glasgow in September 1855, a difference of opinion with regard to the House of Refuge emerged between McCallum and James McClelland. While McCallum extolled the virtues of his institution, McClelland said he had toured foreign reformatories which had convinced him that the Refuge was inferior to those abroad. He referred primarily to the lack of emphasis on agricultural training, stating that he had offered to join in the purchase of a farm but that no one had taken up his suggestion. McCallum retorted that only lack of funds had prevented the purchase of a farm, and reiterated the need for outdoor labour in his 1857 Report, as 'no Institution can be complete without this...'.[62] Eventually, a separate farm school was established on the outskirts of the city at Riddrie as a branch of the House of Refuge. But, judging from Turner's reports, the experiment was not conducted with much enthusiasm. In 1865 he noted that the farm could hold fifty boys but only twenty-five were living there, while in 1866 he remarked that it was still 'an appendage rather a substantial branch of the institution'.[63] In 1862 Turner 'urged on Mr. McCallum the expedience of not keeping the boys too long in the Institution',[64] and wrote of the Girls' House that 'Plants are not the stronger or better prepared for the vicissitudes of ordinary out-door weather for being kept too long in the greenhouse'.[65] Out of 543 boys discharged from Duke Street during the five years up to 1864, only 65 were released under three years.[66]

An independent investigation confirmed the opinion of the government inspector. In 1866 James Greig and Thomas Harvey, Assistant Commissioners appointed by the Royal Commission on Education in Scotland, published a *Report on the State of Education in Glasgow*. Their opinions are of particular value since, as R.R. Bone points out, they investigated not just reformatories but every type of school, whereas the inspector could only compare one reformatory or industrial school with another.[67] Like Turner, Greig and Harvey noted the lack of agricultural training. When they visited the fifty-five-acre Riddrie farm there were only half a dozen boys there.[68] Similarly, the structure of authority in the institution was criticised; there were too many boys for the governor to know each one personally. He therefore had to rely on his assistants, but this inevitably meant that the governor could not be aware of everything that happened. Consequently, Greig and Harvey cast doubts on the claimed success of the Refuge in reforming juvenile offenders. McCallum maintained that of 975 boys released from the institution between 1854 and 1864, 828 were 'doing well', leaving only 147 to be accounted for. Yet on an examination of his figures, Greig and Harvey discovered 479 whose whereabouts could not be traced. Again, of 329 girls released from the Girls'

Refuge between 1850 and 1860, 55 had escaped and as many as 133 were sent back to their relatives – in other words, to the same environment which had started them on a criminal career.[69]

It is therefore not surprising that trouble once more erupted, this time on a more serious scale than in 1861. An officer of the Boys' House claimed he had been unfairly dismissed by McCallum and wrote to the Home Office, revealing that 'immoral and indecent practices had prevailed long and largely among the boys, especially the oldest and more trusted ones...'[70] It transpired that McCallum had played down these evils and he was compelled to resign in February 1867.[71] Admissions were suspended and the running of the House reviewed and investigated.[72] Turner's comments again give an insight into the conditions which had given rise to abuses:

> To the student of reformatory principles the case gives a valuable lesson on the dangers of associating large numbers of boys in an inclosed institution without family division: of keeping boys till they are almost adults, and employing them on only indoor occupations; of almost exclusively employing men as officers and servants; of the over use of boy monitors; and especially of too much confidence in religious mechanism and routine.[73]

The fears expressed by Greig and Harvey were thus shown to be justified. In the ten years from the passing of the Reformatory Schools Act, the institution had become subject to the criticisms which had formerly been made of prisons. Greig and Harvey observed that 'what seems to be wanted is an established connexion between the inner and the outer world during the probationary period over which the sentence extends'.[74] The remark demonstrates how far the Refuge had departed from its original aims, for the institution had been intended by William Brebner to provide precisely the transition to the everyday world which Greig and Harvey claimed was lacking. The Refuge had degenerated into a self-enclosed mechanical regime, and McCallum's boast that the institution was 'a world on a small scale' was given an ironic twist – it had become a world in itself, rather than equipping young offenders to take their place in society. By 1867 there were iron grates in the passages and bars on the windows, and the Refuge had now become virtually a penal institution.[75] As the Refuge was now more like a prison, it became as difficult to reform a child there as it had been in prison. Turner's words after the inquiry of 1866–1867 were the final proof of failure: 'It is a painful justification of the measures taken for the reform of the House of Refuge, that 74 boys formerly inmates of that school were found in prison during the year.'[76]

The origins of this decline can be directly traced to the effects of the 1854 legislation which altered the character of the institution. The Act which at first appeared to encourage the Refuge in reality contained the seeds of its decline, so that by 1867 changes in the city's ways of dealing with convicted juvenile delinquents were as necessary as they had been in 1829.

Glasgow industrial schools

Like the Juvenile Delinquency Commissioners in charge of the Refuge, the managers of the Glasgow industrial school had been quite specific in their expectations from the 1854 legislation: 'Let us ... hope that power may be given to the magistrates to send the child to an industrial school, and to order him there to be maintained at the expense of the parent who has neglected him.'[77]

The power was desired because experience had shown that children stopped attending or were withdrawn by their parents and sent out to work or beg. In 1852, for instance, seventy-six boys and eight girls attended the school for only a few days.[78]

Since the Act supplied the hoped-for powers, it was well received in Glasgow and immediate steps were taken to put it into effect. In October 1854 a meeting of magistrates, representatives of industrial schools, Houses of Refuge and parochial boards was held to consider how to achieve this objective, while the appointment of a committee of the City, Govan and Barony parochial boards augured well for a smooth working of the clause relating to the maintenance of poor law cases in industrial schools. The school was quick to provide sleeping accommodation for warrant cases and, in contrast to Edinburgh and Aberdeen, no disagreement over this is recorded. £500 was spent on the purchase of a building next door to the school for conversion into a dormitory. The Industrial School Society changed its name to the 'Glasgow Industrial and Reformatory School Society', the day scholars being referred to as industrial cases and those committed by magistrates as reformatory cases, although there was no difference in the treatment applied to both classes of pupil.

In the first year of the Act's operation, ninety-six children were sent by magistrates. Before long, however, the shortcomings of the Act in relation to the poor law became evident, as happened in Aberdeen and Edinburgh. Over the first few years the number of commitments by magistrates declined, to just thirty in 1858.[79] But, as Bailie Clouston, one of the magistrates, pointed out at the 1859 annual meeting, this was not due to any disapproval of the institution on the part of the magistrates, but rather to the fact that the Act permitted poor-law authorities or parents to take charge of the child.[80] The City parish, which had been instrumental in setting up the industrial school in 1847, continued to co-operate, but as the Superintendent of Police, Captain Smart, said, 'with one of the other parishes [i.e. Barony] every petty obstacle has been thrown in the way to prevent its operation'.[81] For instance, in April 1859 the Barony inspector of the poor, Mr. Beattie, complained that Bailie Playfair had refused to accept security offered by a parent for her child's good behaviour, and had sent it to the industrial school. This Beattie considered to be an unwarranted violation of parental rights; to Playfair the good of the child was the most important matter and his response was to ask: 'what was the value of the security of a drunken mother who sent her child out to beg, and who watched for the copper she received that she might spend it in liquor!'[82] The case illustrates how local poor-law authorities could still affect the implementation of the national Act.

Nevertheless, when the magistrates received wider powers under the 1861 Act[83] the number of commitments to the school increased again: in 1861, fifty boys and twenty-six girls; in 1862, sixty-eight boys and thirty-one girls. The field of operation of industrial schools was expanded further in 1866 when children under twelve charged with crime could be sent there. The Refuge thus lost even more potential inmates, 'as the Magistrate, having now an asylum that can be reached direct, will no doubt prefer it to one, the only access to which is through prison'.[84] Consequently, the industrial school required larger premises, opening another school three miles outside the city at Mossbank with accommodation for 350 and facilities for agricultural work.

Another extension of industrial school provision occurred with the certification in November 1862 of St. Mary's R.C. School, Abercrombie Street. This was under the management of the Catholic churches and it seems likely that it was the availability of state aid which prompted them to open a school at this stage, as it appears to have been paid for largely from grants and industrial earnings, with any shortfall being made up by contributions from the chapels.[85] After the school's director, a Mr. McCulloch, resigned on the grounds that the clergy were interfering with his running of the school, magistrates were less willing to send children there. McCulloch opened another boys' school at Slatefield, certified in December 1867, which was run more efficiently, the result being that magistrates were more inclined to commit Catholic boys there in preference to Abercrombie Street.[86]

The position by 1868, then, was that the two Houses of Refuge had 213 inmates – admissions to the Boys' House having stopped because of the previous year's enquiry – while the industrial school had over 600 and was preparing to accommodate 1,000.[87] The Refuge was never to recover its former importance. The national Acts thus started the process of expanding industrial schools at the expense of reformatories, and as legislation was now uniform for the whole country, similar trends were evident in the Glasgow institutions as elsewhere. But there were added complications in the city, as the 1841 local Juvenile Delinquency Act remained in force after the national system had been set up. There continued to be a number of children in the Houses of Refuge under the terms of the local Act, that is, voluntary inmates who may not have been in prison. This was particularly true of the Girls' House: even in the 1870s about half of its inmates were voluntary and, as Turner commented, were in reality industrial school cases. The developments which have been considered brought the city increasingly into line with national trends, with the result that the existence of the local Act in its original form became more and more of an anomaly. In the post-1872 Education Act era the city's reformatory and industrial school provision required complete reorganisation and a new local Act was passed in 1878. This will be considered in the next chapter.

Conclusion

Though Aberdeen, Edinburgh and Glasgow had all developed their own approaches to the treatment and prevention of delinquency in the 1840s, the passage of legislation from 1854 onwards led to standardised provision of reformatory and industrial schools across the whole of the UK. With increasing powers of detention, the Scottish industrial schools evolved from being preventive agencies attended by day scholars into what the government inspector called 'reformatories of a milder sort'. While prison now played an ever-diminishing role in the treatment of young offenders, reformatory and industrial schools became more penal in character. Eventually, this would lead to a further radical change of approach in the early twentieth century which aimed at keeping children out of institutions altogether.

Table 9.1 Children on the roll of the United Industrial School, Edinburgh, 1847–73

	Number in school (at time of Annual Meeting in Nov/Dec)	Detained under industrial schools legislation	Voluntary cases (average)
1847	50		
1848	100 (approx.)		
1849	140		
1850	142		
1851	133		
1852	138		
1853	141		
1854	116*		
1855	111		
1856	114		
1858	126*		
1859	118		
1860	121		
1861	98	1	
1862	130	27	
1863	154	77	
1864	161	103	41
1865	156	103	44
1866	145	82	44
1867	146	89	40
1868	147	92	42
1869	156	101	40
1870	164	104	38
1871	176	119	35
1872	170	127	33
1873	149	104	32

Note: *Average for year
Source: Annual Reports

Notes

1 J. Carlebach, *Caring for Children in Trouble* (London, 1970), pp. 66–70.
2 E.g. 1853–4 report of the Aberdeen Industrial Schools Association.

3   *Aberdeen Herald*, 1 February 1861.
4   Watson, *Chapters*, p. 23.
5   W. Watson, *National Education* (Manuscript).
6   Frederic Hill, *An Autobiography of 50 Years in Times of Reform* (London, 1893), p. 223.
7   Tenth Report, RIS, PP XXXVI (3889) 1867, p. 89.
8   Paper on the Aberdeen Industrial Feeding Schools.
9   W. Watson, 'Letter to the Manager of Industrial Schools' (*c.*1862), p.8.
10 Figures compiled from RIS.
11 Eighteenth Report by the Committee of Directors of the Aberdeen House of Industry and Refuge, 1853–4, p. 5.
12 Report to the Directors of the Aberdeen House of Industry and Refuge by a Committee of their number appointed to take steps for carrying into effect the Industrial And Reformatory objects of Institution (n.d.).
13 Ibid.
14 Ninth Annual Report of the Oldmill Reformatory School, 1865.
15 Third Report, RIS, 1860, p. 55.
16 Seventh Annual Report of the Oldmill Reformatory School, 1863, p. 10.
17 W. Watson, 'Crime in Aberdeenshire', Manuscript of a lecture read to the Social Science Association, Aberdeen, in 1863.
18 Seventh Report, RIS, 1864, p. 48.
19 P. Seed, 'Types of Conceptualisation of Ascribed Client Need in Social Service Provision' (Aberdeen University, Ph.D. thesis, 1976), p. 159.
20 See p. 82.
21 *Edinburgh Evening Courant*, 10 January 1860.
22 *The Scotsman*, 26 December 1859.
23 *Edinburgh Evening Courant*, 30 December 1865.
24 *The Scotsman*, 20 January 1863.
25 *The Scotsman*, 20 December 1864.
26 Ibid.
27 Fifteenth Report, RIS, 1872, p. 147.
28 'Triennial Report of the Dean Bank and Boroughmuirhead Institutions, for the Reformation of Juvenile Delinquents', 1853, p. 3.
29 Triennial Report, 1841–44, p. 2.
30 *The Scotsman*, 28 December 1859.
31 Fourth Report, RIS, 1861, p. 59.
32 SC 1852-3, para. 560.
33 *The Scotsman*, 17 December 1858.
34 *The Scotsman*, 18 March 1859.
35 Reports on the Wellington Reformatory Farm School, Edinburgh, for 1859, 1860 and 1861 (Edinburgh, 1862), p. 6.
36 Fifth Report, RIS, 1862, p. 59.
37 *The Scotsman*, 23 November 1866.
38 *Edinburgh Evening Courant*, 31 March 1864.
39 Eleventh Report, RIS, 1867–8, p. 60.
40 *The Scotsman*, 27 October 1864.
41 *North British Daily Mail*, 8 June 1855.
42 Third Report, RIS, 1860, p. 57.
43 Report of the Glasgow Reformatory Institution, Boys House of Refuge, Duke Street (Glasgow, 1856), p. iii.
44 Report of the Glasgow Reformatory Institution, 1858, p. 18.
45 Journal of the Statistical Society of London, XVIII, December 1855, p. 359.
46 *Reformatory and Refuge Journal*, No. 1, 1861, p. 10.
47 Report of the Glasgow Reformatory Institution, 1857, p. 14.
48 Third Report, RIS, 1860, p. 57.

49 Eighteen out of thirty-five in 1855. For further details, see Rev. A.K. McCallum, 'Juvenile Delinquency – Its Principal Causes and Proposed Cure, as adopted in the Glasgow Reformatory Schools', *Journal of the Statistical Society of London*, XVIII, December 1855, pp. 356–363.
50 Third Report, RIS, 1860, p. 46.
51 Ibid.
52 Boys' House of Refuge, 1856 Report, p. 31.
53 Ibid, p. vii.
54 Females' House of Refuge. Report, in order to an Improved System of Classification and Management, by a Committee of Directors, June 1850 (Second ed., Glasgow, 1854), p. 9.
55 Ibid., p. 7.
56 The Glasgow Girls' Reformatory, or Juvenile Department of the Females' House of Refuge. From 1840 to 1860 [Glasgow, 1860], p. 6.
57 Extracts from Minute-Book of the Commissioners of the Glasgow Houses of Refuge, in Reference to Certain Claims of the Roman Catholic Clergy [Glasgow] 1858, p. 12.
58 Ibid., p. 14.
59 *North British Daily Mail*, 19 February 1868.
60 24 September 1855.
61 Fourth Report, RIS, 1861, p. 61.
62 Boys' House of Refuge, 1856 Report, p. 11.
63 Ninth Report RIS, 1866, p. 60.
64 Fifth Report RIS, 1862, p. 61.
65 Seventh Report RIS, 1864, p. 50.
66 James Greig, C.S., and Thomas Harvey, M.A., *Report on the State of Education in Glasgow* (Edinburgh, 1866), p. 102.
67 R.R. Bone, 'History of the Scottish Approved Schools' (Glasgow University B.Ed Thesis, 1966), p. 58.
68 Greig and Harvey, op. cit., p. 99.
69 Ibid., pp. 100–101.
70 Tenth Report RIS, 1867, p. 7.
71 Not long after leaving the Refuge, McCallum was again involved in controversy: shortly after he became minister of Millport Baptist Church in April 1869 a split occurred in the congregation.
72 Under the Home Office destruction schedule of 29 July 1912, provision was made for papers relating to reformatory and industrial schools and ships to be destroyed twenty years after their creation.
73 Tenth Report RIS, 1867, p. 7.
74 Greig and Harvey, op. cit., p. 101.
75 Eleventh Report RIS, 1867–8, p. 62.
76 Twelfth Report RIS, 1868–9, p. 10.
77 *Glasgow Herald*, 10 May 1850.
78 *Glasgow Courier*, 27 January 1853.
79 *North British Daily Mail*, 25 January 1859.
80 Ibid.
81 *North British Daily Mail*, 26 September 1860.
82 *North British Daily Mail*, 15 April 1859.
83 See pp. 123–124.
84 Report to the Board of Commissioners of the Glasgow House of Refuge, by a Committee of their number (1869), p. 6.
85 Greig and Harvey, op. cit., p. 106.
86 *North British Daily Mail*, 7 December 1868.
87 Report to the Board of Commissioners of the Glasgow House of Refuge, by a Committee of their number (1869), p. 6.

10 Schooling for all

Industrial schools and the 1872 Education Act

A Scottish industrial school in the 1870s was a very different institution from an industrial school in the 1840s: few of the children attended the school voluntarily, and fewer still returned to their homes at nights. Furthermore, the whole educational landscape had changed with the passing of the Education Acts (1870 in England and 1872 in Scotland) which aimed to provide basic schooling for all children. Yet the concept of the day industrial feeding schools pioneered thirty years earlier by Watson and Guthrie proved to have a continued relevance in the era of universal education.

The 1872 Education (Scotland) Act set up a system of state schooling, with control of parish, church and burgh schools being transferred to local school boards, although Catholic and Episcopalian churches continued to run their own schools. The system was overseen by the Scotch Education Department, initially based in London, and made schooling compulsory for children aged between five and thirteen.[1] As T.M. Devine has pointed out,

> This overwhelming dominance of the state in Scottish elementary education contrasted with England where schooling was not at first compulsory and a large voluntary sector survived that had higher status that the public schools, which were virtually confined to the poorer classes.[2]

Thomas Guthrie proved to be strongly in favour of a national, secular system of education of this kind – in contrast to some of his Free Church colleagues, who continued to support the idea of denominational schools. Such was his reputation as a social reformer that, according to one biographer, Guthrie's stance was sufficient to sway the opinion of many who were not fully conversant with all the complex issues involved. When introducing one of his numerous bills for educational reform, Lord Advocate James Moncrieff (1811–1895)[3] wrote to Guthrie:

> I must press upon you the importance – to you I may not say the duty – of giving decided utterance to your real opinions. You have only to make one of your manly, fearless addresses and you will confirm more waverers in the House [of Commons]...[4]

Guthrie played an important part in the National Education Association of Scotland, founded in 1850 to promote a system of schooling which would replace the role of the heritors and presbyteries with locally elected school boards. These efforts were consistently thwarted by the Established Church, which did not want to relinquish its power, and by English MPs who, wishing to protect the role of the Church of England in education, saw reform of the Scottish system as a threat.[5] It was eventually agreed that 'religious education, without being either "prescribed or proscribed" by the Education Act, should be left to the decision of local boards'.[6] It might appear surprising that Guthrie would be in favour of this, particularly in the light of his uncompromising stance regarding religious teaching in the Edinburgh ragged schools, but his confidence in the elected school boards was such that he did not foresee that a non-sectarian system of schooling would in the long term lead to the Bible playing an ever-decreasing role in Scottish education. 'Can any man in his senses believe that the Bible-reading, Bible-loving people of Scotland will thrust the Word of God out of their schools?'[7]

The boards had not been in existence for long before it was discovered that there were still children who could not attend their schools. 'The "Arab class" of children cannot be reached by the powers and provisions of the Education Act as it now stands, or by the purely instructional machinery which it recognises', observed Sydney Turner.[8] The Edinburgh school board, for example, estimated that there existed over 300 boys and girls in the city who were unable to go to school on account of 'poverty, wilful neglect by parents, or want of control by parents'.[9]

By this stage the certified industrial schools were no longer suitable for neglected children found wandering the streets. Whereas in the early days such schools had to be situated in the areas of towns in which poor children lived in order to secure their daily attendance, this was no longer necessary when the vast majority of pupils were committed by magistrates and in the 1870s it was found more appropriate to move to premises in suburban or rural areas. Turner gives three reasons for this: considerations of health; the need for more careful custody; and the necessity of improved facilities for industrial and agricultural employment. In 1869 the boys' department of the Glasgow Industrial School, the Perth Girls' School of Industry and the Paisley Industrial School all moved to the suburbs; in 1878 the Dundee Boys' School transferred to premises at Baldovan, three miles outside the town, and in 1882 the Girls' House of Refuge, Glasgow, moved out to East Chapelton, Bearsden. Another aspect of this trend was the growing advocacy of training ships, of which Scotland had two: the 'Mars', situated on the River Tay near Dundee, and the 'Cumberland', on the Clyde near Dumbarton. Certified under the Industrial Schools Act in September and June 1869 respectively, the 'Mars' received many of its inmates from Edinburgh and the 'Cumberland' from Glasgow.[10] These were in effect floating industrial schools, with the nature of the training being of a specialised nautical type.

The consequence of the reduction of industrial school provision inside the city areas was a still greater diminution of day scholars. Yet it was for children such as these that Watson and Guthrie had set up day industrial schools in the 1840s, and it was to this type of institution that the school boards now turned. The earlier experiments were cited as proof of the utility of day feeding schools: Mary Carpenter, arguing in favour of such schools in 1872, pointed out that 'The same experiment was tried a quarter of a century ago by Sheriff Watson in Aberdeen, and Dr. Guthrie in Edinburgh, and with *entire success*'.[11] Watson, too, when commenting on an Edinburgh school board proposal to run an industrial school, answered criticisms by referring to his experience in the 1840s. The very same objections being raised in Edinburgh, he said, had been raised thirty years previously in Aberdeen, and he answered each of them in the way he had always done: allowing children home at night would mean that they would influence their parents for good; the ordinary working class was not disadvantaged by the school – in fact, they had contributed generously to its upkeep; and, while the expense of the schools had to be borne by the public, 'it certainly would be much more for their benefit to feed the [children] in school than to allow them to procure the means of feeding themselves by begging, stealing or selling small wares on the street'.[12] Even at the age of eighty-eight, three years before his death, Watson appeared before the 1884 Royal Commission on reformatory and industrial schools arguing for a return to his original idea of day feeding schools.

Though the concept of an industrial school as a residential institution to which children were committed was firmly established, some day feeding schools did begin to reappear, initially in England. Edinburgh was the first city in Scotland to consider the matter after the passing of the 1872 Education Act and a Memorandum to the Lord Advocate was submitted, requesting the power to set up feeding schools financed by the rates.[13] This power was given to English school boards by the 1876 Elementary Education Act but was not extended to Scotland until 1893 [Day Industrial Schools (Scotland) Act, 56 & 57 Vict., c. 12]. An earlier opportunity did emerge in 1879 when the directors of the Edinburgh United Industrial School offered the school board their property without compensation. However, the objection in the way of this plan was that the United School wished to retain its distinctive policy of allowing separate religious education for Protestant and Catholic children; if the school board were to take it over on these terms a demand might arise for similar arrangements to be extended to other board schools. Since the outbreak of typhus in 1865, the United School had been pressed by the inspectorate to move to a healthier location but it lacked the funds, hence its willingness to hand over control to the school board. It was even in danger of losing its certification at one stage and it eventually closed in 1900.

In the interim, the Edinburgh school board decided to provide food and clothing at selected centres attached to existing schools, and aided about one thousand children in this way during 1882–1883 until it was in a position to establish St. John's Hill Day Industrial School in 1898. By contrast, in Glasgow, several day industrial schools opened between 1878 and 1912, by which time the city had seven such schools. Other Scottish towns did not, however, take up the idea, presumably because their smaller size enabled poor children to be absorbed into ordinary board schools.

In order to explain the wholehearted adoption of day industrial schools in Glasgow compared to elsewhere, it is necessary to examine the complicated evolution of the city's own local Juvenile Delinquency Act, originally passed in

1841 with the aim of supporting the House of Refuge. From 1867 onwards, this arrangement was increasingly subject to criticism. The inquiry into the running of the Refuge which led to the resignation of its governor had highlighted the dangers of keeping boys under confinement and in the 1880s most of the reformatory and industrial schools in Glasgow, as elsewhere, moved out of the built-up area. In February 1868, there was an indication of future trends when admissions to the Refuge were suspended and some of the boys transferred to the Stranraer Reformatory, where they spent a greater proportion of their time in agricultural work.[14]

In spite of the Refuge's diminished field of operation, the assessment of a penny in the pound was still levied in the city for its upkeep. Not only had the rental of the city dramatically increased (by nearly 50 per cent between 1851 and 1861), with the result that there were more buildings on which the rate was charged, but the assessment had been collected twice since admissions to the Refuge were stopped, raising about £18,000.[15] Meanwhile, the industrial schools managed on donations and a grant of four shillings and sixpence per pupils, took in seventy-seven more children in 1867 than in the previous year, had just opened a new school at Mossbank and were soon to establish the 'Cumberland' training ship as a branch institution – all without receiving any share of the proceeds of the assessment. Similarly, the Roman Catholic reformatories catered for a combined average of 297 children in 1869 but were given nothing from the rates, although – as a correspondent of the *North British Daily Mail* who signed himself as 'a compulsory subscriber to the Houses of Refuge' pointed out – Catholics nevertheless had to pay the assessment, despite the fact that children of their persuasion were hardly ever admitted to the institutions.[16]

A review of Glasgow's reformatory facilities was therefore long overdue. In 1869 even the Commissioners in charge of the Houses of Refuge admitted that 'causes have been coming into operation tending to limit their usefulness'[17] and a number of solutions were proposed, such as a single governing body for all the local institutions dealing with destitute and delinquent children. For the moment, it was decided that no changes to the Refuge would be undertaken as its vacant accommodation was likely to be taken up soon, 'as crime, unfortunately ... never fails to grow with the increase of population'.[18]

However, an adjustment was made to the assessment by an Amending Act in 1870 [33 & 34 Vict. c. xlii] allowing an annual grant of fifty-two shillings per inmate to be given to the managers of the other city reformatory and industrial schools out of the surplus of the previous year's assessment. Even this failed to redress the inequalities of the local Act. The prediction that the excess space in the Refuge would sooner or later be needed proved to be wrong: at the end of 1869 the Boys' House had 171 inmates; six years later it had only 134.[19] Moreover, the continued increase in the rental of Glasgow again left the Refuge Commissioners with an embarrassingly large surplus from the assessment at a time when the industrial schools had continued to grow and require more money.[20] By December 1876 there were 458 boys and 232 girls connected with the schools, but public subscriptions were £40 less than the previous year[21] and the government had rejected the schools' application for a weekly grant of five shillings per pupil, as in England, instead of four shillings and sixpence. Even more significantly, the 1872 Education Act, by dealing with many potential delinquents at an earlier stage of their evolution, further narrowed the field of operation not only of the Refuge, but of the industrial schools too.

Accordingly, the idea proposed by the 1869 Committee was taken up again: a union of the institutions under a single body. The school board appointed its own committee to meet with representatives of the Refuge and industrial schools since it had an interest in the review of reformatory and industrial school arrangements, having quickly discovered that many of the children attending its schools were in need of food and clothing as well as education. The School Attendance Officer, William Mitchell, revived the idea of day industrial schools to meet this need, under the superintendence of the Juvenile Delinquency Commissioners rather than the school board. He argued that if children could be fed and clothed by the school board in day industrial schools irrespective of whether or not they were entitled to poor relief, this would soon lead to contributions to voluntary agencies drying up and would consequently increase the burden on the rates. The school board thus asked for a clause to be included in the proposed Juvenile Delinquency Bill by which the Board of Commissioners could set up and contribute to the running of day industrial schools.[22]

A bill was therefore prepared giving 'a fresh constitution of the bodies connected with these institutions ... so as to more fully meet the requirements of the times'.[23] The 1878 Juvenile Delinquency Act [41 & 42 Vict. c. cxxi] entrusted the running of the Refuge to a body entitled 'The Directors of Houses of Refuge and Reformatory and Industrial Schools in the City of Glasgow', to which properties of the Refuges and the industrial schools at Mossbank and Rottenrow were transferred. The directors were given full powers to run the institutions and appoint higher officers and superintendents, dividing into separate committees to be in charge of each school. Although the Roman Catholic reformatory and industrial schools continued to be managed separately, a capitation grant was given to them and grants were to be paid to a day industrial school should one be set up.

The Act went a considerable way towards achieving the 'more united action' and 'greater efficiency and economy' for which it was designed.[24] For instance, accommodation was re-allocated to give the most room to the agencies which needed it. The proportion of voluntary inmates in the Girls' Refuge had always been greater than in the Boys',[25] though, as Turner's reports consistently pointed out, these were destitute children who should have been in an industrial school. Thus, in 1881 the Girls' Industrial School in Rottenrow moved to the Maryhill premises formerly occupied by the Girls' Refuge; the Girls' Refuge in turn transferred to the Riddrie premises which had been an annexe of the Boys' House, and the following year moved to new and smaller buildings outside the city boundary at East Chapelton, Bearsden.[26] Each institution was now housed in premises more suited to its needs in more healthy surroundings. The Boys' Refuge fell gradually into disuse, its accommodation being far too large, and it finally closed in May 1887. Of the forty-four boys remaining, twenty-two were sent to Canada under the charge of the superintendent, Mr. Rae. Boys convicted at Glasgow courts were thereafter received by other reformatories.[27]

The new arrangements meant that the city was again at the forefront of the development of institutions which met contemporary needs. Evidence from the annual returns published by Glasgow Police from 1857 onwards appears to indicate that the city's various reformatory and industrial schools were making some impact on juvenile crime. Table 10.1 shows that the number of juvenile offenders fluctuated during the period 1860–1880 but did not increase overall.

When these returns are correlated with population figures, a decrease in the number of juvenile offenders per head of population can be seen. In 1851 there were 67,090 children under the age of fifteen in Glasgow, and 587 were charged with crime – a ratio of 114:1. The corresponding figures in 1861 were 79,015 and 390 (202:1) and in 1871 100,691 and 254 (396:1). It was the opinion of Chief Constable McCall in 1871 that 'The Reformatory and Industrial schools, by snatching from incipient vice hundreds of young Arabs in town and country, but especially the pariahs of our large cities, have exercised most important and beneficial moral results…'[28]

By the 1880s the residential institutions were supplemented by various day industrial schools of the type pioneered in Scottish cities in the 1840s. The Glasgow Act of 1878 contained the same provisions for day industrial schools as the English Elementary Education Act of 1876. The board's first school of this kind

Table 10.1 Number of children in Glasgow under fifteen brought before magistrates charged with crime, 1860–80

1860	307
1861	390
1862	271
1863	305
1864	291
1865	277
1866	252
1867	302
1868	349
1869	482
1870	Missing
1871	254
1872	368
1873	477
1874	440
1875	404
1876	399
1877	432
1878	474
1879	370
1880	485

Source: Criminal Returns, City of Glasgow Police, 1857 onwards

was opened in 1879 in Green Street in the Calton district, for the children of poor widows, or those whose parents were both working. 'Many of them', comments the first annual report, 'had already got into bad and truant habits, through the want of home influences, and doubtless many of them were fast becoming fit subjects for the ordinary Industrial Schools or Reformatories'.[29]

The same preventive ideas which had given rise to Glasgow's original industrial school in 1846 were therefore behind the provision of similar institutions which met the needs of the post-Education Act era of the 1880s. Further day industrial schools were established in Rottenrow (1882) and Rose Street (1889), each providing for about 250 pupils. The 1878 legislation was an effective solution because it provided at a local level a financial and administrative back-up to national legislation. The local arrangements of 1841 were not done away with – the assessment remained, but it was modified to meet the needs of the day. The various schools had grown up separately; now their functions were co-ordinated, they were housed in suitable premises and finance was more equitably distributed so that the operation of reformatory and industrial schools in Glasgow could justifiably be described as a 'system'.

The suitability of these arrangements may be judged from the fact that a later Reformatory and Industrial Schools Act in 1890 provided for a contribution from local rates as well as from central government, thus extending to the country at large a practice which Glasgow had followed for many years. When the subject was debated at the 1890 Conference of Managers of Reformatory and Industrial Institutions – held, appropriately enough, in Glasgow – the representatives of the Glasgow schools did not raise the objections which were made by other delegates, for the city's local authorities had supported the Refuge for the past half-century. It is a measure of the success with which the local system finally merged with the national one in Glasgow that the financial provisions of the 1841 Act still continued to work satisfactorily when the House of Refuge for which they were originally designed no longer existed.

Notes

1 See W.W. Knox, 'The Scottish Educational System, 1840–1940' (www.scran.ac.uk/scotland/pdf/SP2_1Education.pdf).
2 T.M. Devine, *The Scottish Nation, 1700–2007* (London, 2012), p. 397.
3 Moncrieff was MP for Leith Burghs (1851–59) and later for Edinburgh (1859–68).
4 Oliphant Smeaton, *Thomas Guthrie* (London and Edinburgh, 1900), p. 110.
5 For a full discussion of the process leading to the 1872 Education Act, particularly the part played by the churches, see John Stevenson *Fulfilling a Vision, The Contribution of the Church of Scotland to School Education, 1772–1872* (Eugene, Oregon, 2012), p. 90 ff.
6 Smeaton, op. cit., p. 111.
7 Ibid., p. 111.
8 Sixteenth Report RIS, PP 1873 XXXI (817), p. 21.
9 'Edinburgh School Board: Report as to CHILDREN not receiving ELEMENTARY EDUCATION, as required by the Education Act for Scotland, Scotland, 1872' (in *Reports, etc. on Education of Destitute Children, 1875–1883,* Edinburgh Central Library).
10 The 'Cumberland' was destroyed by fire in 1889 – said to have been a result of boys

deliberately setting fire to a straw mattress – and was replaced by the 'Empress', which was withdrawn from service in 1923, followed by the 'Mars' six years later.
11 Mary Carpenter, 'Day Industrial Schools for Neglected and Destitute Children', *Reformatory and Refuge Journal*, 1872, LV, p. 273.
12 William Watson, 'Neglected Children' (unpublished manuscript).
13 The 1872 Education Act already gave school boards the power to set up certified industrial schools but these were not suitable for children who had not been convicted in a court and who did not require dormitory accommodation.
14 *North British Daily Mail*, 10 February 1868.
15 *North British Daily Mail*, 22 February 1868.
16 *North British Daily Mail*, 21 March 1868.
17 'Report to the Board of Commissioners of the Glasgow Houses of Refuge by a committee of their number', p. 3.
18 Ibid, p. 8.
19 Glasgow Houses of Refuge: Report by Special Sub-Committee (Glasgow City Archives), undated (c. 1876–7).
20 The term 'rental' here refers to the valuation of the properties on which the assessment was levied. The rental of Glasgow in 1877–1888 was £3,295,888: W.W. Watson, *Report upon the Vital, Social, and Economic Statistics of Glasgow, for 1877* (Glasgow, 1878), p. 97.
21 *Glasgow Herald*, 6 February 1877.
22 *Glasgow Herald*, 13 February 1877.
23 Glasgow Houses of Refuge Bill: Statement for the Promoters (Glasgow City Archives).
24 Glasgow Houses of Refuge, &c. Bill: Memorandum, p. 4 (Glasgow City Archives).
25 Admission of these voluntary 'refuge' cases ceased after 1878.
26 Report of the Glasgow Reformatory and Industrial Schools, 1888 (Glasgow, 1889), p. 6.
27 Ibid., p. 7.
28 Criminal Returns, City of Glasgow Police, 1871, p. 4.
29 Juvenile Delinquency Board. Report of the Day Industrial School, Green Street, Calton (Glasgow, 1880), p. 9.

11 Change and continuity

Nineteenth-century approaches in context

The year after the passing of the Scottish Education Act, Thomas Guthrie died. Around 30,000 people lined the streets as the funeral procession made its way to Edinburgh's Grange Cemetery, and the children of the Original Ragged School sang the hymn 'There is a happy land, far, far away' at the graveside.

It was indeed the end of an era as far as child welfare was concerned. This study took as its starting point the 1812 Tron Riot, when young offenders were portrayed by the authorities as culpable criminals deserving severe punishment; less than forty years later, blame had shifted to the social and economic circumstances which inevitably led children of what Mary Carpenter called 'the perishing and dangerous classes' into crime. 'During the course of the nineteenth century', says Lynn Abrams, 'a "modern" notion of the child was gradually formulated so that by the 1870s the concept of the child, as distinct from the adult, by nature of his or her ignorance, innocence and dependence, was firmly in place'.[1] New methods of treatment, aiming at reformation and, later, prevention, were determined largely by the practices and institutions already in existence; the schools developed in Scotland therefore differed from their English counterparts insofar as these previous practices and institutions were different. While the state's acceptance of responsibility for the welfare as well as punishment of both delinquent and potentially delinquent children was an innovation, this change, like so many other aspects of government growth in this period, took place from what William C. Lubenow called an 'incrementalist perspective': a gradual 'effort to effect change without violating accepted assumptions and traditions…'.[2]

Initially, the connection between old and new approaches would appear to have been a negative one, the shortcomings of existing methods of treatment of delinquents – which usually consisted of no more than imprisonment – leading to attempts to provide alternative facilities. The Glasgow House of Refuge, for example, was designed to supply 'what the Bridewell leaves defective'. Again, the Scottish industrial schools must be seen in the context of previous methods of dealing with poor children. One of their most distinctive features – the attendance of children during the day only, returning to their families at night – arose as a reaction against the hospital system which produced a disapproval of institutionalisation among social reformers that was not so apparent in England. Once again, this varied in different localities: as the hospital system had been most prevalent in

Edinburgh and Aberdeen, it was in these cities that its shortcomings were most evident and non-residential industrial schools were set up; in Perth there had been no poor's hospital, so that when Sheriff Barclay sought to imitate Watson's school there he saw no reason why dormitory accommodation should not be provided.

However, the connection between old and new methods of treatment was more than a negative reaction against the drawbacks of the penal system and poor law. Many pioneering efforts were influenced by the strengths as well as the weaknesses of previous approaches, making positive use of penal or poor law precedents, adapting them to suit their needs. The idea of an industrial school in Edinburgh originated as part of poor law provision, while other schools were not only influenced by but incorporated in existing institutions. The Glasgow industrial school, for example, was originally run in the premises of the Night Asylum and the Girls' House of Refuge as part of the Magdalene Asylum; the Aberdeen industrial schools formed an integral part of a social welfare network at first centred around the city's House of Refuge for the Destitute which itself was eventually to evolve into the Old Mill Reformatory School.

Bearing in mind the importance of existing facilities in shaping these institutions, change was inevitable after 1854 when the schools were certified under Acts which had not been designed primarily to meet Scottish aspirations, even though the influence of the Scottish schools had been an important stimulus behind the passing of legislation in the first place. The effect of legislation in Scotland was consequently different from what had been hoped for. The aim of Reformatory and Industrial School Acts – shared by schools and government alike – was stated by C.B. Adderley, MP for North Staffordshire, in 1858: 'The general principle at present recognized was, that of subsidising local efforts rather than undertaking the whole charge on the part of the State.'[3]

In practice, however, acceptance of government aid diminished public support so that the schools became increasingly dependent on children committed under the Acts and supported by government allowances, to the detriment of the local flexibility which had formerly pertained. This was especially true of the industrial schools legislation passed between 1854 and 1866 so that the Acts which had been viewed by the schools as a consolidation of the Scottish approach in fact made it impossible for them to continue in their original form and began a process which changed them into a different sort of institution altogether.

The reformatories, meanwhile, became increasingly penal institutions for hardened offenders, with young delinquents starting on a course of crime being committed to industrial schools. Thus by the 1870s the reformatories were subject to the criticisms made of prisons in the 1840s, while the Scottish industrial schools had developed into residential institutions that in effect were, as Sydney Turner said, reformatories of a milder sort. The legislation on Day Industrial Schools in 1876 (England) and 1893 (Scotland) saw the re-emergence in the post-Education Act era of a limited number of day feeding schools of the original non-residential type pioneered in the 1840s.

The post-1854 developments outlined above illustrate the well-known pattern of state intervention postulated by Oliver MacDonagh:[4] an 'intolerable' social evil was discovered; legislation, albeit in a compromised form, was passed and responsibility assumed; government inspectors were appointed, leading to centralisation and further legislation. It is not, of course, surprising that parallels exist with other areas of government intervention in social welfare, since, as we have seen, the treatment of delinquency overlapped considerably with the treatment of these problems. In some ways the Reformatory and Industrial Schools Acts, although setting a precedent, were not a new departure or an extension of state intervention in the sense of, for instance, the clauses relating to children in the 1833 Factory Act. Delinquent children were already dealt with by the state; the Acts simply provided for the same children in a different way. Furthermore, as their supporters constantly argued, there would be no increase in state expenditure, as (in theory, at least) it was cheaper to reform a child than to punish him in a prison and allow him to grow up into an adult criminal. Nevertheless, the Acts were of vital importance as they marked the extension of government responsibility to include potentially delinquent children and, in the longer term in conjunction with other forces, to the provision of elementary education for all in 1872.

A comparison of juvenile justice in the nineteenth century with subsequent changes up to the present day reveals that the genesis of many of the developments of the last hundred years can be traced to the 1840s and 1850s. In *Punishment and Welfare*, David Garland argues that the roots of current approaches are to be found later, in the period between 1895 and the start of the First World War. Nevertheless, he concedes that 'even the new institutions which emerged in this period such as probation, Borstal, preventive detention and "individualisation" have obvious precursors and parallels in the previous period or even earlier'.[5]

The trend towards dealing with juveniles apart from adults, outside the penal system and within the community, has been the theme of much legislation over the past century and a half. Linda Mahood has designated the period from 1885 to 1932 'the protective era', as these years saw major pieces of legislation such as the 1907 Probation Act and the 1908 Children's Act which set up separate juvenile courts. The abolition in 1899 of the requirement for a period of imprisonment prior to admission to a reformatory meant that there was effectively little difference between reformatory and industrial schools other than the age of the children sent to them. In 1932 the new term 'approved school' was adopted, though by this stage institutionalisation was falling out of favour and other options such as probation were being employed. The long and gradual progress towards a welfare-based approach culminated in the setting up of children's hearings by the Social Work (Scotland) Act of 1968 following the recommendations of the Kilbrandon Report of 1964, which 'did not think that any form of judicial procedure was the best way of going about meeting the needs of the children, which it believed were mainly educational and social in nature'.[6] All these developments could be interpreted as part of a continuum stretching back to the pioneering experiments of reformers like Watson and Guthrie in the 1840s. Kilbrandon's vision is in essence the same as that of the Edinburgh detective James McLevy (1796–1875), who had hoped 'to see the time when jails and penitentiaries will be changed into ragged and industrial schools'.[7]

Debate in more recent years has continued to echo many of the views expressed in the mid-nineteenth century, with the pendulum regularly swinging between what is perceived as either a 'tough' or a 'lenient' approach. In the 1980s social worker and children's campaigner Baroness Faithfull (1910–1996) – in many ways a twentieth-century Mary Carpenter – strenuously opposed moves to deal with children in 'training centres' attached to prisons, arguing instead for earlier intervention in family situations. Her belief was that

> Some juveniles require residential care, which should be well resourced with a good complement of skilled and highly valued staff. But for most young offenders we need more schemes based in the community, which can involve juveniles in constructive activities and enable them to form relationships with stable adults.[8]

At the other extreme, politicians regularly feel compelled to respond to public demands for a 'tougher' approach of the kind favoured by former Metropolitan Police Commissioner Sir David McNee, who began his career as a beat constable in Glasgow: 'The majority of young offenders do not need to be treated as welfare cases. They need merely to be given a sharp reminder that what they have done was wrong…'.[9]

That suggestion was condemned as 'a return to the nineteenth century' by Dennis Gower, Scottish officer of the British Association of Social Workers, who argued that 'ceasing to look at children as young criminals … is not new. It is something which was started 70 years ago'.[10] In the 1990s Tony Blair's Labour party made much of the slogan 'tough on crime, tough on the causes of crime'; this was the era of the ASBO (Anti-Social Behaviour Order), a tactic extended to Scotland for children aged over twelve from 2004 onwards. A recent review of Youth Justice in Scotland notes that 'In this period the Kilbrandon philosophy was subjected to a rigorous test. Welfare and justice came to be presented almost as dichotomous variables and the belief that "needs" and "deeds" formed two sides of the same coin was challenged'.[11]

Current Scottish government policy supports the children's hearings procedure and reaffirms the principle that 'the system considers all those who come within it, either on welfare or offending grounds, as being children in need and facing risk either from their own behaviour or the behaviour of others'.[12] Recent reductions in the number of children referred to the hearings system have been attributed to a policy of early intervention and the encouragement of greater co-ordination between the education system and other agencies working with young people through approaches such as GIRFEC ('Getting It Right For Every Child') and WSA ('Whole System Approach').[13] All of this, of course, is part of a growing worldwide consensus on the need for a holistic approach to young people, enshrined in the United Nations Convention on the Rights of the Child (1989), which states that 'the best interests of the child must always be the primary consideration and that custody should only be used as a last resort'.[14]

Even though there is broad international acceptance of these principles, it can be argued that a distinctively Scottish dimension to juvenile justice remains. In terms of processes, a clear difference exists between the hearings system employed in Scotland and the youth courts favoured in England. As recently as 2009, the Howard League for Penal Reform criticised the imprisonment of minors in England and pointed to Scotland as a model. According to the Chief Executive, Frances Crook,

> Scotland does not demonise children the way we do, punishing young people as individuals for what amount to failures in social policy. Scotland recognises that appalling juvenile re-offending rates – over three-quarters in England and Wales – show that prison is no place for children.[15]

As for the future, Professor Bill Whyte of the University of Edinburgh, in a lecture reviewing the legacy of Kilbrandon over the past fifty years, concluded that 'It now needs a new generation of practitioners, managers and policy makers to own, maintain and develop this legacy in line with international standards'.[16]

One point that emerges from this study of reformatory and industrial schools in nineteenth-century Scotland is that many supposedly modern ideas, when divested of their twenty-first-century associations, are not in fact new. The attempt to tackle the causes rather than the results of crime through a welfare-based approach, the provision of training for employment, dealing with a child in a way which avoids the stigma of criminalisation – these and many similar ideas were part of the Victorian reformers' vision. Over the past 150 years many schools have opened and some prisons have closed,[17] yet it remains as true as ever that 'In terms of policy, the authoritarian, the retributive, the restorative and the protective continually jostle with each other to construct a multi-modal landscape of youth governance'.[18]

Notes

1. Lynn Abrams, *The Orphan Country* (Edinburgh, 1998), p. 24.
2. William C. Lubenow, *The Politics of Government Growth* (Newton Abbot, 1971), p. 185.
3. Quoted in Twelfth Annual Report of the Edinburgh Original Ragged School, 1858, p. 18.
4. Oliver MacDonagh, 'The Nineteenth-Century Revolution in Government: A Reappraisal', *Historical Journal*, I, I (1958), pp. 52–67.
5. David Garland, *Punishment and Welfare* (Aldershot, 1985), p. 5.
6. Peter Boss, *Social Policy and the Young Delinquent* (London, 1967), p. 79.
7. James McLevy, *The Sliding Scale of Life* (Edinburgh, 1861), p. vi.
8. Quoted in *The Herald*, 1 February 1980.
9. Quoted in *The Sunday Times*, 9 July 1978.
10. Quoted in *The Herald*, 10 July 1978.
11. Claire Lightowler, David Orr and Nina Vaswani, *Youth Justice in Scotland: Fixed in the Past or Fit for the Future?*, p. 9 (www.cycj.org.uk/wp-content/uploads/2014/09/Youth-Justice-in-Scotland.pdf). For an interpretation of the competing trends in Scottish youth justice in the period up to 2010, see Lesley McAra, 'Scottish youth justice: convergent pressures and cultural singularities' in *The Criminalisation of Youth: Juvenile Justice in Europe, Turkey and Canada*, edited by Francis Bailleau and Yves Cartuyvels (Brussels, 2010), pp. 93–110.

12 *Children and the Scottish Criminal Justice System*, Scottish Parliament Information Centre, July 2011, p. 5.
13 See www.gov.scot/Topics/Justice/policies/young-offending/whole-system-approach.
14 Quoted in Neal Hazel, *Cross-national Comparison of Youth Justice*, p. 5 (see dera.ioe.ac.uk/7996/1/Cross_national_final.pdf).
15 Quoted in *The Guardian*, 10 February 2009.
16 *Scottish Journal of Residential Child Care*, Vol. 13, No. 3, December 2014, p. 16.
17 In 2016 Her Majesty's Young Offenders Institution at Polmont, near Falkirk, had capacity for 712 male offenders between the ages of sixteen and twenty-one.
18 John Muncie, quoted in Neal Hazel, op. cit., p. 22.

Bibliography

Manuscript sources

Aberdeen Central Library:

Papers of William Watson: The Church and the School; Crime in Aberdeenshire; English and Irish Industrial Schools; National Education; The Spread of the Aberdeen System in Scotland; Visitation of Industrial Schools 1866.

Edinburgh City Archives:

Minutes of Police Commissioners, General Commissioners, 13 Vols., 1803–1856.
Minutes of Police Commissioners, Watching Committee, 5 Vols., 1827–1856.

New College Library, Edinburgh:

Papers of Alexander Thomson of Banchory: Draft Report to Prison Board; Paper on the Aberdeen Industrial Feeding Schools.

Scottish Records Office, Edinburgh:

Register of Criminal Prisoners [Edinburgh], 1841–61.
Kirk Session Minutes, St. John's Church, Edinburgh, Vol. I.

Glasgow City Archives:

Glasgow Bridewell. Minutes and Accounts of Commissioners, 1820–1845. Council Act Book, Vol. 57.

Printed sources

1. Parliamentary papers

(a) Reports

Report from the Select Committee appointed to inquire into the state and description of Gaols and other places of confinement, PP 1819, VII (579).

Report from the Select Committee appointed to inquire into the state of Prisons in Scotland, and into the means of maintaining Prisoners confined therein under criminal warrants, PP 1826, V (381).
Report from the Select Committee appointed to inquire into the cause of the increase in the number of Criminal Commitments and Convictions in England and Wales, PP 1826–7, VI (534).
Second Report, PP 1828, VI (545).
Reports of the Inspector of Prisons for Scotland, Northumberland, and Durham, PP 1836–1857.
Reports of the Inspectors of Prisons for the Northern District, PP 1857–8 until 1878.
Reports from the General Board of Directors of Prisons in Scotland, PP 1840–1861.
Second Report from the Select Committee of the House of Lords appointed to inquire into the Execution of the Criminal Law, especially respecting Juvenile Offenders and Transportation, PP 1847, VII (534) [Referred to in footnotes by the abbreviation SC 1847].
First Annual Report of the Board of Supervision for the Relief of the Poor in Scotland, PP 1847, XVIII (767).
Report from the Select Committee on Prison Discipline, PP 1850, XVII (632).
Report from the Select Committee on Criminal and Destitute Juveniles, PP 1852, VII (515) [Referred to in footnotes by the abbreviation SC 1852].
Report from the Select Committee on Criminal and Destitute Children, PP 1852–3, XXIII (674) [Referred to in footnotes by the abbreviation SC 1852–3].
Report from the Select Committee on the Public Prosecutors Bill, PP 1854–5, XII (481).
Reports of the Inspector, appointed under the provisions of the Act 5 & 6 Will. 4, c. 38, to visit the different Reformatory Schools of Great Britain, PP 1857–8 until 1878 [Referred to in footnotes by the abbreviation RIS].
Report from the Select Committee appointed to inquire how the education of destitute and neglected children may be most efficiently and economically assisted by any public fund, PP 1861, VII (460).
Report of the Commissioners appointed to inquire into the State of Popular Education in England, Vol. I, PP 1861, XII Part 1 (2794).

(b) Accounts and papers

Minutes of the Committee of Council on Education, dated 2nd June 1856, offering grants for the promotion of schools wherein children of the criminal and abandoned classes may be reformed by industrial training, PP 1856, XLVI (259), p. 399.
Return of all reformatories which have been certified in England and Scotland, and of reformatories refused certification, with the grounds of refusal, PP 1856, XLIX (47), p. 329.
Return of children in industrial, ragged, and reformatory schools, assisted within the past year as schools of industry by the Committee of Council for Education, showing the number in each schools, and the amount of the grant in each case, PP 1856, MX (164), p. 323.
Minute of the Committee of Council on Education on certified industrial and ragged schools, dated 31st December 1857, PP 1857–8, WTI (2315), p. 377.
Amount of grants made in reformatories, ragged industrial schools, & c. in England and Scotland, in accordance with the Privy Council minute, dated 2nd June 1856, PP 1859, XXI (227. Sess. 1), Part II, p.125.

2. Newspapers

Aberdeen Banner
Aberdeen Herald
Aberdeen Journal
Edinburgh Evening Courant
Glasgow Argus
Glasgow Constitutional
Glasgow Courier
Glasgow Herald
Greenock Advertiser
North British Daily Mail
The Scotsman
The Witness

3. Annual reports and other documents relating to industrial and reformatory schools in Edinburgh, Aberdeen and Glasgow [for details, see individual citations in footnotes]

4. Nineteenth and early twentieth-century books, articles and pamphlets

Alison, A., *Principles of the Criminal Law of Scotland* (Edinburgh, 1832).
Alison, W.P., *Observations on the Management of the Poor in Scotland, and Its effects on the Health of the Great Towns* (Edinburgh, 1840).
Angus, M., *Sheriff Watson of Aberdeen: The Story of his Life, and His Work for the Young* (Aberdeen, 1913).
[Anon.] 'Reasons for Establishing a Public System of Elementary Instruction in England,' *Quarterly Journal of Education*, I (1831), pp. 213–224.
[Anon.] *The Poor of Edinburgh; or, Recollections of the Canongate in 1842* (London, 1842).
[Anon.] 'The Criminal Statistics of Aberdeen for Twenty Years', *Journal of the Statistical Society of London*, XXVII (1864), pp. 413–421.
[Anon.] *The History of the Workhouses or Poor's Hospital of Aberdeen* (Aberdeen, 1865).
Antrobus, E.E., *The Prison and the School* (London, 1853).
Baird, C.R., *Report on the General and Sanatory Condition of the Working Classes and the Poor in the City of Glasgow* (London, 1841).
Barclay, H., *Juvenile Delinquency, Its Causes and Cure. By a Country Magistrate* (Edinburgh and London, 1848).
Beggs, T., *Juvenile Delinquency and Reformatory Institutions: A Lecture delivered to the members of the Leeds Mechanics' Institution* (London, 1857).
Bentley, J., *State of Education, Crime, etc.* (London, 1842).
Bell, G., *Blackfriars' Wynd Analyzed* (Edinburgh, 1850).
Bell, Sir J. and Paton, J., *Glasgow. Its Municipal Organization and Administration* (Glasgow, 1896).
Brebner, W., *Letter to the Lord Provost, on the Expediency of a House of Refuge for Juvenile Offenders in Glasgow* (Glasgow, 1829).
Broun, A., *Reports of Cases before the High Court and Circuit Courts of Justiciary in Scotland in 1844 and 1845* (Edinburgh, 1846).

Bryce, J.D., *The Glasgow Magdalene Asylum, Its Past and Present: With Relative Facts and Suggestions* (Glasgow, 1859).
Burns, Rev. R., *Historical Dissertations on the Law and Practice of Great Britain, and particularly of Scotland, with Regard to the Poor* (Glasgow, 1819).
Burns, Rev. R., *Memoir of the Rev. Stevenson Macgill D.D.* (Edinburgh, 1842).
Butler, D., *The Tron Kirk of Edinburgh* (Edinburgh and London, 1806).
Carpenter, M., *Reformatory Schools, for the Children of the Perishing and Dangerous Classes, and for Juvenile Offenders* (London, 1851).
Carpenter, M., *Juvenile Delinquents: Their Condition and Treatment* (London, 1853).
Carpenter, M., 'Day Industrial Schools certified by the Secretary of State: A Paper read before the repression of crime section of the Social Science Association, Liverpool, October 1976' (Bristol, 1876).
Carpenter, M., 'Juvenile Delinquency in Its Relation to the Education Movement', in A. Hill (ed.), *Essays upon Educational Subjects Read at the Educational Conference of June 1857* (London, 1857), 320–333.
Clay, Rev. W.L., *The Prison Chaplain: A Memoir of the Rev. John Clay, B.D.* (Cambridge and London, 1861).
Cleland, J., *Annals of Glasgow* (2 Vols., Glasgow, 1816).
Cleland, J., *Glasgow Bridewell or House of Correction* (Glasgow, 1835).
Cornwallis, C.F., *The Philosophy of Ragged Schools* (Small Books on Great Subjects, No. XVIII, London, 1851).
Day, S.P., *Juvenile Crime, Its Causes, Character and Cure* (London, 1858).
Dunlop, A.M., *The Law of Scotland regarding the Poor* (Edinburgh and London, 1854).
Forsyth, W., 'Criminal Procedure in Scotland and England', in *Essays Critical and Narrative* (London, 1874).
Fraser, Rev. W., *Memoir of the Life of David Stow* (London, 1868).
Greig, J. and Harvey, T., *Report on the State of Education in Glasgow* (Edinburgh, 1866).
Goodwin, J., *History of the Glasgow Night Asylum for the Houseless, from Origin to Jubilee* (Glasgow, 1887).
Gurney, J.J., *Notes on a Visit Made to Some of the Prisons in Scotland and the North of England in company with Elizabeth Fry* (London, 1819).
Guthrie, Rev. T., *A Plea for Ragged Schools* (9th Ed., Edinburgh, 1847).
Guthrie, Rev. T., *A Second Plea for Ragged Schools* (Edinburgh, 1849).
Guthrie, Rev. T., *A Plea on Behalf of Drunkards and Against Drunkenness* (Edinburgh, 1851).
Guthrie, Rev. T., *Autobiography of Thomas Guthrie, D.D., and Memoir by his sons*, Rev. David K. Guthrie and Charles J. Guthrie, M.A.
Hanna, Rev. W., *Memoirs of Thomas Chalmers. DD. LL.D.* (2 Vols, Edinburgh, 1854).
Hill, A., *Train up a Child in the Way he should Go: A Paper on the Industrial Schools of Scotland, and the Working of Dunlop's Act* (London and Bristol, N.D.).
Hill, Florence, *Children of the State* (London, 1866).
Hill, Frederic, *Crime: Its Amount Causes, and Remedies* (London, 1853).
Hill, Frederic, *An Autobiography of Fifty Years in Times of Reform* (London, 1894).
Hill, M.D., *Suggestions for the Repression of Crime* (London, 1857).
Hume, D., *Commentaries on the Law of Scotland Respecting Crimes* (2 Vols., Edinburgh, 1819).
Kay, J., *The Condition and Education of Poor Children in English and in German Towns* (London, 1853).
Kingsmill, J., *Chapters on Prisons and Prisoners* (London, 1852).
Knighton, W., *Training in Streets and Schools* (London, 1855).

Lewis, Rev. G., *Scotland a half-Educated Nation, both in the Quantity and Quality of her Educational Institutions* (Glasgow, 1834).

Liddell, A., 'Letter on Industrial Schools addressed to the Convenors of Committees on Schools of Industry' (Glasgow, 1846).

Linton, T., *Report and Returns as to Crimes, Offences, and Contraventions, within the Limits of the Police of the City of Edinburgh* (Edinburgh, 1862–72).

Logan, W., *The Moral Statistics of Glasgow* (Glasgow, 1849).

McCallum, Rev. A.K., 'Juvenile Delinquency – Its Principal Causes and Proposed Cure, as adopted in the Glasgow Reformatory Schools', *Journal of the Statistical Society of London* XVIII (1855), pp. 356–363.

McClelland, J., *On Reformatories for the Destitute and the Fallen* (Glasgow, 1856).

MacGregor, J., *Shoe Blacks and Broomers* (London, 1853).

MacGregor, J., *The Law of Reformatories* (London, 1856).

Maclagan, A., *Ragged School Rhymes* (Edinburgh, 1851).

McLennan, J.F., 'Scottish Criminal Statistics', in *Transactions of the National Association for the Promotion of Social Science* (Edinburgh Meeting, 1863) (London, 1864), pp. 384–394.

McLevy, J., *The Sliding Scale of Life* (Edinburgh, 1861).

Mathieson, W.L., *Church and Reform in Scotland 1797–1843* (Glasgow, 1916).

Miller, H., *Papers relative to the State of Crime in the City of Glasgow, with Observations of a Remedial Nature* (Glasgow, 1840).

Mitchell, W., *Twelve Years' Experience of Day Industrial Schools in Glasgow* (London, 1886).

National Reformatory Union, The Authorized Report of the First Provincial Meeting of the National Reformatory Union, Held at Bristol on the 20th 21st and 22nd of August 1856 (London, n.d.).

The New Statistical Account of Scotland, XII (Edinburgh and London, 1845).

Nicholls, G., *A History of the Scotch Poor Law* (London, 1856).

Paterson, J., *A Compendium of English and Scotch Law* (Edinburgh, 1860).

Plint, T., *Crime in England* (London, 1851).

Rae, J., *Reformatories: Their History, Management and Results* (Glasgow, 1867).

Ragged Schools in relation to the Government Grants for Education, The Authorized Report of the Conference held at Birmingham, January 23rd., 1861 (London and Birmingham, N.D.).

Renwick, R. (ed.), *Extracts from the Records of the Burgh of Glasgow, Vol. X* (Glasgow, 1915).

Shuttleworth, Sir J.K., *Public Education* (London, 1853).

Skelton, Sir J., *The Boarding-out of Pauper Children in Scotland* (Edinburgh, 1876).

Smeaton, Rev. G., *Memoir of Alexander Thomson of Banchory* (Edinburgh, 1869).

Smeaton, O., *Thomas Guthrie* (Edinburgh and London, 1900).

Smiles, S., *Self-Help* (London, 1903).

Smith, J., *The Grievances of the Working Classes; and the Pauperism and Crime of Glasgow* (Glasgow, 1846).

Spens, W.C., *Jurisdiction and Punishments of Summary Criminal Courts* (Edinburgh, 1875).

Stark, J., *Inquiry into some points of the Sanatory State of Edinburgh* (Edinburgh, 1847).

Strang, J., *The Progress of Glasgow in Population, Wealth, Manufactures & c.* (Glasgow, 1850).

Strang, J., *Economic and Social Statistics of Glasgow, 1851–61* (Glasgow, 1852–63).

Symons, J.C., *Tactics for the Times as Regards the Condition and Treatment of the Dangerous Classes* (London, 1849).

Tancred, T., 'House of Refuge for Juvenile Offenders, Glasgow', *Journal of the Statistical Society of London*, VI (1843), pp. 252–255.

Thomson, A., *Industrial Schools; their Origin Rise and Progress, in Aberdeen* (Aberdeen, 1847).

Thomson, A., *Social Evils: Their Causes and Their Cure* (London, 1852).
Watson, W., *The Juvenile Vagrant and the Industrial Schools* (Aberdeen, 1851).
Watson, W., *Chapters on Ragged and Industrial Schools* (Edinburgh and London, 1872).
Watson, W., *Pauperism, Vagrancy Crime, and Industrial Education in Aberdeenshire, 1840–75* (Edinburgh and London, 1877).
Watson, W., *Should I Subscribe to the Industrial School? or Reasons for the Education of Pauper Children* (Aberdeen, 1850).
Watson, W.W., *Report upon the Vital, Social, and Economic Statistics of Glasgow, for 1877* (Glasgow, 1878).
Wilson, J.H., *The Bon-Accord Repository of Local Institutions, Municipal, Educational, Ecclesiastical, and Commercial* (Aberdeen, 1842).
Wood, J., *Account of the Edinburgh Sessional School* (Edinburgh, 1830).

5. More Recent Books and Articles

Abrams, L., *The Orphan Country* (Edinburgh, 1998).
Adams, T.H., *The Making of Urban Scotland* (London, 1978).
Bailleau, F. and Cartuyvels, Y. (eds), *The Criminalisation of Youth: Juvenile Justice in Europe, Turkey and Canada* (Brussels, 2010).
Barrie, D.G., and Broomhall, S., *Police Courts in Nineteenth-Century Scotland*, 2 Vols. (Farnham, 2014).
Bone, R.R., 'History of the Scottish Approved Schools', Glasgow University B.Ed thesis, 1966.
Boss, P., *Social Policy and the Young Delinquent* (London, 1967).
Carlebach, J., *Caring for Children in Trouble* (London, 1970).
Checkland, O., *Philanthropy in Victorian Scotland* (Edinburgh, 1980).
Clark, E.A.G., 'The Superiority of the "Scotch System": Scottish Ragged Schools and Their Influence', *Scottish Educational Studies*, IX (1977), pp. 29–39.
Clokie, H.M., and Robinson, J.W., *Royal Commissions of Inquiry* (Stanford, 1937).
Craigie, J., *A Bibliography of Scottish Education before 1872* (London, 1970).
Curtis, S.J., *History of Education in Great Britain* (London, 1948).
Daiches, D., *Edinburgh* (London, 1978).
Devine, T.M., *The Scottish Nation, 1700–2007* (London, 2012).
Donajgrodski, A.P. (ed.), *Social Control in Nineteenth Century Britain* (London, 1977).
Drummond, A.L., and Bulloch, J., *The Scottish Church 1688–1843* (Edinburgh, 1973).
Drummond, A.L., *The Church in Victorian Scotland, 1843–1874* (Edinburgh, 1975).
Ferguson, T., *The Dawn of Scottish Social Welfare* (London, 1948).
Finer, S.E., *The Life and Times of Sir Edwin Chadwick* (London, 1952).
Finlayson, G.B.A.M., *The Seventh Earl of Shaftesbury, 1801–85* (London, 1981).
Foucault, M., *Discipline and Punish* (London, 1977).
Fox, L.W., *The English Prison and Borstal System* (London, 1952).
Garland, D., *Punishment and Welfare* (Aldershot, 1985).
Gatrell, V.A.C., and Hadden, T.B. 'Criminal Statistics and their Interpretation', in E.A. Wrigley (ed.) *Nineteenth-century Society: Essays in the Use of Quantitative Methods for the Study of Social Data* (Cambridge, 1972), pp. 336–396.
Gillis, J., 'The Evolution of Juvenile Delinquency in England, 1890–1914', *Past and Present*. 67 (1975), pp. 96–126.
Handley, J.E., *The Irish in Modern Scotland* (Cork, 1947).
Hawes, J.M., *Children in Urban Society: Juvenile Delinquency in 19th Century America* (New

York, 1971).

Henriques, U.R.Q., 'The Rise and Decline of the Separate System of Prison Discipline', *Past and Present*, 54 (1972), pp. 61–93.

Heywood, J., *Children in Care* (London, 1959).

Hinde, R.S.E., *The British Penal System* (London, 1951).

Ignatieff, M., *A Just Measure of Pain: The Penitentiary in the Industrial Revolution* (London, 1978).

Knell, B.E.F., 'Capital Punishment: Its Administration in Relation to Juvenile Offenders in the Nineteenth Century and its Possible Administration in the Eighteenth', *British Journal of Criminology*, V (1965), pp. 198–207.

Knox, W.W., 'The Attack of the "Half-Formed Persons": The 1811–2 Tron Riot in Edinburgh Revisited', *The Scottish Historical Review*, Vol. XCI, No. 232, October 2012, pp. 287–310.

Knox, W.W., 'The Scottish Educational System, 1840–1940' (www.scran.ac.uk/scotland/pdf/SP2_1Education.pdf).

Koestler, A., *Reflections on Hanging* (London, 1956).

Lindsay, J., *The Scottish Poor Law: Its Operation in the North-East, from 1745 to 1845* (Ilfracombe, 1975).

Lubenow, W.C., *The Politics of Government Growth* (Newton Abbot, 1971).

MacDonagh, O.O.G.M., 'The Nineteenth-Century Revolution in Government: A Reappraisal', *Historical Journal*, I (1958), pp. 52–67.

MacLaren, A.A., *Religion and Social Class. The Disruption Years in Aberdeen* (London and Boston, 1974).

Mackie, J.D., *A History of Scotland* (Harmondsworth, 1964).

Mackie, P., 'The Foundation of the United Industrial School of Edinburgh: A Bold Experiment', *The Innes Review*, Vol. XXXIX, No. 2, Autumn 1988, pp. 133–150.

Mackie, P., 'Inter-denominational Education and the United Industrial School of Edinburgh, 1847–1900', *The Innes Review*, Vol. XLIII, No. 1, Spring 1992, pp. 3–17.

Mahood, L., *Policing Gender, Class and Family: Britain 1850–1914* (London, 1995).

Manton, J., *Mary Carpenter and the Children of the Streets* (London, 1976).

May, M. 'Innocence and Experience: The Evolution of the Concept of Juvenile Delinquency in the Mid-nineteenth Century', *Victorian Studies*, XVII (1973), pp. 7–29.

McCaffrey, J.F., *Scotland in the Nineteenth Century* (London, 1998).

McGowan, J., *A New Civic Order: The Contribution of the City of Edinburgh Police, 1805–1812* (Musselburgh, 2013).

Mechie, S., *The Church and Scottish Social Development 1780–1870* (London, 1960).

Murray, I.H., 'Thomas Chalmers and the Revival of the Church', *Banner of Truth Magazine*, No. 198 (March 1980), pp. 1–32.

Philips, D., *Crime and Authority in Victorian England* (London, 1977).

Pinchbeck, I., and Hewitt, M., *Children in English Society*, Vol. II (London, 1973).

Poverty in the Victorian Age. Debates on the Issue from 19th Century Critical Journals. Volume IV, Scottish Poor Laws 1815–1870 (Farnborough, 1973).

Radzinowicz, L., *A History of English Criminal Law and Its Administration from 1750* (4 Vols., London, 1948–1968).

Ralston, A.G., 'The Tron Riot of 1812', *History Today*, May 1980, Volume 30, Issue 5, pp. 41–45.

Ralston, A.G., 'The Development of Reformatory and Industrial Schools in Scotland, 1832–1872', *Scottish Economic and Social History*, 1988, Volume 8, Issue 1, pp. 40–55.

Rose, G., *Schools for Young Offenders* (London, 1967).

Rothman, D.J., *The Discovery of the Asylum* (Boston and Toronto, 1971).
Saunders, L.J., *Scottish Democracy 1815–40* (Edinburgh and London, 1951).
Scotland, J., *The History of Scottish Education* (2 Vols., London, 1969).
Seed, P. 'Types of Conceptualization of Ascribed Client Need in Social Service Provision: Based on a Case Study of the "Aberdeen System" of Industrial Feeding Schools and the Associated Social Movement, 1841–1884', Aberdeen University Ph.D thesis, 1976.
Stevenson, J., *Fulfilling a Vision: The Contribution of the Church of Scotland to School Education, 1772–1872* (Oregon, 2012).
Tobias, J.J., *Crime and Industrial Society in the 19th Century* (London, 1967).
Wilson, A., *The Chartist Movement in Scotland* (Manchester, 1970).
Young, A.F., and Ashton, E.T., *British Social Work in the Nineteenth Century* (London, 1956).

Index

Aberdeen House of Refuge 63–5, 132, 136
Aberdeen Industrial Schools 64–72, 129–31
Aberdeen Police Act, 1829 60
Aberdeen Reformatory and Industrial Schools Act, 1885 134
Act for the more speedy Trial and Punishment of Juvenile Offenders, 1847 10, 97
Adams, John 4, 6, 8, 10
Adderley, C.B. 10, 15, 163
Alison, Dr. W. P 34, 101
Antrobus, E.E. 17

Barclay, Sheriff Hugh 91, 163
Barnardo, Dr. Thomas 16
Bedford, Peter 12
Beggs, Thomas 4, 6
Bentham, Jeremy 11
Black, Adam 9, 83, 122
Boroughmuirhead Reformatory, Edinburgh 140–1
Brebner, William 45, 46, 102
Burns, Rev. Robert 99

Cameron, David x
capital punishment 7, 28–9, 97
Carlebach, J. J. xi 129
Carpenter, Mary 7, 14, 18, 68, 94, 123, 162
Carter, Rev. Thomas 9
Chadwick, Edwin 9, 45
Chalmers, Rev. Dr. Thomas 45, 100, 108
Checkland, O. xiii, 83
Clay, Rev. John 9, 12, 14, 47
Cockburn, Lord Henry 78
Cornwallis, C.P. 3
'Cumberland' Industrial Training Ship 155

Day Industrial School, Calton, Glasgow 160

Day Industrial Schools (Scotland) Act 1893 156
Day, S.P. 15
Dalry Refuge, Edinburgh 38, 40
Dean Bank Institution, Edinburgh 40, 65, 93, 139–41
Denman, Lord Chief Justice 18
Dickens, Charles 94
Disruption of 1843 xiv, 79, 101, 106, 107
Dunlop, Alexander Murray 112, 114, 115
Dunlop's Act 112, 114–19, 129–31, 136–9, 149–150

Edinburgh House of Refuge for the Destitute 39–40, 101, 103
Edinburgh Police Act 1812 30
Edinburgh Police Act 1832 40
Education in Scotland 105–9
Education Act 1870 19
Education (Scotland) Act 1872 107, 154–60
Ewing, James 46, 47

Faithfull, Baroness 165
Free Church of Scotland xiv, 63, 65–6, 75, 79, 84, 88
First Book of Discipline 105

Glasgow House of Refuge 47–54, 93, 94, 96, 143–8, 157–8
Glasgow Industrial Schools 51–2, 149–50
Glasgow Juvenile Delinquency Act 1841 44, 50
Glasgow Juvenile Delinquency Act 1878 158–60
Glasgow Night Asylum for the Houseless 51, 103
Glasgow Roman Catholic Reformatory Schools 146

Glasgow Society for the Encouragement of Penitents 45
Glasgow Society for Repressing Juvenile Delinquency 47
Guthrie, Rev. Dr. Thomas xi, 1, 4, 13, 75–88, 92, 95, 103, 112, 121, 136–7, 154–5, 162

Hackney Wick Asylum 13, 14
Hanbury, Robert 122–3
Heriot's Hospital 81
Hill, Alfred 95
Hill, Frederic 17, 20, 40, 45, 46, 100, 102, 103, 130
Hill, Matthew Davenport 8, 11, 14, 17
Howard Association for Penal Reform 17
Howard League for Penal Reform 166
Hume, David 31

imprisonment of young offenders 12–15, 45–7, 164
industrial schools: Aberdeen 64–72, 129–31; Edinburgh 83–8, 125, 136–9, 156; Glasgow 51–2, 149–50, 158–60; other UK cities 94–6
Industrial Schools Act 1857 113
Industrial Schools Consolidating and Amending Act (Scotland) 1861 119–20
Industrial Schools Act 1866 124
industrial training 9, 11, 79, 82, 86–7, 130–1, 133, 144

Jameson, Sheriff Andrew 38, 84
Jebb, Sir Joshua 4
juvenile delinquency: causes 2–6; legal aspects 7–10, 96–9; investigations by Select Committees 10–15; in relation to education 16–20

Kingsmill, Rev. Joseph 14, 18, 19
Koestler, Arthur 7

Lewis, Rev. George 31, 106
Liddell, Andrew 45, 51
Locke, William 94

Mack, Bailie James 82, 136
Malthus, Rev. T.R. 106
'Mars' training ship 155
McCallum, Rev. A. K. 48, 144, 146–8
MacDuff, Rev. Dr. J.R. 109
Macgill, Rev. Stevenson 45
MacGregor, John 4, 13
Maclagan, Alexander 83

McLevy, James 164
Mettray, France 143
Millbank Penitentiary 9
Miller, Captain Henry 51, 100
Mount Street Reformatory, Aberdeen 134
Moncrieff, Lord James 154
Mure, David 124
Murray, Lord John 84

Newcastle Commission on the Education of the Poor 16
Nicholls, Sir George 101

Oldmill Reformatory School, Aberdeen 118, 131–3, 163
Original Ragged School, Edinburgh 83–8, 136–9

Pakington, Sir John 118
Parkhurst Prison 12–13
Pearson, Charles 8
penny theatres 3–4
Philanthropic Society 12, 93
Philips, David 7
Playfair, Bailie James 53
Plea for Ragged Schools 75, 79, 92, 95
Plint, Thomas 6
Poor Law Amendment Act 1834 15, 101, 104
Poor Law Act (Scotland) 1845 51, 101–4
Poor Relief in Scotland 99–105
Pounds, John 18
Power, David 10

Ragged School Rhymes 83, 87
Ragged School Union 18, 95
Redhill, Surrey 46, 143
Reformatory and Refuge Union 14, 119
Reformatory Schools Act 1854 *see* Youthful Offenders Act
Reformatory and Industrial Schools (Scotland) Act 1854 *see* Dunlop's Act
Reformatory Schools Act, 1866 124
Robertson, Rev. William 75, 81
Rolfe, R. M. 17
Royal Commission on Reformatory and Industrial Schools 1884 156

Sanspareil Theatre, Liverpool 4
Shaftesbury, Lord 6, 95
Smith, John 9, 81
Society for Investigating the Causes of the Alarming Increase of Juvenile Delinquency in the Metropolis 11–12

Society for the Improvement of Prison Discipline and the Reformation of Juvenile Offenders 8
Speirs, Sheriff Graham 40, 78, 84
St. John's Hill Day Industrial School, Edinburgh 156
St. Mary's Roman Catholic School, Glasgow 150
Stark, Dr. James 34
Stevenson, R.L. 34
Stow, David 47, 108
summary jurisdiction 10, 35, 97–8
Symons, Jelinger C. 19

Tancred, Thomas 103
Thomson, Alexander 13, 60–3, 71–2, 98, 131
Tron Riot, Edinburgh xi, 24–32

Turner, Rev. Sydney 19, 95, 104, 108, 114–16, 125, 131, 140, 144–7, 155, 158

United Industrial School, Edinburgh 85–8, 125, 136–9
United Nations Convention on the Rights of the Child 165

Watson, Sheriff William xi, 57–72, 82, 94–5, 108, 116, 130, 135–6
Wellington Farm School, Edinburgh 118, 141–3
Williams, Captain W. J. 8, 9, 94
Wood, Rev. J. J. 81–2

Youthful Offenders Act 1854 15, 112, 131–48